Literature Instruction

Literature Instruction

A Focus on Student Response

Edited by
Judith A. Langer
State University of New York at Albany

National Council of Teachers of English
1111 Kenyon Road, Urbana, Illinois 61801

Staff Editor: William Tucker

Cover Design: Carlton Bruett

Interior Book Design: Tom Kovacs for TGK Design

NCTE Stock Number 33185–3050

Preparation of these reports was supported in part by a grant number G008720278, which is cosponsored by the U.S. Department of Education, Office of Educational Research and Improvement (OERI/ED), and by the National Endowment for the Arts (NEA). However, the opinions expressed herein do not necessarily reflect the position or policy of OERI/ED or NEA, and no official endorsement of either agency should be inferred.

Library of Congress Cataloging-in-Publication Data

Literature instruction : a focus on student response / edited by
   Judith A. Langer.
      p.   cm.
   Outgrowth of a variety of projects of the Center for the Learning
and Teaching of Literature, State University of New York at Albany.
   ISBN 0-8141-3318-5
   1. Literature—Study and teaching—United States. I. Langer,
Judith A. II. State University of New York at Albany. Center for
the Learning and Teaching of Literature.
LB1575.5.U5L58   1992
807—dc20   91–38081
                                                        CIP

Contents

Introduction

Judith A. Langer
State University of New York at Albany

This book is not only the outgrowth of a variety of projects of the Center for the Learning and Teaching of Literature, but also an ongoing part of its continuing mission to stimulate national reform in the teaching of literature. Among the Center's major emphases has been a revitalization and reconceptualization of the teaching of literature with a particular emphasis on the special kinds of creative and critical thinking that separate literary experiences from others. Thus, the exploration of possibilities, the welcome of ambiguity, the tolerance for multiple interpretations, as well as the quest to separate the indefensible from the theoretically sound have been at the heart of our instructional concerns. This has placed students' growing ability to develop and ponder their own and others' understandings at the center of instruction.

Some of the chapters that follow are reports of research carried out during the first three years of the Center's existence, from 1987 through 1990. Other chapters were prepared for a teacher's conference the Center sponsored called "New Directions in the Teaching of Literature." Still other chapters were commissioned to provide additional issues for consideration. All have appeared as part of the Center's Report Series, and have been read by a small but loyal following. This NCTE publication provides the first opportunity for these ideas to be presented as a related whole and to reach a wider readership.

Together, the chapters provide an overview of the latest thinking on response-oriented instruction, pointing to new and needed directions for instructional change. Chapters 1 and 2 provide the argument for change in literature education, and point to particular concerns that need to be addressed. In the first chapter, Arthur Applebee discusses the findings from a series of surveys and classroom studies of literature instruction across the United States, using what he learned to raise a number of issues he feels must be addressed as starting points for any meaningful reform. In the next chapter, Alan Purves discusses his studies of formal and informal literature testing and describes the limitations he found in the conceptualization as well as presentation of present-day tests. He then suggests several dimensions that should be considered in the future. Both Applebee and Purves argue that instruction and assessment in literature continue to be based on theories of criticism and of learning that are no longer current in their respective fields, and consequently call for a new theory of effective teaching and learning of literature to guide both day-to-day practice and longer range curriculum planning. In chapter 3, Judith Langer discusses her two complementary strands of research that underlie a student-response-based view of the learning and teaching of literature. First, she examines the nature of literary understanding and the ways it develops during reading and discussion, and contrasts it with meaning making when reading other types of material—for other purposes. Then, she describes findings from a series of collaborative studies that explored the effective ways in which literature instruction could support students' literary understanding—supporting their ability to arrive at and go beyond their initial responses.

Each of the remaining chapters suggests a particular approach to literature instruction from a student-response perspective—one that supports students not only in coming to understand the texts they are reading, but in learning to engage in the kinds of creative and critical thinking that underlie the literary experience. In chapter 4, Robert Probst, from a reader-response perspective, discusses ways in which literature instruction can reflect the literary experience as a coming together of reader and text, as a significant event in a reader's intellectual and emotional life. He describes five kinds of reader-knowledge the teacher can tap in supporting such transactions. In chapter 5, Susan Hynds focuses on the use of questions, suggesting that by reflecting on the cognitive, social, and cultural dimensions of the questions they ask, teachers can gain insight into the kinds of thinking they prompt their students to experience. She then addresses questions and classroom contexts that support student thinking. In chapter 6, Jayne DeLawter focuses on the elementary classroom, contrasting the skills-oriented teacher's role as "curriculum clerk" with the student-response-oriented teacher as "explorer." She then describes instructional patterns that go beyond the basalization of literature and organize classrooms to support students' engagement in the lived-in literary experience. In chapter 7, Patrick Dias suggests issues to be considered when rethinking instructional practice and provides a portrait of what response-based classrooms might look like. He describes one instructional procedure in detail in order to illustrate the ways in which particular roles and tasks promote authentic thinking and invite readers to create their own poems. In the last chapter, Anthony Petrosky argues against teaching models that support unidimensional and restricted thinking on the part of teachers and students alike, and contrasts them with the multiplicity of viewpoints that are actively considered and reconsidered in a "field of play." As an example of his position that continuous conversation supports rethinking and reformulation, he uses the comments of the reviewers of his chapter as a voice that caused him to reconsider his original paper about his own approaches to literature instruction. Thus, his original paper is presented intact, bounded by a prologue and epilogue. The prologue presents theoretical ideas he developed in response to the reviewers' comments, and the epilogue presents his realization that his original lesson was driven by his own idiosyncratic experiences. Thus we are led to see how the reviewers' comments provided him with the perspective to move beyond his first position. This demonstration becomes part of his argument that literary understanding is always subject to reconsideration, based on one's own ideas or others'./

In all, this book discusses possibilities for student-response-based literature instruction from elementary grades through college. Although it is no longer the case, original funding for the Literature Center limited the scope of its activities to the middle and high school grades. While the majority of chapters in this volume reflect this focus, DeLawter's is the only one to deal expressly with elementary and Petrosky's with college classes. However, the theoretical notions underlying response-based instruction and the teaching practices that support it are ageless, cutting across both grade and "achievement levels."

This volume is offered to stimulate dialogue leading to principled reform—one that is anchored in new conceptualizations of what student response entails, how to teach it, how to determine what counts as knowing from this perspective, and how to create educational environments in which student response can grow and thrive.

1 The Background for Reform

Arthur N. Applebee
State University of New York at Albany

During the past few years, the teaching of literature has received increasing attention both within the profession and from the public at large. This attention stems from a concern that traditional cultural values are not receiving sufficient emphasis (e.g., Hirsch, 1987), from attempts to reinforce the academic curriculum (e.g., Bennett, 1988), and from teachers who have begun to question whether recent changes in writing instruction may have implications for the teaching of literature as well. Though some of these discussions have been intense, they have lacked a solid base of evidence about the characteristics of literature instruction as it is currently practiced in American schools. What goals do teachers propose to guide their teaching of literature? What selections do they use? How are these selections presented? To what extent are curriculum and instruction differentiated for students of differing interests or abilities? What, in fact, are the most pressing issues of theory and practice in the teaching of literature?

To answer questions such as these, the Center for the Learning and Teaching of Literature has been carrying out a series of studies of the elementary and secondary school curriculum. These have included a survey of the book-length works that are required in the secondary school (Applebee, 1989a), an analysis of the role of literary selections in published tests (Brody, DeMilo, and Purves, 1989), case studies of programs in schools with reputations for excellence in English (Applebee, 1989b), analyses of the place of literature in elementary school programs (Walmsley and Walp, 1989), a content analysis of the selections and teaching apparatus included in secondary school literature anthologies (Applebee, in press), and a survey designed to provide a broad portrait of methods and materials in representative samples of schools nationally (Applebee, 1990). Together, these studies have been designed to provide a rich portrait of current instruction—the background against which any reform will take place.

Competing Models of the English Language Arts

Since the 1970s, a variety of movements have affected the teaching of the English language arts in general and the teaching of literature in particular. One important set of movements affecting the teaching of English has come from outside the profession. In the 1970s, public concern about students' abilities to perform successfully in the job market led to a widespread emphasis on "basic skills." This, in turn, led to the institutionalization of a variety of forms of minimum competency testing in the majority of states, and reinforced a "language skills" emphasis in the teaching of the English language arts. The emphasis on basic skills prompted its own reaction during the following decade, in the form of a reassertion of the traditional values of a liberal, academic curriculum. Calls for a return to "excellence," for a more academic curriculum, and for the preservation of "cultural literacy" are all rooted in this liberal (and paradoxically, in this context, conservative) tradition. Like the emphasis on basic skills that preceded it, this emphasis also came largely from outside the professional education community but has led to a widespread reexamination of curriculum and materials in the teaching of the English language arts.

Even as these external calls have been shaping the teaching of English, leaders of the profession have been searching for a new basis for the curriculum. The difficulty of that process was evident in a report from the NCTE Commission on the English Curriculum. Its report, *Three Language Arts Curriculum Models* (Mandel, 1980), did not attempt to reconcile the many competing models within the profession, but instead presented three alternative, comprehensive curriculum models for prekindergarten through college. The three models represent long-standing traditions in the English language arts: one was student centered, emphasizing "personal growth"; one was content centered, emphasizing the preservation of a cultural heritage; and one was skill centered, emphasizing the development of language competencies.

In contrast to the eclecticism represented by the Curriculum Commission volume, the most fully developed models to be offered for language arts instruction in recent years have been based on constructivist theories of language use and language development. Constructivist approaches have a variety of roots, with related frameworks emerging in fields as seemingly diverse as linguistics, psychology, history of science, sociology, and philosophy (on constructivist theories, see Langer and Applebee, 1986; Applebee, in press). What scholars in this tradition share is a view of knowledge as an active construction built up by the individual acting within a social context that shapes and constrains that knowledge, but that does not determine it in an absolute sense.

Thus constructivist theory involves an important shift in what counts as knowledge, and by implication what should be taught in schools. From a constructivist perspective, notions of "objectivity" and "factuality" lose their preeminence, and are replaced by notions of the central role of the individual learner in the "construction of reality" (Berger and Luckmann, 1966). Instruction becomes less a matter of transmittal of an objective and culturally sanctioned body of knowledge, and more a matter of helping individual learners learn to construct and interpret for themselves. There is a shift in emphasis from content knowledge to processes of understanding that are themselves shaped by and help students to become part of the cultural communities in which they participate. The challenge for educators is how, in turn, to embed this new emphasis into the curricula they develop and implement.

In the English language arts, constructivist frameworks have been particularly appealing to scholars who have emphasized the skills and strategies that contribute to ongoing processes of language use. During the 1970s and early 1980s, process-oriented approaches dominated writing instruction and affected reading instruction as well, particularly through the whole language movement, which sought an integrated approach to all aspects of the language arts. Although process-oriented approaches developed first in the teaching of writing and reading and have been slower to develop in the teaching of literature, teachers and scholars who have been convinced of the value of process-oriented approaches to the teaching of writing have begun to look for ways to extend these approaches to other areas of the curriculum (Applebee, 1989b; Langer, 1984, 1989, 1990; Purves, 1990).

Responding to the tension between external calls for basic skills and for a traditional liberal curriculum, and the emerging focus within the profession on process-oriented approaches, NCTE, the Modern Language Association, and five other organizations concerned with the teaching of English as a first or second language formed an English coalition to consider common problems and issues. As one part of their activities, they jointly sponsored a three-week conference during which some sixty educators met daily to find common ground for their teaching of the language arts. Their report, *The English Coalition Conference: Democracy through Language* (Lloyd-Jones and Lunsford, 1989), is firmly within a constructivist tradition. The conference emphasized the role of students as "active learners," and argued, as the introduction to the report explained, that learning "inevitably unites skills and content in a dynamic process of practice and assimilation" (xxiii). Although conference participants found themselves in some agreement about goals and directions for the teaching of the English language arts, they failed to provide clear guidelines for curriculum. Caught in a reaction against prescriptive "lists"—whether of texts to read or skills to learn—the conference found no broader structuring principles to offer. Instead of a unifying framework, the report presents a variety of alternatives and options, each of which is valuable in itself, but the total of which does not provide a sense of unity and direction. In this regard, the report abandoned the eclecticism of the earlier volume (Mandel, 1980) without offering a viable alternative.

The Literature Center studies of current practice, then, have taken place against a background of considerable movement within the teaching of the English language arts. Constructivist approaches have made a large contribution to the theory guiding the teaching of writing and reading, but have a less clearly developed relationship to the teaching of literature. Older frameworks, stressing basic skills, liberal education, and personal growth, continue to assert themselves. Newer frameworks, derived from constructivist principles, have gained considerable influence but have yet to result in well-articulated guidelines for curriculum and instruction.

The most recent of the Literature Center studies of current practice (Applebee, 1990) was a questionnaire survey of five national samples of schools: representative samples of public, Catholic, and independent secondary schools, and complete samples of two sets of schools that had been singled out for excellence in their English programs (schools that consistently had winners in the National Council of Teachers of English [NCTE] Achievement Awards in Writing competition, and schools that had been designated as Centers of Excellence by NCTE). Five staff members in each school were asked to complete questionnaires designed to provide information about different aspects of the literature program: the department chair, the school librarian, and three "good teachers of literature" were chosen as representative of the literature program across grades and tracks. A total of 650 schools, representing 82 percent of those contacted, responded to the survey.

In the present chapter, I will provide an overview of secondary school literature instruction as it emerges from this study, and will look across the whole set of Literature Center studies to outline a series of continuing issues that represent the current growing points in current theory and practice in the teaching and learning of literature.

Current Practice in the Teaching of Literature:
An Overview of Results from the National Survey

The Schools and Their Teachers

One set of questions included in the survey examined the general context in which literature instruction takes place, including such factors as teacher preparation, teaching load, and strengths and weaknesses of the English program as a whole. Responses to these questions indicated that, in general, teachers of English are experienced and well prepared. On average, public school teachers reported over fourteen years of teaching experience, and 95 percent reported an academic concentration in English or a related field. Some 61 percent had a master's degree. Reports of teaching conditions show some improvement when compared with earlier studies (Squire, 1961; Squire and Applebee, 1968), but even today only 28 percent of public-school teachers reported loads that reflect the NCTE-recommended maximum of 100 students per day.

The three greatest strengths that teachers noted in the English programs in their schools reflect their professionalism and competence: they valued the freedom to develop their own style and approach, the overall preparation of the faculty, and the support of the department chair. The program in literature and the program for the college bound were also highly rated.

Teaching load led the list of weaknesses cited by the public-school teachers, but it was considered a weakness by only 36 percent of those responding. Teachers' perceptions of the degree of community support and of programs for nonacademic students came next among the weaknesses the teachers noted.

Reports from the award-winning schools indicated a number of consistent differences between them and the random sample of public schools. Compared with the random sample, the award-winning schools were disproportionately suburban, had more resources available to support a program in literature, hired teachers with more experience and more graduate preparation for teaching, kept teaching loads lighter, and offered more special programs and extracurricular activities related to the teaching of English. They also tended to be more content with the quality of their students and the level of community support for the program in English.

Teaching conditions in Catholic schools were similar to those in public schools, though overall school size was considerably smaller.

Teaching loads in the independent schools were by far the best, with fully 70 percent of the teachers reporting loads that met the NCTE-suggested maximum of 100 students per day.

The Curriculum as a Whole

Another set of questions included in the survey focused on the organization of the English curriculum as a whole, including the relationships between literature and the other components of English instruction. Results from these questions suggest that literature has maintained the central place in the English curriculum that it has had at least since the turn of the century (Applebee, 1974), in spite of recent reforms focusing on the teaching of writing. Approximately 50 percent of class time is devoted to literature in high school English classes; when the interrelated nature of the English language arts is taken into account, as much as 78 percent of class time may be devoted to literature-related activities. The emphasis on literature is highest in the upper grades and college preparatory tracks, and lower in middle school and non-college preparatory classes.

Teachers report emphasizing a broad range of text- and student-centered goals for their teaching of literature, and do not see these emphases as being in conflict with one another. Their expectations are highest for their college-bound students; for the non-college bound, they place less emphasis on both student-oriented and text-oriented outcomes.

The curriculum as a whole tends to be organized around genres in grades 7 through 10, American literature in grade 11, and British literature in grade 12. Recent attempts to add courses in world literature introduce some variation into this pattern, particularly at the tenth- and twelfth-grade levels. Within these broad organizational patterns, the most highly rated approach to organizing the curriculum was the study of individual major works (rated highly by 78 percent), followed closely by study of genres (72 percent). The most highly rated approaches to literature study all involve techniques that work well with whole-class study. Guided individual reading received lower ratings than any other approach, though it was somewhat more popular in the junior high/middle school grades than it was in the high school.

The most important influences on the organization of the curriculum take place at the departmental level, whether because of the influence of a formal course of study or through informal consensus. Many department chairs, however, receive very little compensation for the organization and supervision of the work in English. They were most likely to receive some form of support (usually released time or a salary increment) in the award-winning schools, and least likely to do so in Catholic and independent schools. Even in large schools, 21 percent of the department chairs reported receiving no support at all for their duties.

The curriculum in literature was very similar across the various samples studied here, and also seems very stable. The majority of department chairs expected that there would be *no* changes in content or approaches to the teaching of literature in their departments during the next few years.

The Texts Students Read

Another aspect of the national survey focused on the selections that were chosen for study. In this case, teachers were asked to list all selections which students dealt with in class or as homework during the previous five days. The titles they reported suggest a curriculum dominated by familiar selections drawn primarily from a white, male, Anglo-Saxon tradition. In most classrooms, these selections are chosen by the teacher from a literature anthology and from class sets of book-length texts. As earlier surveys have suggested (Tanner, 1907; Anderson, 1964; Applebee, 1989a), William Shakespeare is by far the most popular author, followed in the present study by John Steinbeck and Langston Hughes.

While it is encouraging to see Hughes emerging high in the list of frequently taught authors, the overall proportions of selections by minorities and by women remain low. Across genres, only 8 percent of the selections that had been taught in the past five days were written by a minority author, and only 16 percent were written by a woman. In using works by women and minorities, teachers report more success with poems and short stories than with novels and plays, but this success does not seem to have had much influence on the works they chose to teach.

Teachers report three sets of influences on their choices of selections to teach: departmental policies, community reaction, and teacher judgment (including their familiarity with specific selections). Taken together, their reports suggest that when it comes to broadening the canon to include more works by women and minorities, teachers may be unsure of the literary merit of new selections, as well as personally unfamiliar with them, thus making them initially less teachable, and worried about community reaction—as a result the curriculum changes with glacial slowness.

Instructional Approaches

Just as important as what is taught is how it is taught. Teachers' approaches to particular texts—the questions they ask and the responses they expect to receive—can have a profound influence on what students learn. Responses to a variety of questions in the national survey indicate that the typical high school literature class places heavy emphasis on whole-class discussion of texts that all students have read. These discussions are most likely to focus on the meanings of the text, both in terms of students' experiences and in terms of careful questioning about the content. They are less likely to emphasize line-by-line analysis or extended discussion of the authors' literary techniques.

Taken together, teachers report a dual emphasis: on techniques that are loosely related to reader-response theories and on those that are associated more directly with close analyses of text. Rather than standing in opposition to one another, these broad theoretical orientations to literary study are frequently treated in complementary fashion: in our earlier case studies, concern with reader response seemed most typically used as a way into texts, while a focus on analysis of the text itself emerged as a later but ultimately more central feature of classroom study.

Teachers' approaches to texts are quite consistent across the major genres that are taught, though with some shifts in emphasis in response to the particular characteristics of each genre. Thus poetry and plays were more likely to be read aloud, novels and plays were more likely to involve the use of study guides, and plays (predominantly Shakespeare's) were more likely to include background lectures (presumably to help with the difficulties of Shakespearean language and theatre). Across all genres, however, whole-class discussions focusing on meanings and interpretations remained the primary means of instruction.

Teachers' reports on assessment techniques reflected this emphasis, with evaluation of participation in discussion being rated as the most frequent measure of progress in literature. Formal measures of progress were dominated by quizzes, unit tests, and essays, with the balance shifting toward essays in the upper grades and in college preparatory classes, and toward quizzes and study guides in the lower grades and in non-college tracks.

In general, there was considerable consistency between the goals teachers cited for the study of literature, and the particular techniques that they reported emphasizing in their classrooms. Means of assessment seemed more neutral, with essays, for example, being adaptable to a variety of different emphases depending upon the teachers' goals.

Essays, however, were rarely used for non-college-bound students—who seem in general to receive more emphasis on narrowly defined comprehension skills and less on response and interpretation.

Literature and Writing

If writing and literature are often treated as independent components of the teaching of English, teachers' responses to the present survey suggest that separation is unrealistic. In the junior high and middle school, some 58 percent of the writing students do is writing about literature—a figure that rises to 80 percent by the senior high grades. Clearly, these two aspects of the teaching of English are closely intertwined.

It also seems clear that two decades of discussion of process-oriented approaches to the teaching of writing have had some impact on the majority of schools. Two-thirds of the department chairs reported that the majority of their teachers were familiar with such approaches. They also reported that changes in writing instruction had led to more writing about literature, and also to some changes in the ways that literature was taught. These reports are more optimistic than those from classroom observers in our previous study (Applebee, 1989b), though that study also found that changes in literature instruction were often being led by teachers who had previously been active supporters of process-oriented approaches to writing.

Reports on the kinds of literature-related writing students do, however, are somewhat less optimistic. When examined within the context of a variety of classroom activities, essays and comprehension questions both receive heavy emphasis in the teaching of literature. And when teachers are asked to list their most common writing assignment, rather than to report on the variety of activities in their classrooms, researchers find that text-based essays dominate by a wide margin over essays that stress a reader's personal response or inter-pretation. Instruction in college-bound classes places greater emphasis on essay writing, while that in non-college tracks places more emphasis on exercises.

Teachers' reports indicate considerable variety in the techniques that they regularly use when teaching writing, including such techniques as multiple drafts and peer response. The most frequently used evaluation techniques, however, remain very traditional, emphasizing written comments, assignment of a grade, and correction of errors in mechanics. Thus, although it is clear that process-oriented instruction is broadly recognized as an appropriate approach to the teaching of writing, it does not seem to have led to drastic reformulation of what teachers do, at least in the context of writing about literature.

The School Library

The school library can provide an important complement to the program in literature, providing resources for classroom instruction as well as for independent reading. Reports on library resources available to support the program in literature suggest that school library collections have been strengthened since Squire and Applebee (1968) examined them in the early 1960s, but that considerable room for improvement remains. Less than half of the English teachers in the present study rated their school library as an "excellent" resource in the teaching of literature.

Teachers' ratings of the library were related most directly to the size of the library collection and to the availability of specific titles. Ratings were lower for libraries that restricted access to some materials, but were higher for those where the library staff met regularly with the English department to coordinate use of materials. Computer and media resources, though part of most library collections, were not important factors in teachers' ratings of the library's usefulness.

Libraries were used most frequently for research papers and for films or videotapes; surprisingly, they were used much less frequently to encourage wide reading or as part of individualized reading programs, though such uses increased in schools where the teachers gave higher ratings to the library collection. The majority of the teachers supplemented resources available in the school library with a classroom book collection, particularly in the junior high/middle school grades.

When librarians were asked for suggestions for broadening the curriculum to include a better representation of women and minorities, they offered a wide variety of titles and authors. It is perhaps revealing of how much collection development needs to be broadened that the three authors the librarians reported being asked specifically about were available in fewer than half of their libraries.

The Program as a Whole

As it emerges from our national surveys of current practice, the teaching of literature is a relatively traditional enterprise. The typical literature classroom is organized around whole-group discussion of a text everyone has read, with the teacher in front of the class guiding the students toward a common or agreed-upon interpretation. Teachers recognize a variety of text- and student-centered goals, and rely on activities and techniques that reflect these two broad sets of goals. Rather than being treated as strongly divergent alternative approaches, emphases on students or on texts are treated as legitimate and complementary, to be drawn upon at different times for different purposes. Student-centered approaches are often used as motivational techniques, the lead-in to more formal, text-centered study.

Selections for study are drawn most often from a commercial literature anthology, although in schools that have the economic resources to provide them, considerable emphasis is also placed on separately bound class sets of novels and plays. The selections chosen for study, whether drawn from the anthology or from other sources, tend to be traditional. William Shakespeare remains the single most popular author, and the vast majority of the selections that are taught are from a white, male, Anglo-Saxon tradition. Contemporary literature, at least when defined as selections from the past thirty years, receives a reasonable amount of attention, particularly contemporary novels.

Overall, there is considerable complacency about the teaching of literature. The majority of department chairs do not expect to see major changes in their programs or approaches within the next few years, and the majority of teachers rate their teaching of literature as a particular strength of their English programs.

The lack of concern about the program in literature should not be surprising. The profession as a whole has focused its attention over the past twenty years on the teaching of writing, pointing out problems and urging reforms. Throughout that period, the teaching of literature has continued unchanged and unexamined. The only serious challenges to current approaches have come from a reaction against a broadening of the canon of texts (e.g., Hirsch, 1987)—a reaction that the findings from the current study suggest may be unwarranted—and, more indirectly, from changes in writing instruction.

Continuing Issues in the Teaching of Literature

The results from this survey, as well as from the related studies of current practice that have been conducted at the Center for the Learning and Teaching of English, suggest a series of issues that need to be addressed in the teaching of literature. These issues reflect the growing edges of theory and practice, and the starting points for any meaningful reform. They offer another way in which to place the results from the national survey into a broader perspective.

Issue 1. We need to develop programs that emphasize students' ability to develop and defend their interpretations of literary selections, rather than ones that focus only on knowledge about texts, authors, and terminology. As I noted earlier, the conventional wisdom about the teaching of language has shifted increasingly toward an emphasis on constructivist approaches. Rather than treating the subject of English as a subject matter to be memorized, a constructivist approach treats it as a body of knowledge, skill, and strategies that must be constructed by the learner out of experiences and interactions within the social context of the classroom. In such a tradition, to know a work of literature is not to have memorized someone else's interpretations, but to have constructed and elaborated upon one's own within the constraints and conventions of the classroom discourse community.

Teachers' goals for the teaching of literature as revealed in the national survey seem caught between constructivist and earlier traditions. On the one hand there is considerable concern with text-centered goals that are in part a legacy of New Critical techniques and in part a legacy of skill-oriented instructional approaches. On the other hand there is also considerable emphasis on student-centered goals, and on the critical frameworks offered by reader-response criticism. These latter goals are more in keeping with a constructivist framework for teaching and learning, though as currently implemented they seem more closely related to earlier traditions of concern with students' motivation and "personal growth."

The traditional teacher-centered classroom that is reflected in the results of the present study is an effective means of conveying a large body of information in a relatively short period of time. However, it is not a particularly effective or efficient framework for instruction within a constructivist framework. Rather than helping students develop their own strategies for and approaches to the reading of literature, the teacher-centered classroom is much more likely to stress shared interpretations and group consensus. It is also likely to rely upon discussions in which some or all of the students are invited to respond to the teacher's questions, rather than upon discussions that engage each student in an extended exploration of his or her own ideas, developing those ideas by comparing them with the views of others. (Note that the quarrel here is not with class discussions or with instruction centered around shared experiences of books; it is with the presumption that such experiences should *begin* from the teacher's knowledge of correct interpretations and *end* when those interpretations have been effectively conveyed to the group as a whole.)

The patterns of instruction revealed in the national survey reflect an English classroom divided against itself. In the teaching of writing, teachers are more likely to emphasize the development of students' meaning-making abilities. Even if not fully accepted, process-oriented approaches to writing instruction are at least widely understood. But in the teaching of literature, on the other hand, the focus on the student is likely to stop after an initial emphasis on developing motivation and interest. At that point, a focus on the text, with the attendant concern with common interpretations, the "right answers" of literary study, comes to the fore.

Issue 2. We need to develop a theory of the teaching and learning of literature to guide the rethinking of high school instruction. If we are to shift the emphasis in instruction from the teacher and the text to the student and the process of understanding, then we need a much clearer set of theoretical principles to guide instruction. Recent developments in critical theory have for the most part ignored pedagogical issues, and teachers in the national survey, like those in our earlier study (Applebee, 1989b), found little in current theory to revitalize their instructional approaches. Instead, they rely for their curriculum planning and day-to-day instruction on traditional organizational concepts such as genre, chronology, and themes, on reader-response theory to foster student involvement, and on New Critical approaches to provide techniques for the study of individual texts.

What is lacking is a well-articulated overall theory of the teaching and learning of literature that will give a degree of order and coherence to the day-to-day decisions that teachers make about what and how to teach: What text should we choose? How should we decide what questions to ask first about a literary work? How should a student's response be followed up? What kinds of writing about literature will lead to the development of more comprehensive interpretations? What does a "good" interpretation consist of? Questions such as these need to be considered within a more comprehensive theoretical frame.

Relatively well-established traditions have begun to provide such frameworks for writing and reading within the English language arts. The teaching of literature, however, has until recently remained largely outside of recent movements in those fields. One of the most comprehensive attempts to develop such a framework for the literature curriculum has been carried out by Judith Langer (1989, 1990) and her colleagues. In a series of studies, they have been reexamining the process of understanding from the reader's point of view, using the results of that examination to rethink how literature instruction can best support students' efforts as they learn to become more effective readers. Such careful examination of the processes of teaching and learning is a necessary first step to the articulation of the principles of an effective constructivist framework for teaching and learning.

Issue 3. We need to revitalize instruction for non-college-bound students. One of the clearest patterns to emerge from the present national survey is the extent to which non-college-bound students are given a more skills-oriented, and less interesting, program of study than their college-bound peers. Compared with literature instruction for the college bound, that for the non-college bound entails lower overall teacher expectations, more emphasis on worksheets and study guides, less composition of coherent text, more quizzes and short-answer activities, less reading, more language study (i.e., grammar and usage), less individualized reading, and less use of the library.

Surprisingly, perhaps, the one place in which the curriculum of students not planning to attend college does *not* differ much from that of the college-bound student is in the selection of texts. Their curriculum is just as traditional as that of their peers, with Shakespeare's plays leading the list of most frequently taught texts.

Problems with programs for the non-college-bound student are hardly a recent development; they were also one of the major findings of the Squire and Applebee (1968) study of exemplary programs in the early 1960s. For the most part, general or vocational programs in English are simply derivative of the college preparatory program, with more emphasis on "skill and drill" and less on literature and the humanities. That teachers find these courses uninteresting to teach and students find them dull to take is hardly surprising. What is surprising is that we have let the problems continue so long without a serious attempt to find remedies that would make them more interesting, and more effective, for students and teachers alike.

Issue 4. We need to broaden the canon of selections for study. The recent revival of interest in the literature curriculum, and with it of interest in research in the teaching and learning of literature, has been due in no small part to concerns about a watering down of the traditional cultural content of the English course. Critics such as William Bennett (1984) and E. D. Hirsch (1987) have called for a reassertion of a focus on texts of cultural importance, the "great works" of Western civilization that have been replaced by less important writings by women or minorities, or drawn from non-Western traditions.

In that context, it has been surprising to find in this and our earlier studies (Applebee, 1989a, 1989b) that the selections that are actually taught remain very narrowly defined. In the present survey, only 16 percent of the selections chosen for study were written by women, and only 8 percent were by non-white authors.

The narrowness of the reading lists is particularly troublesome given some twenty years of commentary in the professional literature on the need to move beyond the traditional selections, to better recognize the diverse cultural traditions that contribute to contemporary American life. The strategies that have been adopted so far have centered on providing resource lists of titles from various traditions and on broadening the materials included in the literature anthologies. Clearly, however, new strategies are needed. The responses from the teachers in the present study suggest a variety of factors that may contribute to their reluctance to expand the selections they teach. These include a lack of familiarity with the selections they might use, doubts about the literary quality of much of the available material, and worries about community reaction. If the canon is really to be broadened, these problems and concerns are going to have to be more directly confronted.

Issue 5. We need to provide supportive institutional contexts for our programs in literature. Teachers of English do not work alone. In our earlier case studies of programs with reputations for excellence, we found that the best programs were characterized by strong departmental leadership, with an awareness of and trust in the professionalism of the classroom teacher. Many of the outstanding programs could also boast of abundant resources within the English department and in the school at large.

The national survey also highlighted the extent to which schools in all five samples could rely upon experienced and well-trained teachers to carry out the program in literature, and the quality of the faculty led the list of program strengths that teachers themselves cited. Also among the strengths that teachers cited were support from the principal and department chair.

Nonetheless, when the various samples of schools in the national survey are compared, one of the major differences that emerges between the award-winning schools and the others is the level of available resources. The award-winning schools tended to have better libraries, more abundant resource materials, a larger array of literature-related extracurricular activities, and lighter teaching loads. Their teachers were also more likely to rate the support of the community as a strength, and to have continued their own training beyond the master's level. Resources alone do not make for excellent programs, and many of the differences between schools in the present study reflect socio-economic differences in the communities they serve. Nonetheless, when schools do not have adequate resources, it becomes much more difficult to provide students with a challenging program in literature.

Supportive institutional contexts consist of more than just money, however. They also consist of institutional structures at the school and district level that support teachers in their professionalism rather than constrain their power to make educationally sound decisions about the instruction they offer. The support of the department chair, the principal, and the community at large are all important to the development of a strong program in literature. This support involves not only the endorsement of what teachers wish to do in their classrooms, but also the establishment of appropriate systems of evaluation (of students and of teachers) so that curriculum and assessment can work together to support student learning. Support at these levels will be particularly critical as teachers begin to change their approaches to literature, moving away from the teacher-centered whole-class discussions toward more innovative approaches.

A Janus Look

The teaching of literature as we know it is only about one hundred years old, having entered the schools in the late nineteenth century. Some aspects of literature instruction have remained remarkably constant, even as it has been reshaped in light of new demands placed on schools in general and on teachers of English in particular. From the beginning, literature instruction has constituted the central part of the teaching of English, the core around which other components are orchestrated. From the beginning, it has focused on a body of major texts that get reconfigured around themes, genres, or chronology, but that continue to play a central role in teachers' conceptions of the curriculum. From the beginning, instruction has centered around whole-class instruction focused on these core texts. And, from the beginning, literature instruction has been justified for its contribution to other objectives (mental discipline, vicarious experience, reading skill) rather than for any particular, unique contribution that the study of literature may make in its own right.

As we begin a second century of the teaching of literature, it is time to examine these enduring characteristics of literature instruction, asking ourselves which are appropriate and essential, and which have continued only because they have remained unexamined. I believe we are finally moving to a point where we can state the values of a literary education more clearly and forcefully, in terms that will justify just as much attention to literary study as our nation periodically invests in math, science, and "basic" literacy skills. And I believe that as we make that statement, we will also provide the rationale for our more carefully considered choices from among the many competing approaches to teaching and learning that are now manifest in our school programs.

References

Anderson, S. (1964). *Between the Grimms and the group*. Princeton, NJ: Educational Testing Service.

Applebee, A.N. (1974). *Tradition and reform in the teaching of English: A history*. Urbana, IL: National Council of Teachers of English.

Applebee, A.N. (1989a). *A study of book-length works taught in high school English courses* (Report Series 1.2). Albany, NY: Center for the Learning and Teaching of Literature, SUNY at Albany.

Applebee, A.N. (1989b). *The teaching of literature in programs with reputations for excellence in English* (Report Series 1.1). Albany, NY: Center for the Learning and Teaching of Literature, SUNY at Albany.

Applebee, A.N. (in press). Environments for language teaching and learning: Contemporary issues and future directions. In *Handbook of research on teaching the English language arts*. New York, NY: Macmillan.

Bennett, W.J. (1984). *To reclaim a heritage*. Washington, DC: National Endowment for the Humanities.

Bennett, W.J. (1988). *American education: Making it work*. Washington, DC: U.S. Government Printing Office.

Berger, P.L., and Luckmann, T. (1966). *The social construction of reality: A treatise in the sociology of knowledge*. New York, NY: Anchor Books.

Brody, P., DeMilo, C., and Purves, A.C. (1989). *The current state of assessment in literature* (Report No. 3.1). Albany, NY: Center for the Learning and Teaching of Literature, SUNY at Albany.

Hirsch, E.D., Jr. (1987). *Cultural literacy*. Boston: Houghton Mifflin.

Langer, J.A., and Applebee, A.N. (1986). Reading and writing instruction: Toward a theory of teaching and learning. *Review of Research in Education, 13*, 171–194.

Langer, J.A. (1984). Literacy instruction in American schools: Problems and perspectives. *American Journal of Education, 93*, 107–132.

Langer, J.A. (1989). *The process of understanding literature* (Report Series 2.1). Albany, NY: Center for the Learning and Teaching of Literature, SUNY at Albany. (Also appeared Oct. 1990 as The process of understanding: Reading for literary and informative purposes, *Research in the Teaching of English, 24*, 228–260.

Langer, J.A. (1991). *Literary understanding and literature instruction* (Report Series 2.11). Albany, NY: Center for the Learning and Teaching of Literature, SUNY at Albany.

Lloyd-Jones, R., and Lunsford, A. (1989). *The English coalition conference: Democracy through language*. Urbana, IL: National Council of Teachers of English.

Mandel, B.J. (1980). *Three language arts curriculum models: Pre-kindergarten through college*. Urbana, IL: National Council of Teachers of English.

Purves, A.C. (1990). *The scribal society: An essay on literacy and schooling in the information age*. White Plains, NY: Longman.

Squire, J.R. (1961). *The national interest and the teaching of English*. Champaign, IL: National Council of Teachers of English.

Squire, J.R., and Applebee, R.K. (1968). *High school English instruction today: The national study of high school English programs*. New York, NY: Appleton Century Crofts.

Tanner, G.W. (1907). Report of the committee appointed by the English conference to inquire into the teaching of English in the high schools of the middle west. *School Review, 15*, 32–45.

Walmsley, S. and Walp, T. (1989). *Teaching literature in the elementary school* (Report Series 1.3). Albany, NY: Center for the Learning and Teaching of Literature, SUNY at Albany.

2 Testing Literature

Alan C. Purves
State University of New York at Albany

All of the critical and scholarly emphasis on reader response to literature, on reception theory, and on student-centered learning that has taken place over the past twenty years would suggest that literature teaching and testing dealt with the vast range of potential readings of texts, with humane and tentative probings into the minds and responses of students. But an examination of the tests that are in print denies this. Such were the findings of a recent report of the Center for the Learning and Teaching of Literature (Brody, DeMilo, and Purves, 1989), which showed that most tests given in the state assessments or by commercial testing companies concentrate on the content of a literary work and on relatively low-level comprehension. The end-of-unit textbook tests are much the same. The tests of literature faced by secondary school students in the United States use an approach like that of the old drama "Dragnet": "Just the facts, ma'am." This is unfortunate because we know that these tests influence not only the curriculum but also the beliefs and attitudes of teachers and students. They are the tail that wags the dog.

Further, while the nation's testing programs devote a great deal of energy to testing reading and writing, they fail to treat literature and cultural literacy seriously. The artistic aspects of literature and the cultural heritage of our society are not reflected in the nation's tests, and, as a result, this has led to their neglect by the schools. The tests concentrate on prose fiction and exclude poetry and drama; they tend to ignore cultural literacy and various critical methodologies. All of these tendencies add up to a monotonous view of learning in literature.

Almost universally, the focus of these tests is on the comprehension of content, particularly on the meaning of specific parts or on the main idea or theme of a passage which is given to the student to read. A typical test will have a two-paragraph excerpt from a novel or story and follow it with three or four questions like these fictitious examples:

In line 10, the word *rogue* means: (a) stranger, (b) out of control, (c) colored with red, (d) falling apart

The two people are: (a) father and son, (b) brothers, (c) husband and wife, (d) strangers

This selection is about: (a) the end of an adventure, (b) the relationship between people and animals, (c) the climax of a journey, (d) the break-up of a family

Such questions hardly tap the imaginative power of literary works; in fact, they reduce them to the level of textbooks where the knowledge is factual. Some of the published tests go so far as to ask students whether statements such as "Huckleberry Finn is a good boy" or "Hamlet is mad" are true or false. As a result, students find that they do not have to read the selection; they can turn to plot summaries or simplified study guides.

In summary, our team found that the tests focus student attention on text comprehension at a relatively low level of understanding. They do so without a clear differentiation between reading a literary selection and reading a nonliterary one; any text is viewed as having a content that can be easily summarized into a single main idea, point, gist, or theme.

Is this the way we want our children to view literature? Literature is a complex and artistic use of words that stimulates readers' imaginations. Reading and studying literature should make readers aware of the beauty and power of the language, and the richness of the cultural heritage from all parts of the world. Literature has the ability to take readers out of their world and into other worlds, to make them laugh or cry, to challenge their beliefs, to make them wonder.

Is Huck Finn a good boy? Whose standards are we to use? Those of his society or those of the author? Is Hamlet mad? What is madness and what is acting? Can a mad person make such clever remarks or be so deliberate in his actions? These are questions to explore, to ponder, to challenge us. Literature and its teaching should offer our students intellectual challenges such as how they should interpret and evaluate words and language and poetry. Literature and its teaching should bring our students the pleasures of emotion and of the mind. Literature and its teaching should open our students to the beauty of words and expression and ideas. But how do they view it?

How Students See Literature Learning

One of the most useful sources of information on the topic of what constitutes school achievement comes from those who receive instruction, the students themselves. These people are expert in one subject if they are indifferent in others—they are expert in being students and knowing the rules of the game. The Center undertook another study (McCarry, Purves, and Henkin, 1991), using a survey instrument parallel to one already perfected in the analysis of written composition instruction (Takala, 1987). In that study students were asked to give advice on how to do well in school composition. In this study, we asked secondary students to write on the following topic:

> Write a letter of advice to someone two years younger than yourself who is intending to attend your school and who has asked you to explain how to do well in literature classes in your school. Write a friendly letter and include in it five specific pieces of advice.
>
> From an analysis of over a thousand responses by juniors and seniors at a national sample of schools considered excellent, there emerged the following general categories of advice: Reading Strategies, Writing Strategies, Classroom Strategies, and General Admonitions, as well as a large number of sub-categories.

The results indicate that the largest category of advice to prospective literature students dealt with strategies and tactics which tend not to be part of the announced curriculum. A large proportion of these responses dealt with reading strategies, followed by classroom strategies, particularly test-taking strategies. A relatively large number of these responses dealt with such procedures as reading on an empty stomach, how to sit while reading, or where to read. Yet another segment dealt with whether or not to skim first, whether to underline or take notes. The second most frequent category dealt with ancillary aids. Some of the writers advised calling a friend who had read the book, talking to one's parents, or, most frequently, using *Cliffs Notes*.

Another large category of advice fell into the area of classroom and test-taking strategy with particular emphasis on such strategies as where to sit or whether to be called on or to volunteer. Much of the advice in this category concerns strategies for homework ("You should get it in on time"), and test-taking ("It's better to have English second period so you can get the questions from the first-period students"). All of this advice was eminently practical.

By contrast, relatively few responses dealt with literary matters or even with the mental activities used while reading. The results appear to confirm the findings of our study of tests (Brody, DeMilo, and Purves, 1989).

By and large, the power of literature to capture the imagination of the reader remains unexplored by most assessments. Literature is treated as if it were no different from articles in encyclopedias or research reports. This is a critical problem in English education because these tests are ubiquitous and powerful. They dominate the lives in the school, and, despite what curriculum guides might say, the tests call the tune of the real world of the schools. This being so, it would seem difficult for teachers and their students to see literature, as a school subject, as anything but dead and lifeless.

Perhaps students see successful work in school literature as part of a "game" of reading to take comprehension tests, either formal ones, or practice tests given by the teacher as part of the day's lesson. They do not read for enjoyment, for enlargement of their understanding, or from a desire to appreciate the classics. The results of our student-advice study showed clearly that students focused upon issues of format, spelling, grammar, and other surface features rather than on content and organization. The implications for instruction appeared clear: with their red pencils teachers were signaling their real concerns, which were at variance with their professed concerns. Literature in schools appears to be a serious business clearly related to grades and achievement, rather than related to the lofty aims which literature and literature education set for themselves in curriculum guides and professional publications.

Fortunately, some people are beginning to take a renewed interest in the teaching of literature as an important part of children's education. There is a greater interest in using good literature in elementary school reading programs, although poetry and drama are still omitted. In the secondary schools, teachers and curriculum planners are also more aware of the importance of literature to the psychological and intellectual well-being of students and society, as the other chapters in this volume plainly attest.

How might we better enable schools and students to take a more active role in the learning of literature? I think we can do so through reconstructing our tests. We need to consider two issues: what do we mean by learning in literature, and what is the nature of difficulty in literature learning? Through such a rational process, we can begin to say what sorts of things would best constitute evidence that students have developed in the ways that literature teachers see as most valuable.

The Domain of Literature Learning in School:
A Proposed Model

A review of the various statements about the goals and aims of literature teaching (Purves, Shirk, and Li, 1990) showed that there were three complementary or competing views: that literature is an adjunct of the language arts, that it comprises a distinct body of knowledge, and that it is an aspect of aesthetic perception. Thus literature is seen alternatively as a stimulus for reading and writing, as an aspect of the humanities, and as one of the arts.

School literature has often been fitted—rather uncomfortably—into "the language arts," which are defined as reading, writing, speaking, and listening. Since literature involves texts that people read or write, and since literature instruction often involves writing, literature is often seen as simply a subset of reading and writing, with an occasional nod to speaking and listening. Literature study fits into the program as something pleasant to read and interesting to write about. This view seems to prevail in the basal reading approach of elementary schools (see Walmsley and Walp, 1989), and it carries on into the secondary school curriculum. Literature becomes a content, used to promote skills in reading and writing or to promote individual growth, depending upon the ideology attached to the language arts. In the current world of tests, literature is usually a vehicle for reading comprehension tests or for measures of writing proficiency.

A second perspective views literature as a school subject with its own body of knowledge. This body consists primarily of literary texts, often specified by genre, date, theme, author, and other classifications, as determined by experts, by those who purvey textbooks, or by teachers and curriculum planners. There are three other broad areas of literature content besides the texts: (1) historical and background information concerning authors, texts, and the times in which they were written or that form their subject matter; (2) information concerning critical terminology, critical strategies, and literary theory; and (3) information of a broad cultural nature such as that emerging from folklore and mythology, which forms a necessary starting point for the reading of many literary texts. This perspective has been criticized as focusing too much on things external to the text; at the same time, many have argued that such knowledge is crucial to the acts of reading and writing. In the world of testing, there are a few current commercial tests that concentrate on this sort of knowledge (usually at the college level), although it formed the basis of the 1987 study of cultural knowledge (Ravitch and Finn, 1987; Applebee, Langer, and Mullis, 1987).

There is yet another perspective. A growing and vocal minority sees the domain of literature learning as the development of a different kind of reading from that used with other texts. This kind of reading is called "aesthetic" and is opposed to the reading that one does with

informational texts (see Langer, this volume). Recent literary theory
has come to view literature less in terms of the writer and more in
terms of the reader, for it appears to be the reader, particularly the
informed and trained reader, who defines a text as literary and reads
it not for the information but for the experience of its nuances. Such
a definition follows the strand of thinking that developed from I. A.
Richards's *Practical Criticism,* where the idea that the reader helped
form the meaning of the text was given cogent voice. The summary
of the position is best expressed by Louise Rosenblatt, in *The Reader,
the Text, the Poem* (1977), who says that literary texts are grounded in
the real world of writers who may intend them to be seen poetically
or not. Once written, texts become alive only when they are read, and
they become literary when a sufficient body of readers choose to read
them as aesthetic objects rather than as documents. These readers
bring a great deal of background knowledge concerning the substance,
structure, and style of the texts in order to ascertain their meaning
and significance. The meaning is that which can be verified by other
readers and by recourse to the historical grounding of the text if such
is available. The significance is personal or perhaps communal.

In this perspective, a major function of literature education is the
development of what one might call preferences or habits of mind in
reading and writing. One must learn to read aesthetically and to switch
lenses when one moves from social studies to poetry. In addition,
literature education is supposed to develop something called "taste"
or the love of "good literature," so that literature education goes
beyond reading and writing in the inculcation of specific sets of
preferred habits of reading and writing about that particular body of
texts that is termed literature.

Many see these views of the teaching of literature to be in conflict,
but for many teachers they can be held in balance. Rather than being
forced to choose among the three views, I would argue that the domain
of school literature can be divided into three interrelated aspects:
knowledge, practice, and habit. The interrelationships are complex in
that one uses knowledge in the various acts that constitute the practices
and habits, and that the practices and habits can have their influence
on knowledge. At the same time, one can separate them for the
purposes of curriculum planning and, as we shall see, testing. I would
schematize the three subdomains as indicated in figure 1.

Knowledge is divided into that contained in texts, including allusions
to myths and folk tales, and that about the world surrounding the
writing and criticism of texts. Practice is divided into responding, to
cover reading, watching, and listening; and articulating, to cover

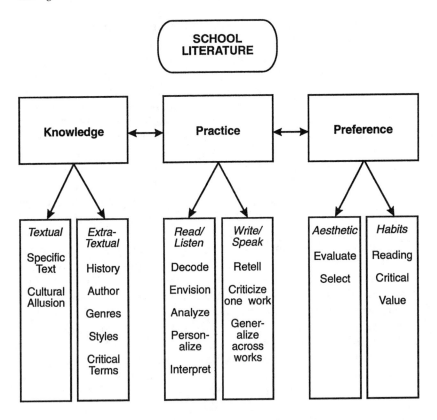

Fig. 1. A model of the domain of school literature.

speaking and writing about individual texts or about literature in general. "Responding" includes decoding or making out the plain sense of the text or film, envisioning or coming to some whole impression and recreation of what is read (Langer, 1990), and the more detailed activities of analyzing, personalizing, and interpreting. Often people envision without analyzing or interpreting.

"Articulating" covers a wide variety of ways by which students let people know what their response is. This is the key to the curriculum in many ways. The study of literature is not just reading in a closet but bringing out into the open an envisionment of what is read. Like any school subject, literature involves public acts in which the student must be articulate about procedures and strategies as well as about conclusions that might be true of the subject outside of school. Proofs are not necessary in mathematical applications outside of school; essays about one's reading of a text are not required after reading every library book.

"Preferred Habits" refers broadly to the set of attitudes, stances, and beliefs encouraged through literature instruction. In order to preserve the aesthetic nature of the text, and treat a work of literature like *Moby Dick* as a novel and not as a treatise on whales, students must learn how to perform this kind of reading, and they must be encouraged to read this way voluntarily. The curriculum, then, must seek to promote habits of mind in reading and writing. One set of these habits concerns the way people make aesthetic judgments about the various texts read and how they justify these judgments publicly.

Since literature education is supposed to develop something called "taste" or the love of "good literature," the curriculum looks beyond reading and writing to the formation of specific sets of preferences and habits of reading and writing. It may include the development of a tolerance for the variety of literature, of a willingness to acknowledge that many different kinds and styles of work can be thought of as literature, and an acceptance that just because we do not like a certain poem does not mean that it is not good. The development of such habits of mind should lead students to acceptance of cultural diversity in literature, and, by, extension, in society.

The curriculum can also lead students to developing a taste based on an awareness of the meretricious or shoddy use of sentiment or language. Experienced readers of literature can see that they are being tricked by a book or a film even when the trickery is going on—and they can enjoy the experience. Like advertising and propaganda, literature manipulates the reader or viewer. The conscious student can be aware of such manipulation and value the craft at the same time as discerning the motives that lie behind it.

I should note that these habits and preferences are culture specific. A dramatic example of the clash of cultural values has occurred over Salman Rushdie's *Satanic Verses*. It is clear that the literary and aesthetic habits of mind in most of the West are not shared by some in the Islamic world. It is also clear that many writers such as Wole Soyinka were themselves torn when they defended Rushdie on Western terms only to find themselves the targets of a group viewing literature in other terms. This issue, writ large in a global scene, also divides the citizens of the United States, as the many censorship cases have attested.

Putting the pieces of the model together rationally would suggest that if we want to measure our students' learning in literature, we will have to attend not only to issues of comprehension and writing about literary texts, but also to knowledge, attitudes, and judgments. This means asking students what they think and feel about what they have read and also asking them whether they know something about literature as an art. Asking these questions might well alert students to our strong belief in the power of literature to move the mind and to affect our lives. We might also ask them how they value literature and the ideals concerning literature which the society professes to hold under the First Amendment and under its other protestations concerning the value of literature and the arts in our society. When we ask these questions as well as the "cognitive" ones, we find that we can better see the effects of our teaching. One study (Ho, 1988) has shown that there is little difference in the "cognitive" outcome of a traditional critical program and a response-centered one; the difference lies in the positive effect the latter has on habits, attitudes, and beliefs.

Difficulty and Growth in Literature Learning

Having established something of the nature of the domain of literature learning, we must confront a second question. What do we know about growth and development? In the knowledge segment of the domain it is easy to talk about knowing more names and facts as being "better" than knowing fewer. The problem is that we haven't reached a clear consensus on the body of important information. That issue would form the topic of a whole volume.

We seem to have greater consensus as to what constitutes growth in habits and preferences. What we, as teachers, value as habits and preferences with respect to literature are generally agreed upon within the profession, even if they are not shared by many of those outside of it. We prefer our students read classics rather than trash, we don't want them to be book-burners, we want them to be tolerant of the opinions of others, and we want them to be consumers of the literary culture if not creators of it.

That leaves for consideration only the area of development in the practice of reading and writing. How do we want our students to develop? One answer is that we want them to be able to read increasingly more difficult works with understanding. But just what does that mean? At the Center, we asked a group of experts to help define the limits of "difficulty in literature" (Purves, 1991, in press). Some were critics, some were linguists, some were classroom researchers. Each wrote from his or her own perspective, yet there was a general consensus that there is no objective criterion by which we can

say that *Heart of Darkness* is more difficult than *The Pearl*. One reason
is that we want students to not simply read the text but articulate
their understanding of it. The reading and the articulation work hand
in hand. The consensus of the experts was that the standards for
learning in literature are those of the community into which a given
individual is entering.

It is not enough for a high school senior to read a poem like "Nikki-
Roosa" by Nikki Giovanni and simply say in class, "Gee, I like it."
That might be all right for the seventh grader. In the classroom
community, the senior is expected to be able to say something about
the theme and its relation to the African American experience and
about the structure and use of language. In an honors class, that senior
might be expected to say something about the switch in point of view
and whether it is a real or apparent switch. In college, as an English
major, the student might be expected to add something about the
historical context of the poem.

Given this idea of differing expectations, I would argue that the
nature of difficulty is a combination of the complexity and detail of
(1) the requisite knowledge to be a member of the community, (2) the
use of that knowledge in responding and articulating, and (3) the use
of that knowledge in making appropriate aesthetic judgments and
distinctions between personal and communal standards in the exercise
of preferences and habitual behaviors with respect to texts. Such a
conception also allows for works to be difficult, not based on some
intrinsic characteristics, but in terms of the reader's community. Shakespeare may be harder or easier depending upon the nature of the
community and its standards concerning knowledge, practice, and
preferred habits and upon the intellectual distance an individual must
travel to enter that community.

The Role of the Community in Literature Learning

This view suggests the importance of literature learning as related to
the idea of community, where the literature curriculum serves the
function of bringing the individual into the community. That is, it
provides the student with the requisite knowledge of the communal
canon as well as the ways of reading that preserve the appropriate
view of the functions of texts in the community. From this experience,
the student also acquires a communal set of values concerning literature
and, perhaps, values arising from the content of the literature that
was read. This has long been the thought of those who create literature

programs in the schools as well as those who write. Shelley claimed poets were the unacknowledged legislators of mankind. Emerson sought to create an American literature that would solidify American values. The community decides what literature is and should be for the reader. The students learn to accept these values as they become members of the community.

The difficulty of a text (D), then, varies with the amount of knowledge concerning the text and its context (K) presumed by the academic community as sufficient for an individual to demonstrate an "adequate" (A) and "appropriate" (A^1) articulation of a response to that text. It may be expressed in the formula: $D = K (A + A^1)$.

Thus, no text is easy or difficult outside of the norms and standards of the community that determines (1) what is necessary and sufficient knowledge, (2) what is an adequately framed discussion of that text or generalization about the text within a larger discussion of literature, and (3) what is an appropriate aesthetic disposition toward the text. The more deeply an individual becomes a member of that community, the easier any text becomes for that individual. Testing, therefore, needs to account for the manifold standards of the community that determine the criteria for success.

Implications for Assessment

In order to make a comprehensive assessment of literature learning, then, a classroom testing program needs to cover the whole of the domain—or at least sample selectively from it. There should be some measure of the knowledge that teachers expect the students to have acquired. This means that teachers must decide which knowledge is important. Is it names and dates? Is it themes, movements, and ideas? Is it critical terms and critical procedures?

The teacher must also set the terms for defining the difficulty of the texts they ask students to read and write about. Is the difficulty to be one of the obscurity of the text or its remoteness from the lives of the students? Is it to be in terms of the subtlety of the emotions or the complexity of the metaphors? On another level, is the difficulty to be with the complexity of what the student is to say about the text? Certainly it is hard to read an unfamiliar text and immediately answer some brief questions about it; how much harder is the task when the student is asked to compose a formal essay judged on content, organization, and style? Should a teacher ask students what general principles they have discovered about literature?

The teacher must also determine what attitudes, interests, and habits to measure. Should one ask about the students' taste, or the premises underlying that taste? Should the teacher find out if the students have become more intense readers, making deeper connections with their reading? Should the students be measured for their interest in reading and viewing, for their beliefs about the role of literature in society? All of these are questions that need to be asked in framing a comprehensive assessment program for literature learning.

The Center has been conducting a series of pilot tests of our model and its assessment to come up with a program that might be used by a school—or a state for that matter (Purves, Shirk, and Li, 1990; Li, Purves, and Shirk, 1991). The principle behind the testing is that knowledge, practice, and preference are related but not highly inter-related aspects of the construct of literature learning. A comprehensive measure of student performance, therefore, should address each of the three areas. From the pilot tests we found that within the knowledge domain, textual knowledge and knowledge of critical terms are distinct, particularly in their relationship to the practice of reading and respond-ing. Within the domain of practice, more than one passage is needed to get some estimate of a student's performance across text types. It seems to make little difference whether one uses open-ended or multiple-choice questions, but one can argue on other grounds that open-ended questions probably present somewhat more of a challenge to students than multiple-choice questions (Hansson, 1990), and would therefore be a more exacting measure of the ability to read and shape a response to what is read.

It is clear that an extended response is also desirable, but the question might be phrased to allow the student some preparation for writing a fully developed composition. A stark question is less desirable than a question that builds upon another sort of task, one that gets the student to consider the text in question (Hansson, 1990). A combination of multiple-choice and essay, or scale and essay, might be the optimum measures.

In the realm of preference, it would appear important to separate the student's criteria for judging a text from the judgment itself. It would also appear to be important to get a depiction of the general attitudes towards literature, including censorship, since, clearly, these appear to be related to cognitive performance (whether in an antecedent or consequent role remains unclear).

From these conclusions we derived an assessment of student learning in literature that would include the following measures:

1. Measures of background knowledge—terminology and cultural information: these may include matching, and supplying or generating items.

2. Measures of the ability to read and to articulate a written response to at least two texts that differ in genre, the measures to include both supplying and constructing items, with the latter taking the form of extended discourse.

3. Measures of preference including aesthetic judgment of specific texts, and general habits and beliefs concerning literature and its place in the world.

Such an assessment provides a more comprehensive picture of student learning and also of program effectiveness than does any one measure taken alone.

If we consider the criteria attached to these measures, we could offer the following definition of an "ideal" United States secondary student of literature. Giving the test can help teachers find out whether such a student exists. A good literature student is clever, articulate, knowledgeable, and committed to literature and the literary experience. Such a student can read a text and answer specific questions concerning its content, structure, and form; can write an extended response to a text; knows something of the cultural matrix of literature and of the nature of the language used in discussing literature. And such a student is a reader who becomes involved in the text, likes to read, and respects literature enough to be chary of the censor's red pen.

A recent study (Ho, 1988) showed that a complex measure such as this also served best to validate a type of instruction. If the intention of the instruction is to make classroom exploration of literature more open and to use more "real" and thought-provoking questioning than normal instruction, its validation must include measures of both practice and preference.

In the most recent phase of the work of the Center, we gave a comprehensive test to nearly a thousand secondary school students in New York, California, and Wisconsin. The experience of creating a domain-referenced evaluation of literature learning at the secondary school level brought with it some conclusions both about testing and about literature learning. The test results confirm that the three subdomains of knowledge, practice, and habits or preferences are distinct yet related. Knowledge affects practice but is not a substitute for it; the same can be said for interests and qualities of reading. Within the field of practice, there seems to be a distinction between demonstrating one's understanding of a text and articulating a sustained response to a text. Reading and writing, indeed, are related, but they are not equivalent.

When we examined the results of our testing, we found that few ideal students exist in the sample we tested. The composite student in our sample is more complex. Students who can answer the critical questions may not be the best writers of extended prose, nor can they be unless helped with some mediated response. These same "good readers" do possess background knowledge, but they are not necessarily readers who get deeply involved in what they read, nor are they particularly interested in reading literature. The "total" literature student is a fiction rather than a reality. The students can compartmentalize themselves. It may in fact be true that to be a clever reader, it is better not to be a committed one. It may also be that we in the schools have placed a premium on cleverness rather than commitment.

This inference is supported by several students commenting that they thought it inappropriate for teachers to ask for their beliefs and opinions in a test. To ask for cognitive performance is all right, they said, but not to ask what they think. Such an opinion is shaped by their perceptions of appropriate testing and, by extension, appropriate teaching. This finding is corroborated by the parallel study asking students to define the characteristics of a good literature student in secondary schools, which suggests that they see the school placing a premium on cleverness, that literature as a school subject is something to get the right answer about rather than to experience aesthetically or become attached to. For students, only a semblance of interest seems appropriate and only a modicum of knowledge is useful to test taking.

The tests that we have experimented with are imperfect measures, as all tests are. I would not advocate any district or teacher buying them. In their totality, however, they suggest that a school, a district, or a state is able to get some picture of what students in literature look like. They form the outlines of a portrait of the typical product of our schools. Whether it is a portrait that we like is indeed an issue of concern. We suggest that the actual picture we found is not a flattering one.

Our testing provided a school-by-school profile that enabled the English teachers to see what their students looked like against the national average as well as against the ideal. It is my belief that such profiles present teachers with a better way of seeing what sort of students of literature their students are than is provided by a single score on a reading test. Are our students clever readers or good readers? Are they going to be the impassioned students we sometimes read about? Are they the ones who go for the grade and the right answer without being moved by the passion and artistry of the works they read? Or are they those who can strike an appropriate balance in their encounters with literature? We won't know unless we find out.

References

Applebee, A.N. (1989). *The teaching of literature in programs with reputations for excellence in English* (Report Series 1.1). Albany, NY: Center for the Learning and Teaching of Literature, SUNY at Albany.

Brody, P., DeMilo, C., and Purves, A.C. (1989). *The current state of assessment in literature* (Report Series 3.1). Albany, NY: Center for the Learning and Teaching of Literature, SUNY at Albany.

Goodman, K. (1984). Unity in reading. In A.C. Purves and O. Niles (Eds.), *Becoming readers in a complex society*. Chicago: National Society for the Study of Education, 79–114.

Hansson, G. (1990). *Reading and understanding literature* (Report Series 4.5). Albany, NY: Center for the Learning and Teaching of Literature, SUNY at Albany.

Ho, B. (1988). *An investigation of two methods of teaching poetry to secondary students*. Unpublished masters thesis, National University of Singapore, Singapore.

Langer, J.A. (1990). *Literary understanding and literature instruction* (Report Series 2.11). Albany, NY: Center for the Learning and Teaching of Literature, SUNY at Albany.

Li, H., Purves, A.C., and Shirk, M. (1991). *Prototype measures of the domain of learning in literature* (Report Series 3.3). Albany, NY: Center for the Learning and Teaching of Literature, SUNY at Albany.

Pearson, P.D. and Tierney, R.J. (1984). On becoming a thoughtful reader: Learning to read like a writer. In A.C. Purves and O. Niles (Eds.), *Becoming readers in a complex society*. Chicago: National Society for the Study of Education, 144–174.

Purves, A.C. et al. (1980). *Achievement in reading and literature: The United States in international perspective*. Urbana, IL: National Council of Teachers of English.

Purves, A.C. (1985). The potential and real achievement of U.S. students in school reading. *American Journal of Education, 93,* 82–106.

Purves, A.C. (1987). Literacy, culture and community. In D.A. Wagner (Ed.), *The future of literacy in a changing world*. Oxford: Pergamon Press.

Purves, A.C. (1990). *The scribal society*. White Plains, NY: Longmans.

Purves, A.C., Shirk, M., and Li, H. (1990). *A tentative model for the assessment of learning in literature* (Report Series 3.3). Albany, NY: Center for the Learning and Teaching of Literature, SUNY at Albany.

Ravitch, D. and Finn, C.E., Jr. (1987). *What do our 17-year-olds know*. Boston: Houghton Mifflin.

Richards, I.A. (1929). *Practical criticism: A study of literary judgement*. New York: Harcourt Brace.

Rosenblatt, L. (1977). *The reader, the text, the poem: The transactional theory of the literary work.* Carbondale, IL: Southern Illinois University Press.

Takala, S. (1983). Achievement and the domain of school writing. Urbana, IL: IEA Written Composition Study.

Walmsley, S. and Walp, T. (1989). *Teaching literature in the elementary school* (Report Series 1.3). Albany, NY: Center for the Learning and Teaching of Literature, SUNY at Albany.

3 Rethinking Literature Instruction

Judith A. Langer
State University of New York at Albany

The need to reexamine the role of literature in the educational experience of young people is particularly acute at this time, when the nation as a whole is attempting to redefine its educational goals and objectives. Although the various reform movements have had many dimensions, one central theme has been the need to develop students' thinking abilities—the complex ways of approaching issues that underlie disciplined and reasoned thought. However, too often educators have turned to generic problem-solving approaches as the focus of reform, with identified "critical thinking" strategies applied in similar ways across the different academic subjects (see, for example, Swartz and Perkins, 1990).

In this chapter, I propose a series of ways to think about literature and its teaching that will help us move beyond such notions, making distinctions among meaning-making strategies based upon the different purposes for which people read—in this case whether people read to engage in a literary experience or to gain information. My argument has three parts: (1) that literature is indeed a distinct way of knowing, with its own special orientation toward meaning; (2) that processes of understanding literature have distinct patterns that provide a way to think about the kinds of questions we ask and the support we provide; and (3) that by modifying our approaches to instruction in particular ways, we can more effectively support the teaching and learning of literature.

For the past few years, I have been developing an underlying theory for the teaching of literature. As part of this work, I have been studying the nature of literary understanding and the ways in which it differs from approaches to understanding other course work (see Langer, 1989, 1990a), and have been using this information as a way to rethink literature instruction (see Langer, 1990b, 1991; Roberts and Langer, 1991). Here, I will discuss literature and the process of literary

35

understanding, and then the implications for instruction. I will elaborate my discussion with examples from a multiyear collaborative project involving fifteen teachers from a variety of city and suburban schools.

What Is Literary about Literature?

When contemplating educational reform, it is important that we consider the unique contribution that English language arts instruction can make to students' intellectual development. Over the years, scholars have made distinctions between literary and scientific ways of thinking, suggesting that together they form the multiple sources of reason people draw upon when constructing meaning. In this tradition, Suzanne Langer (1942; 1967) speaks of subjective and objective realities, Louise Rosenblatt (1978) speaks of aesthetic and efferent readings, James Britton (1970) speaks of spectator and participant roles, and Jerome Bruner (1986) speaks of narrative and paradigmatic thought. Although developed for different purposes, each set of distinctions focuses on qualitative differences between experiences that have literary and informative purposes. Each conceives of two kinds of approaches to reasoning that are available within the human consciousness: on the one hand, a situation where the language user engages in a lived-through experience, and, on the other hand, a situation where the language user holds meaning apart in quest of a more rational or logical understanding. One is more subjective, focusing inward on personal meanings, the other more objective, focusing outside of the individual's personal life-world. Each of these commentators views subjective experience (such as that involved in literary meaning making) as a natural and necessary part of the well-developed intellect— different from, but as valued as, objective experience.

Although the development of logical thought has tended to be the primary focus in school course work, there is growing evidence that the processes involved in understanding literature are also productive and important in dealing with problems of everyday life and work. For example, a growing body of study indicates that doctors, physicians, lawyers, and computer repairers use both modes of thought to solve problems (e.g., Dworkin, 1983; Elstein, Shulman, and Sprafka, 1978; Orr, 1987a; Putnam, 1978). This work describes ways in which professionals who usually take a "logical" approach to problem solving productively turn to storytelling to help them work through difficult problems and develop possible solutions. However, while such work indicates the importance of storytelling as a means of problem solving, the process of storytelling as a way of thinking has been largely unexplored, and the connection between such thinking and the goals and processes of literature instruction needs to be made more explicit.

Orientations toward Understanding—one body of work (see Langer, 1989, 1990a) helps explain some basic distinctions between readers' approaches toward meaning when they are reading in order to engage in a literary experience in contrast to when they are reading in order to gain information. Although both purposes can interplay during any one reading experience (e.g., living through the characters' experiences in a novel, yet learning about particular events in the Civil War), each reading tends to have a primary purpose (in this case to engage in a literary experience) with other goals being secondary. It is this primary purpose that guides readers' overall approach to meaning making, moving them toward one or another of two distinctly different orientations. In both cases the meanings they develop are guided by their sense of the whole—a sense of what the piece is all about. However, it is also this sense of the overall whole that differs when reading for literary and informational purposes, causing readers to orient themselves in different ways because their expectations about the kinds of meanings to be derived when reading for one or the other purpose are different.

When readers engage in a literary experience, their orientations can be characterized as *reaching toward a horizon of possibilities*; they make sense of new parts of the text in terms of their sense of the whole, but they also use the new text to reconsider that whole as well. A literary orientation is one of exploration—where uncertainty is a normal part of response and newfound understandings provoke still other possibilities. Readers contemplate feelings, intentions, and implications, using their knowledge of human possibility to go beyond the meanings imparted in the text and fill out their understandings. In this way, readers explore possibilities on two levels: in terms of their momentary understandings, and in terms of their changing sense of the unfolding whole.

In contrast, when the purpose of reading is primarily to gain information (as is generally the case when reading expository prose, for example), readers' orientation can be characterized as *maintaining a point of reference*. From early on, they attempt to establish a sense of what the topic is or the slant the author is taking toward it. Once done, this sense of the whole—where the piece is going—becomes a relatively steady reference point. Unlike the frequent reconsiderations of the possibilities of the whole that readers engage in during a literary reading, when reading for information, readers attempt to build upon, clarify, or modify their momentary understandings but rarely change their overall sense of the topic or point; their sense of the whole changes only when a substantial amount of countervailing information leads them to rethink their general sense of what the piece is about.

These notions provide us with ways to conceptualize the process of meaning development during the literary experience, and to recognize how it differs from the process of understanding when reading for other purposes. They also can help us rethink the role literature instruction might play in students' intellectual development: students need to learn to use literary approaches to create "poems" in Rosenblatt's (1978) sense, as well as to learn the approaches needed to gain information. As Bruner (1986) argues, we need to call on the strengths of both modes in academic study and in everyday life. The development of students' abilities to engage in literary understanding is a unique contribution that literature education can make.

However, we have ample evidence that across the United States, literature is too often taught and tested in a nonliterary manner. In a series of studies of the questions asked in anthologies as well as on a range of tests, Brody, DeMilo, and Purves (1989) report that literature is usually treated as content (a point of reference), with a particular right answer as the goal of testing. Similarly, studies of classroom discussion indicate that literature tends to be taught in an informational manner (Applebee, 1989), as if there is a point to be gotten or a correct interpretation the reader must move toward. Schooling rarely asks students to share their own understandings of a text, nor does it help students learn to build richer ones through the exploration of possibilities.

Yet, making the distinction between exploring possibilities and maintaining a point of reference has the potential to influence the ways in which literature education is perceived at a policy level—in terms of its contribution to students' general intellectual development, and also in terms of its implications for instruction. On the one hand it suggests that business cannot go on as usual, with reform efforts in critical thinking treating literary instruction similarly to other course work, and on the other it suggests the need for some shifts in goals and apparatus generally associated with literature instruction. For example, the kinds of questions asked of students will need to differ when reading is for literary as opposed to informative purposes, focusing on the possibilities students consider on the one hand and on the content they come away with on the other. The kinds of help given and evaluations made will also need to differ, with teachers, instructional materials, and tests validating different approaches toward meaning-making based upon purpose, as opposed to the unidimensional valuing of informational approaches that presently exists.

Thus, English educators—teachers, policymakers, test developers, and publishers, as well as researchers and teacher trainers—have a job to do. We need to develop a better way of thinking about the process of literary understanding—and a common language to talk about, support, value, and teach it.

What Does It Mean to Understand Literature?

Such changes will need to be guided by a view of meaning development as an act of sense making rather than fact finding. (While the act of locating information is a necessary and often useful activity, the "search and lift out" behaviors needed to accomplish such tasks differ from those used to make overall sense of a piece of text.) Sense-making reading experiences involve a process of meaning change, where understandings flex and grow over time. I use the word "envisionment" (see Fillmore, 1981; Langer, 1985, 1986, 1987, 1989, 1990a, b) to refer to the understanding a reader has about a text at a particular point in time; what the reader understands, the questions that develop, as well as the hunches that arise about how the piece might unfold. A reader has many different envisionments (or text-worlds) throughout the reading of a particular piece—they change because as reading continues some information is no longer seen as important, some is added to the reader's consciousness, and some earlier interpretations are changed. What readers come away with at the end of a reading is a final envisionment. This includes what they understand, what they don't, and the questions they still have. Therefore, the final envisionment is also subject to change with further time and thought.

Although this constructivist view of reading has become fairly well accepted in the research literature (see, for example, Goodman, 1970; Iser, 1978; Rumelhart, 1975; Spiro, Bruce, and Brewer, 1980; Suleiman and Crosman, 1980), its implications for instruction have barely been considered, although they can have considerable impact on the questions we ask students as well as what we consider "acceptable understanding." If we believe that understanding changes as readers move through a text, then we must also accept that what students come away with at the end of a reading are not the bits of information that appeared in the text, but their final envisionments—the text-world they have constructed (see Langer, 1986, 1987a, b). If we wish to discuss students' understandings of the text, literal and inferential questions do not work, nor do activities such as the traditional retracing of the plot line; such questions are text-based and do not reflect the envisionment-building process the student has gone through. Instead, we need to ask questions that tap these final envisionments; although we don't want to end there, it is the most meaningful place to begin.

How Do These Envisionments Develop?

During reading, there are a series of stances or relationships the reader takes toward the text, each adding a somewhat different dimension to the reader's growing understanding of the piece. (See Langer, 1989, 1990a, for a more elaborated discussion of stances.) These stances are recursive (having the potential to recur at any point in the reading) rather than linear and are a function of varying reader/text relationships. They are

- *Being Out and Stepping Into an Envisionment.* In this stance, readers attempt to make contacts with the world of the text by using prior knowledge, experiences, and surface features of the text to identify essential elements (e.g., genre, content, structure, language) in order to begin to construct an envisionment.

- *Being In and Moving Through an Envisionment.* In this stance, readers are immersed in their understandings, using their previously constructed envisionment, prior knowledge, and the text itself to further their creation of meaning. As they read more, meaning making moves along with the text; readers are caught up in the narrative of a story or are carried along by the argument of an informative text.

- *Stepping Back and Rethinking What One Knows.* In this stance, readers use their envisionments of the text to reflect on their own previous knowledge or understandings. Rather than prior knowledge informing their envisionments as in the other stances, in this case readers use their envisionments of the text to rethink their prior knowledge.

- *Stepping Out and Objectifying the Experience.* In this stance, readers distance themselves from their envisionments, reflecting on and reacting to the content, to the text, or to the reading experience itself.

Over time, understanding grows from meanings readers derive from the various stances they take along the way—getting acquainted, using meaning to build meaning, associating and reflecting, and distancing.

Through these shifting relationships between self and text, readers structure their own understandings.

Thus, the notion of stances has the potential to help us understand where and what kind of support to provide in helping students move through the process of coming to understand literature. It suggests the kinds of instruction that will support readers in developing their understandings—where instruction can focus on the reader's process of thinking through the content. In doing so it also raises questions about the efficacy of some instructional procedures widely used in English classes. For example, questions that focus on the concerns readers have as they move through the stances use the students' processes as the starting place in opening discussions, asking questions, offering assistance, and making assignments. From this vantage point, comprehension cannot be conceptualized as either literal or inferential (or as plot summary), since these distinctions are text based, and assume that information presented at different points in the text combines without the visions of possibilities engaged in by the reader. Nor can it be considered in terms of a taxonomy of discrete levels of abstraction where the words and their possibilities do not constantly interplay. Such distinctions simply do not reflect real processes of reading and understanding, where stances shift and horizons evolve as readers' envisionments build (Langer, 1985, 1987).

The stances can also help us understand the particular difficulties that some readers face in their reading. For example, poor readers often spend much more time in the "being out and stepping into an envisionment" stance (see Langer, 1991; Purcell-Gates, in press). Although they enter the other stances at least some of the time, their problem seems to lie more with their ability to develop a depth of understanding—a sufficiently rich envisionment in *any* of the stances to sustain and build upon it. Instead, unexpected events, unfamiliar formats, or new language can cause them to lose their present envisionment, sending them back into the first stance, once again in search of an array of initial information familiar enough to allow them to "step in" again.

Even good readers face similar problems when they are confronted with more difficult texts. At any point where the language or ideas they are reading about are sufficiently discordant with their envisionments, readers might return to a "being out and stepping in" stance in order to gather enough basic knowledge to permit them to continue their move through the piece. In such cases, either their envisionments are too sparse to offer clues, or they do not adequately search their envisionments for clues.

Posing questions that ask students to share and discuss their envisionments can support them through a difficult part of the piece yet still leave room for them to continue building envisionments on their own. Asking questions that help students explore their envisionments, that guide the students to explore possible meanings beyond those they already have considered within a particular stance, have the potential to help them learn ways in which they can enrich their envisionments on their own. Questions that focus primarily on stepping out and going beyond, the kinds of questions that ask students to trace the plot line, analyze characters and events, or focus on the language, organization, or literary elements in the piece (the kinds of questions often asked in English classes), are likely to be helpful only later in the process.

What Might Such an Instructional Context Look Like?

For the past few years, I have been studying what these notions of envisionments, stances, and orientations mean for the teaching of literature (see Langer, 1987, 1990a, 1991; Roberts and Langer, 1991), identifying ways in which classrooms can become environments that encourage students to arrive at their own understandings, explore possibilities, and move beyond their initial understandings toward more thoughtful interpretations. From this work, I have distilled some general principles of instruction that permeate classrooms that encourage students to think.

Students as Thinkers

Students are treated as thinkers, as if they can and do have interesting and cogent thoughts about the pieces they read, and also have questions they would like to discuss. Teachers provide students with ownership for the topics of discussion, making students' understandings the central focus of each class meeting.

The following are examples of questions teachers use to begin a lesson, indicating that they are interested in students' responses rather than predetermined "right" interpretations:

> *Teacher:* How did you feel at the end of the story?
> *Teacher:* What was on your mind?
> *Teacher:* What did it mean to you?
> *Teacher:* Anything you want to talk about?
> *Teacher:* Caly, why don't you start us off?

Prompted in this way, these class discussions begin with the students' envisionments, permitting them to voice their initial impressions, to raise questions, to introduce possibilities, to hear others, and to think beyond.

After the lesson is under way, there are continuing invitations for students to think about and contribute to the ongoing discussion. For example:

> *Teacher:* Would someone like to comment on that point?
> *Teacher:* O.K. Anybody want to add to what Sido . . .
> *Teacher:* . . . And Iris, you said?

Group work also provides students with opportunities to explore their understandings. Sometimes these discussions focus on topics the teacher has set, but most often these work best when students are encouraged to discuss their initial impressions, raise questions, review predictions or responses they have written in their journals, or to address issues they think are interesting for the group to consider. Such discussions provide a forum for students to explore their own ideas, and to help each other move beyond their initial impressions. As one student put it,

> When we have our discussions, we learn a lot from each other. We can really give each other ideas. It's not just one person's ideas, it's all of them together.

Written assignments such as logs, "briefwrites," informal letters, and written conversations, in addition to more formal reviews, essays, and analytical papers, also encourage students to reflect on, state, defend, and rethink their responses. Students can be encouraged to keep literature journals, and also to use them on a regular basis during class discussions, small-group meetings, and when they write alone or with someone else. Among other things, students are asked to jot down any questions they have; to make predictions about how they think characters feel, what might happen next, or how the piece might turn out; to note their ideas about the piece up to that point in their reading; to note what they do or do not like or agree with, and why; or to make notes about anything else they have read or seen that they were reminded of when reading this piece. They are also encouraged to use their journals as discussion starters. For example, one middle-grade remedial reading teacher had her students reread a poem they had read at home (homework assignment), and then suggested, "Jot down any ideas you have about the poem. . . . and what it means to you." The students' comments became the focus of discussion, beginning with the teacher's initial question, "So, what does it mean to you?"

In each case, the continual focus on students' developing understandings—exploring them, talking about them, and refining them—
offers ways in which students are encouraged to realize that acceptable
behavior in this class involves thinking about the piece being read,
focusing on developing ideas, and sharing responses with classmates.

Literature Reading as Question Generating

Teachers who support literary understanding assume that after completing a piece, readers come away with questions as well as understandings, and that responding to literature *involves* the raising of
questions. Thus, teachers continually invite students' questions, in
many contexts. For example, they invite students' questions at the very
beginning of a new work:

> *Teacher:* Look at the title and the picture. Any questions come to
> mind?

They also use homework as an opportunity for students to become
aware of their questions. For example:

> *Teacher:* Read the next chapter. Come in with a question for us
> to discuss.

They also invite questions during class discussion:

> *Teacher:* Is there anything more you'd like to talk about regarding
> these chapters?
> *Teacher:* Do you have any questions about what is so great about
> Gatsby. . . . I know Brig isn't the only one that has that question.
> *Teacher:* Do you have any problems with what's happening?
> *Teacher:* Any questions?

In more traditional classrooms, having questions signifies that a student
doesn't know (the "right" answer) and therefore question asking is
often avoided by students. However, in classrooms that support literary
understanding, it is considered a desirable behavior, indicating that
students who ponder uncertainties and ambiguities and explore possibilities are behaving as *good* readers of literature.

Student Knowledge Taps

In lessons where students were involved in literary thinking, teachers'
questions tap students' knowledge, not the teacher's expected response.
Such questions are concerned with what the students understand or
are concerned with. Student knowledge taps are questions that have

no right answers and prompt extended language and thought. Examples follow:

> *Teacher:* What do you think is happening to his life?
>
> *Teacher:* Ron, how is she more mature?
>
> *Teacher:* What are you making of the book so far?
>
> *Teacher:* Could you continue just a little bit more? Can anyone add to this, expand on this?

Class Meetings as Time to Develop Understandings

When students engage in literary thinking, the relationships they take toward the text recapitulate the stances and orientations toward meaning that characterize the process of literary understanding during reading. Thus, their recursive movements through the stances and exploration of possibilities lead them to a final envisionment after reading that can then become the starting place for exploring further understandings during the class discussion. The following segment, from a few minutes into the class discussion, illustrates this:

> *Sheila:* I didn't like the ending either. Because it just seemed like towards the ending, I mean, at the beginning of the book Lisa wasn't the only person with ideas. But towards the ending, the kids seemed to be like really dumb. And they were just, "We need Lisa, we can't survive without her." And I just, this is like another topic, sort of, but it goes into this, it all seems like that isn't very realistic at all. I mean, I don't see how one person can be smart and have all these ideas, and the rest of them be like frogs.
>
> *Teacher:* So, you're very unhappy with the idea that there's just one person who seems to be able to pick up the leadership and go, and that's not, to use the word, realistic. . . . Kent?
>
> *Kent:* I disagree with her, her, her, and her. (Pointing over and over at one person.)
>
> *Teacher:* What?
>
> *Kent:* Because she says everything wasn't so peachy dandy. . . .
>
> *Charlene:* What about all the other gangs, and the food?
>
> *Kent:* The Chicago gang. Who cares about them?
>
> *Charlene:* What about the other gangs in the city where they used to live? I mean, Tom Logan wasn't the only gang.
>
> *Teacher:* One at a time.
>
> *Gep:* After they demolished Tom Logan's gang, a lot of other gangs did not want to mess with them.
>
> *Charlene:* But what happens if the other gangs join up? You know that is possible.
>
> *Teacher:* O.K. Let's go here with Betsy.

Betsy: I sort of agree with Sheila, because the end is like, unreal, okay? Unreal. . . .

In this instance, a seventh-grade class was discussing their reading of *Girl Who Owned a City* by O. T. Nelson. Sheila makes a stance 4 (stepping out and objectifying the experience) statement, judging the piece and explaining why. Kent makes a 4th-stance response to something Charlene had said earlier, and then shifts to a 4th-stance focus on his view of the ending. Charlene, assuming the 2nd stance (being in and moving through an envisionment), reworks her understanding as she explains it to Kent in her next two turns. Gep continues to work through Charlene's contention that the ending wasn't "peachy," and Charlene adds more for them to think about. Betsy, convinced for the present of the unhappy ending interpretation being developed by Sheila, Charlene, and Gep, does not rework the ideas as they have done, but objectifies the piece by stating her judgment of the ending. Thus, in this section, the students have entered the 4th stance in making judgments about the piece, and have used the 2nd stance to explain and rethink their understandings that underlie these judgments. In addition, the students almost always adopt a literary orientation as they reach toward a horizon of possibilities. For example, Sheila does this with the implicit question "Why did the kids change from having ideas at the beginning of the book to being dumb at the end?" Charlene is explicit as she twice raises the problem of the other gangs, while Gep implicitly opens exploration of the gang's relationship with other gangs. In this way, class discussion serves as a time when the students individually and collectively participate in reworking their interpretations, raising questions, exploring possibilities, and getting deeper into the piece by moving in and out of the four stances.

Instruction as Scaffolding the Process of Understanding

The roles of the teacher and of the student change dramatically in such classrooms, taking the form of a collaborative interaction where the teacher encourages the students to work through their understandings on their own, but also helps them in appropriate ways when this is necessary, accelerating or reducing the complexity of the task in response to what the students are trying to accomplish. In such situations, teachers do not serve as the sole holders of knowledge, and provide almost no evaluating or correcting during class discussion. Instead, they help the students find more appropriate ways to think about and discuss what they read.

Scaffolding Ways To Discuss

Teachers help students learn how to engage in a literary discussion by letting them know what is appropriate to talk about in a literature discussion in their classes (e.g., about students' understandings and questions as opposed to what they think the teacher thinks is "right"). This is done by:

a. Tapping the students' understandings—teachers indicate that students' understandings are the central concern of the discussion by asking questions that invite students to express their ideas and questions. For example, an urban middle school class read the poem "The Duel," by Emily Dickinson, together two times. Then their teacher asked them to read it once again to themselves, and to take five minutes to write their responses in their literature journals. Then they discussed their responses with a partner for about seven minutes. After each pair was finished, they turned their desks in toward the center of the room into a loose circle facing each other, with the teacher seated in the circle as well. Then the discussion began:

Teacher: Let's hear your thoughts. Talk to each other about what you have come up with.

Tish: I heard you (looking at Lenny) talking and I heard you had a question. What was your question?

Lenny: I asked about "I aimed my pebble, but myself" because I didn't understand it.

Tish: He tried to shoot Goliath.

Lenny: No, Up at line 5, "but himself."

Tish: He only fell.

Lenny: (asking Desmond) What have you got?

Desmond: The bully was losing the fight with. . . .

b. Seeking clarification—teachers indicate that clarity of thought is important in class discussions of literature by asking for clarification or restatements when the students' comments are muddy. This can be done in a number of ways. For example:

Teacher: Could you continue just a little bit more, so I get your idea?

Teacher: "Brought out in the open." What is it that we see in the open?

Teacher: Alright, now we have a different interpretation here. Are you saying, even though he didn't do it he would have liked to have done it?

Teacher: O.K., so you think it's made up in his mind?

Teacher: Maybe you need to describe it for more people to understand.

c. Inviting participation—teachers help students learn to "enter" and take their turn in a literature discussion by inviting them to speak and suggesting a direction for their response. For example:

Teacher: Michael, what do you think?
Teacher: What do you think of what Rhonda said?
Teacher: How do you think he's trying to do that?
Teacher: How does he do that, Silvie?

d. Orchestrating the discussion—teachers show students how to "converse"—how to connect ideas, how to agree, disagree, and extend the ideas being discussed by the group, and how to signal this in conversation. Some examples are:

Teacher: Mark, say it so everybody can hear it.
Teacher: Let her finish.
Teacher: But Rick's point is, listen to Rick's point. He's saying it doesn't matter.
Teacher: Raquelle, do you agree with what Tony is saying?
Teacher: . . . But I think if you listen to each other there are a lot of different ways to see what's going on. So, we don't have to take the first answer and say that's it.

Scaffolding Ways to Think

Teachers also help students learn how to think about the content. They do this by indicating alternative (and often more sophisticated) ways to think about the ideas being discussed.

a. Focusing—teachers help students narrow in on the particular concern they wish to discuss instead of moving into a more general commentary that leaves the listener (or reader) uncertain about the student's actual concern. One such example of a teacher's request for clarification which occurred during a discussion of *The Great Gatsby* follows:

Harry: What's so great about Gatsby? That's what I want to know.
Teacher: Do you have any guesses? . . .
Rhonda: . . . It's like because he's throwing all these parties and he's making himself so popular, and it's more or less so far. It's like he's the one who's making himself pretty. Nobody has really, you know, said he's great because you, it's just more or less him throwing these great parties and doing all different kinds of things . . . All his money, nothing to write about (mumble). I'm sure people admire that.

Teacher: Are you saying that that's what may be great about him?

Rhonda: Well, I don't think there's enough information on him. . . .

b. Shaping—teachers help students tighten their presentation, as in the following example:

Teacher: Bob, you said something that was really interesting about Gatsby and trying; he is great because why again?

Bob: Because like he was in the war; he kept trying to get himself killed but it always turned out he did something, you know, beneficial. And got rewarded for it.

Teacher: You said something about his ego?

c. Linking—teachers also show their students how to use information from other parts of the reading, the discussion, or related experiences to enrich their own developing interpretations or to gain new insights. In the following example, Stella's teacher helps her pay attention to what other students have already said in the discussion:

Stella: Maybe he's thinking of something that happened to them in the past. I still think he has a big ego, but maybe he feels really nervous about being around Daisy. Not just any woman, just Daisy.

Teacher: What do you think of what Rhonda said? . . .

Stella: It still doesn't matter. If you have a big ego, it doesn't matter. He'll think, well, that was before; now look at me now (mumble), that was a long time ago. If he had such a big ego, it wouldn't matter. It's like, he would just care about himself. For some reason he cares about her very much and is really worried about what she thinks.

d. Upping the ante—teachers also help students move beyond their already established ways of approaching concerns by providing them with new and sometimes less obvious ways to think about the issues. For example, after the class had explored many of their reasons for not liking the end of the poem "Sign for My Father, Who Stressed the Bunt" because it seemed simplistic to them, this teacher provided them with a new vantage point from which to consider the poem by saying:

Ross: Well, why he was on these teams and he didn't know about, he knew about hunting, but he always wanted, like Brendan was saying, to be in the limelight. He never like really spared his life to get out. . . . He always wanted to be the one to go all the way around.

Teacher: . . . Let me ask this question to see if it helps. . . . Is there a passage of time?

Ross: . . . Alright, there's different leagues, and you start off

like. . . . like there's minors, start with pee wees. . . . It's different age groups.

Brendan: Like six years he's probably talkin' about going from
minors to majors.

In each of these cases, teachers provide students with new ways to
talk about and think about the literature they are reading for class,
helping them become active participants in thoughtful literature lessons.

Transfer of Control from Teacher to Student

To help their students become independent thinkers and learners,
teachers encourage them to take on roles for themselves that their
teacher has previously assumed. In this way, students come to understand and internalize the ways of talking about and thinking about
literature that have already been demonstrated for them. One remedial
student who had provided a particularly thoughtful analysis during a
small-group discussion was asked by his teacher how he knew what
were the most important issues to think about and discuss; he said,
"I knew what you would ask me [even though you weren't there]."
Thus, in a Vygotskian sense, learning how to think and reason about
literature moved from the interpsychological plane (the socially based
interactions where ways to think about literature were modeled by
the teacher) to the intrapsychological plane (where the individuals
internalized the underlying rules their teachers had previously demonstrated for them).

Further, small-group discussions serve as an interim social environment, where students have an opportunity to take over the teacher's
role as they interact with each other. During these small-group work
sessions, they are encouraged to treat each other as thinkers, following
the patterns of thought and interaction that have been previously
demonstrated by their teacher. During these small-group meetings the
teacher often visits each group, taking the role of participant observer—
asking pertinent questions and providing models of how to structure
thought in ways the students are not yet doing.

Thus, in response to instructional support the teacher provides in
the whole-class sessions and the support provided when they are
trying to assume these behaviors on their own, students come to
engage in authentic discussions about literature; they agree and disagree
with each other, challenge each other, and defend their views. In the
following example of a student discussion, we can see how they help
focus, shape, and link what others have said, as well as seek each
others' opinions and challenge each other to rethink.

Student: I want to ask the others if they thought Lisa was city bound.

Student: What about the rest of you. Would you do as she did?

Student: I'm agreeing with those kids, but when things were going well . . .

Student: Show me why you think so. Where did you get it from?

Student: I disagree with her and her and her and him, but I agree with Tom because . . .

Student: What about all the other gangs, and the food?

Student: I felt that in the third part it was a little different . . .

In general, then, when these principles characterize the instructional environment, students are supported to become socialized to engage in the process of literary understanding, exploring, rethinking, explaining, and defending their own understandings. The social structure of such classrooms calls for (and expects) the thoughtful participation of all students, and provides them with the environment in which they can see, learn, and practice these expected behaviors.

Conclusions

In this chapter, I have discussed characteristics of literary understanding and characteristics of English language arts classrooms that support such understanding. The three-part focus (on literature as a distinct way of knowing with its own special orientation toward meaning; on the processes of understanding literature and the patterns they take; and on general principles of instruction that support the process of literary understanding) may prove useful as a framework for reflection and change. While my comments suggest ways to rethink the teaching and learning of literature, they do not propose a wholesale abandonment of what is already familiar. Changes already taking place in classrooms across the country have been motivated by similar concerns; researchers and theorists have explored related issues that are as old as student-centered theory itself. However, a unified way of conceptualizing the goals of literature education and its processes of instruction still eludes us. By and large, the teaching of literature is "rudderless," espousing a focus on thinking and reasoning without a strong and stable conception of what this means in response to literature, and without the contextual anchor that can be provided by a clear understanding of the relationships among the nature of literary understandings and the instructional contexts in which such understandings develop. These are forceful arguments for our need to alter our approach to literature instruction. By being aware of how students make meaning of literary works, and by consideration of the issues raised in other chapters of this volume, we may be moved to rethink the goals as well as practices of literature instruction: to focus on its unique role in students' intellectual development, on its central role in the development of students' critical and creative thinking abilities, and on the concomitant need for national as well as districtwide attention and support for new directions in literature education.

References

Applebee, A.N. (1989). *The teaching of literature in programs with reputations for excellence in English* (Report Series 1.1). Albany, NY: Center for the Learning and Teaching of Literature, SUNY at Albany.

Britton, J. (1970). *Language and learning*. London: Penguin.

Brody, P., DeMilo, C., and Purves, A.C. (1989). *The current state of assessment in literature* (Report Series 2.1). Albany, NY: Center for the Learning and Teaching of Literature, SUNY at Albany.

Bruner, J.S. (1986). *Actual minds, possible worlds*. Cambridge, MA: Harvard University Press.

Dworkin, R. (1983). Law as interpretation. In W.J.T. Mitchell (Ed.), *The politics of interpretation*. Chicago: University of Chicago Press.

Elstein, A., Shulman, L., and Sprafka, S. (1978). *Medical problem-solving: The analysis of clinical reasoning*. Cambridge, MA: Harvard University Press.

Fillmore, C.J. (1981). *Ideal readers and real readers*. Proceedings of the Georgetown University Roundtable Conference. Georgetown University: Washington, D.C.

Goodman, K. (1970). Behind the eye: What happens in reading. In K. Goodman and Olive Niles (Eds.), *Reading process and programs*. Urbana, IL: National Council of Teachers of English.

Iser, W. (1978). *The act of reading: A history of aesthetic response*. Baltimore, MD: Johns Hopkins University Press.

Langer, J.A. (1985). Levels of questioning: An alternative view. *Reading Research Quarterly, 20* (5), 586–602.

Langer, J.A. (1986). *Children reading and writing: Structures and strategies*. Norwood, NJ: Ablex.

Langer, J.A. (1987a). A sociocognitive perspective on literacy. In J. Langer (Ed.), *Language, literacy, and culture: Issues of society and schooling*. Norwood, NJ: Ablex.

Langer, J.A. (1987b). How readers construct meaning: An analysis of reader performance on standardized test items. In R. Freedle (Ed.), *Cognitive and linguistic analyses of standardized test performance*. Norwood, NJ: Ablex.

Langer, J.A. (1989). *The process of understanding literature* (Report Series 2.1). Albany, NY: Center for the Learning and Teaching of Literature, SUNY at Albany.

Langer, J.A. (1990a). The process of understanding: Reading for literary and informative purposes, *Research in the Teaching of English, 24* (3), 229–260.

Langer, J.A. (1990b). Understanding literature. *Language Arts, 67* (8), 812–816.

Langer, J.A. (1991). *Literary understanding and literature instruction* (Report Series 2.11). Albany, NY: Center for the Learning and Teaching of Literature, SUNY at Albany.

Langer, S. (1967). *Mind: An essay on human feeling.* Baltimore, MD: Johns Hopkins University Press.

Orr, J. (1987a). Narratives at work: Storytelling as cooperative diagnostic activity. *Field Service Manager: The Journal of the Association of Field Service Managers International.* June, 47–60.

Orr, J. (1987b). Talking about machines. Report to the Army Research Institute, Xerox Park, Palo Alto, CA.

Purcell-Gates, V. (in press). On the outside looking in: A study of remedial readers' meaning-making while reading literature. *Journal of Reading Behavior.*

Putnam, H. (1978). *Meaning and the moral sciences.* London: Routledge and Kegan Paul.

Roberts, D. and Langer, J. (1991). *Supporting the process of literary understanding: An analysis of classroom discussion* (Report Series 2.15). Albany, NY: Center for the Learning and Teaching of Literature, SUNY at Albany.

Rosenblatt, L. (1978). *The reader, the text, the poem: The transactional theory of the literary work.* Cambridge, MA: Harvard University Press.

Rumelhart, D.E. (1975). Notes on a schema for stories. In D.G. Bobrow and A.M. Collins (Eds.). *Representation and understanding.* NY: Academic Press.

Spiro, R.J., Bruce, B.J., and Brewer, W.F. (1980). *Theoretical issues in reading comprehension.* Hillsdale, NJ: Lawrence Erlbaum.

Suleiman, S.R. and Crosman, I. (Eds.) (1980). *The reader in the text: Essays on audience and interpretation.* Princeton, NJ: Princeton University Press.

Swartz, R.J. and Perkins, D.N. (1990). *Teaching thinking: Issues and approaches.* Pacific Grove, CA: Midwest Publication.

4 Five Kinds of Literary Knowing

Robert E. Probst
Georgia State University

Competing Conceptions of Literature

Consider two points of view on the poem. Wellek and Warren (1956) speak of the "normative character of the genuine poem." It is a "simple fact," they say, that

> it might be experienced correctly or incorrectly. In every individual experience only a small part can be considered as adequate to the true poem. Thus, the real poem must be conceived as a structure of norms, realized only partially in the actual experience of its many readers. Every single experience (reading, reciting, and so forth) is only an attempt—more or less successful and complete— to grasp this set of norms or standards. (pp. 138–139)

What this means, of course, is that we are all deficient, defective readers. "You can read this poem incorrectly," it says, "and you probably will; your experience will be barely adequate, partial, and incomplete; you'll attempt, but fail, to grasp the true poem, the pure meaning." There is a genuine poem; and then, on the other hand, there is your feeble reading. Do what you will, the genuine poem is beyond your scope. In that last verb, "to grasp," we see the desperate reader, fingers clutching frantically, futilely, for any life-ring, any floating timber, any flotsam or jetsam of meaning, and sinking slowly, helplessly, beneath the quiet linguistic surfaces of the text.

Wellek and Warren present, more or less, some fundamental assumptions shared by the New Critics. Perhaps most significant of these is the notion that the literary work sets the standard by which a reading may be judged. They are somewhat vague about what those norms are, and even *where* they are: "The norms we have in mind are implicit norms which have to be extracted from every individual experience of a work of art and together make up the genuine work of art as a whole" (p. 139). Although they seem here to say that the norms are in the collective experience of all the poem's readers, the sum of all their experiences with the text, they have said earlier that the real poem "is not an individual experience or a sum of experiences, but only a potential cause of experiences" (p. 138). Those norms, then, wherever they may be, are less in the readers and their experiences than in the text. The text sets the norms, dictates its own reading. Our task, if we accept that vision of literature, becomes a process of extracting, inferring, interpreting. The text is the container—or at least the arbiter—of meaning, and our goal is to remove that meaning as completely and accurately as we can.

That conception of literature and literary experience has unfortunate consequences for students. First of all, it assures them that they will fail. They may fail more or less badly, but they are doomed to fail. As fallible, imperfect, flawed readers trapped within our own history, limited by what our unique experience has provided for us and withheld from us, we have little hope of achieving that perfect reading postulated by such theories as those of Wellek and Warren. Our individuality, our unique perception and valuation of the world, prevents us from fully grasping those norms—whatever they may be—implicit within the literary work. The conception of the "real poem" as a structure of norms leaves us, like poor Tantalus, clutching at grapes that forever elude us.

And although, by definition, all of us are deficient, some are more deficient than others. The notion of the genuine poem establishes a hierarchy of readers, with the most renowned critic at the top, other published scholars a rung or two below (depending on the number and respectability of their publications), other professors and teachers several steps further down the ladder, and finally, at the bottom, most deficient of all, the student. The concept of the perfect reading, the hierarchy of readers, and the inevitability of failure conspire to diminish the individual reader, especially student readers. Their readings, after all, can be of little significance in this scheme of things. They are novices, uninitiated, and therefore unlikely to approach the ideal reading. Their experiences with the text are thus less meaningful, less significant, less of everything, than is the reading of the established, respected critic.

Only in the readings of the preeminent critics, the authorities, can the genuine poem be approximated. Consequently, university students, predictably and probably wisely, given their assumptions about literature, have depended upon the published criticism and distrusted their own experience with texts. And in the high schools, students have depended upon *Cliffs Notes* or other such eviscerations of literary works rather than the works themselves. The simple outlines and summary judgments offered by such truncations are, after all, what the schools seem to be seeking. These paraphrases have extracted the approved interpretation, summarized the respected critical judgments, and so they represent, in simple, readable prose, the norms toward which students would, in their absence, have to labor. And if those extractions from the texts are, in fact, what we are after, then it makes perfectly good sense to bypass the works themselves in favor of the published summaries and interpretations. Given the choice, most of us would prefer shelled pecans to hours laboring with a nutcracker.

Rosenblatt (1978) offers another point of view. She speaks of the poem as

> . . . an event in time. It is not an object or an ideal entity. It happens during a coming-together, a compenetration, of a reader and a text. The reader brings to the text his past experience and present personality. Under the magnetism of the ordered symbols of the text, he marshals his resources and crystallizes out from the stuff of memory, thought, and feeling a new order, a new experience, which he sees as the poem. This becomes part of the ongoing stream of his life experience, to be reflected on from any angle important to him as a human being. (p. 12)

Rosenblatt flatly contradicts Wellek and Warren, offering us a different conception of literary experience, with drastically different implications for the classroom. The poem, in this vision of literature, does not reside in the text, or in the realm of the ideal. Rather, it is an event, a specific encounter, a momentary happening. It is a meeting of reader and text. The poem is the experience of a particular reader performing with a particular text.

Perhaps this is, and should always have been, obvious. Words, ink on paper, function symbolically, and symbols operate only within the mind. A text in a language we cannot read yields no poetic or literary experience, not because the text is inadequate, but because we are unable to perform symbolically with it. The words remain nothing more than ink on paper. Only when they enter a reader's mind do they come to life. And, since each mind is unique, as anyone who has ever ventured into a seventh-grade classroom—or first-grade, or twelfth-grade, or any other grade—will attest, the life poems take on for each reader is inevitably different. Your poem and my poem *cannot* be the same, though we make them from the same text.

A text does not become a poem until a reader comes along and, by reading it, makes one out of the experience. The notion that the poem is in the reader—or perhaps in the act of reading—rather than in the text or in the ethereal ideal, rearranges matters within the critical community. The poem is now attainable. It becomes mine. And, of course, yours, and our students'. Our readings are no longer the flawed efforts of hopelessly inadequate readers to attain unattainable norms, to seize that genuine poem Wellek and Warren insist is ever beyond our grasp. Rather, our readings *are* the poems; each is the unique literary experience made possible by the encounter of a certain reader with a certain text in certain circumstances.

Rosenblatt's vision insists that we, the readers, are important factors. If the text only becomes a poem when it is read, then we must take the reader into account, as well as the writer and the text, when we wish to speak of literature.

A Text and Its Poems

Consider a short poem—or rather, text, as Rosenblatt would have us use the terms—in light of these two visions of literature. What can we make of Frost's (1949) "The Secret Sits," for example?

> We dance round in a ring and suppose,
> But the Secret sits in the middle and knows.*

What is the perfect, pure, genuine poem, the norm implicit in this text? What would the perfect reading look like, that pure, pristine, crystalline reading uncontaminated, unsullied, by the seamy recesses of our idiosyncratic minds and our unique souls? The text gives us little upon which to work our interpretive charms. Frost's "We" is a bit imprecise; on our students' papers we might complain about the uncertain pronoun reference. And "the Secret" is worse yet. What secret—is there a God; how do salmon find their home; who will win the World Series? And what does this secret know? What possible way is there for us to know whether we have experienced this text "correctly or incorrectly," whether our attempt "to grasp this set of norms" has been more successful, or less so?

Frost's text does not submit happily to the analytic, inferential, interpretive strategies implicit in Wellek and Warren's conception of the "genuine poem." It does not reward our efforts to grasp it in that way. We could argue, of course, that it is an unsuccessful text. And we may very well do that. The critical approaches promoted by Wellek and Warren value complexity and obscurity in texts because those

---

* From *The Poetry of Robert Frost* edited by Edward Connery Latham. Copyright 1942 by Robert Frost. Copyright © 1969 by Holt, Rinehart and Winston. Copyright © 1970 by Lesley Frost Ballantine. Reprinted by permission of Henry Holt and Company, Inc.

features give the critic problems to solve, materials with which to work. Less problematic texts may yield less to the analysis and thus may be seen as less valuable. And more problematic texts, ones that prove too complex and obscure for effective interpretation, may be viewed simply as unintelligible.

Or, on the other hand, we could accept the text as successful and employ intertextual strategies to divine its norms, its meaning. We could examine other Frost writings, read his biographies, talk with his friends. But if we grant that a text ought to have some independent vitality, that a literary text ought to have some life of its own, not totally divorced from other texts, other information, but neither totally dependent upon it, then "The Secret Sits" shouldn't demand all that labor.

If "The Secret Sits" works at all for us, it does so because it invites us in to perform with it. It works, if it does, because we have questions, because we suspect that there are secret answers out there somewhere and that we are dancing futilely around them in circles, never drawing any closer to understanding. If we begin to reflect upon our own confusions, or in some other way engage the text personally, rather than try to figure out precisely what structure of norms lies beneath the words, then we are more likely to consider the reading successful. There would be, in Rosenblatt's terms, a compenetration, a coming-together of reader and text. In responding to the text, we would be marshaling our own resources, crystallizing out of memory, thought, and feeling, a new experience.

Though it isn't a striving for the perfect reading, the structure of norms, Frost might nonetheless approve. Poet James Dickey (1965) surely would. "I am for the individual's reaction," he says, "whatever extraneous material it includes, and against all critical officialdom." In poetry, Dickey (1987) argues, we should hope for

> words to come together into some kind of magical conjunction that will make the reader enter into a real experience of his own— *not* the poet's. I don't really believe what literary critics have believed from the beginning of time: that poetry is an attempt of the poet to create or recreate his own experience and to pass it on. . . . I believe it's an awakening of the sensibilities of someone else, the stranger. (p. 105)

The poem is, then, a unique event in the intellectual life of the reader.

Problems and Implications

By insisting upon the poem as event, Rosenblatt resituates the literary experience, placing it in a social context. The poem becomes a happening, an exchange, a transaction. It occurs between a reader and a text, and among readers. That conception of literature poses some problems for the classroom.

First of all, if the poem is a performance, a unique meeting of reader and text, then the issue of correctness becomes difficult. Welleck and Warren (1956) have said that it is a simple fact that the poem can be read correctly or incorrectly. If there is a norm, a best reading, then the correctness of other readings can be judged by how closely they approximate that best reading. Thus the most persuasive critics become preeminent, their interpretations become the touchstone by which other readings are judged, and students are subtly encouraged to submit to and imitate the thinking of their critical betters. A student's experience with a text is always subject to someone else's evaluation, and it is always, more or less, wrong. But correctness is not so easily assessed if there is no norm, no perfect reading, not even a hypothetical one, to serve as a benchmark.

Correctness becomes, in Rosenblatt's conception of literary experience, a virtually useless concept. It may even be a dangerous concept, because it encourages us to seek standards by which we may measure the rightness of statements about literary experience, by which we may order responses to literature on a scale from better to worse, and standards such as those tend to impose a uniformity or homogeneity that the uniqueness of the human personality does not allow.

That is not to say, of course, that there are *no* aspects of literary experience whose correctness can be judged. If we read the word "proscribe" in a text and think "prescribe," or if we read the word "infer" and think "imply," then we have made a mistake. We are incorrect. But the whole of the literary transaction is not so simply judged.

Similarly, we have to, if not give up, then at least question, the pedagogic and critical goal of interpretive uniformity. To teach the right and proper interpretation, the correct reading, is to ignore the limitless variability of the human experience. If the poem is created in the act of reading, and if each reader—as he or she must—creates the poem not out of the text alone, but out of the encounter between text and personal perspective and circumstance, then there is no right interpretation to teach. One text, ready by thirty students, will yield thirty poems. Though the text may remain constant, unchanging, the minds that engage it must all be unique, and so the poems must be unique.

Granted, we may set confining questions, interpretive questions perhaps, of the sort that do lend themselves to argument and proof. Questions about the attitudes and beliefs of the writer as revealed by a text, about the likely effects of historical events, about the probable borrowings from or influence of other writers—all these can be argued and the arguments judged to be more or less persuasive. But if we accept Rosenblatt's vision of literary experience then we must speculate about the possibility that we may also perform in other ways with texts, that producing interpretations is not the only possibility. We may also admit into the discourse such unique and diverse matters as memories, personal experiences, feelings, images called to mind by, but not contained in, the texts read. And we may accept, as legitimate modes of discourse resulting from literary experiences, poems of our own, letters, adaptations, storytelling, private journal entries, and the like. On such matters as these there is no need to achieve unanimity and consensus—they are personal, individual, unique, but a central part of the literary transaction.

If we accept the idea that the poem is in the reader reading rather than in the text, then we lose, as guiding principles, not only correctness and interpretive uniformity, but also comprehension as it has usually been defined. Traditional views of comprehension—understood as the remembering of information, or as the producing of statements of theme, main idea, and the like, that conform to some predetermined norm—can no longer be considered adequate goals for instruction. Comprehension, as it is traditionally viewed in reading instruction, implies a submission to the text. Students comprehend if they extract information accurately and remember it, if they see the logic or structure of a text, if they draw correct inferences about the author's purpose. All of those are important abilities, but along with them, if we are to allow the full range of possibilities, we must encourage readers to attend to their own conceptions, their own experience, bringing the literary work to bear upon their lives and allowing their lives to shed light upon the work. (Current views of reading comprehension as an interactive and transactional process [see Anderson, Hiebert, Scott, and Wilkinson, 1984, for example] also stress the reader's role in comprehension.)

However, more traditional conceptions of comprehension (upon which many textbooks are based) too easily leave the work as a thing apart from the reader, an object outside of the reader to be worked upon. The reader comes to it, takes something from it, and departs virtually unchanged. It is, perhaps, an adequate model for the reading of some sorts of informational texts, but it is not adequate for the reading of literary works. It neglects the personal experience that is brought to, and that may be reshaped by, the act of reading.

Again, that is not to say that comprehension is irrelevant. Readers who miss major events in a story, who fail to comprehend the rudiments of the plot, are not likely to get as much from the reading as those who catch more of the action. But to remember all that happened—comprehending fully—without engaging the work personally is to miss much of the literary experience as Rosenblatt has defined it. And to encourage students to try to remember all the little details, implying that successful reading can be measured by the recall of massive amounts of trivial information, may well be to shackle their minds so that literary experience becomes virtually impossible.

Purpose and Pattern in Teaching Literature

Response criticism, especially Rosenblatt's work, has suggested a great deal about the methods of teaching both reading and writing appropriate for the literature program. Teachers of literature have always hoped for close and careful reading, of course, but the critical issue raised by Rosenblatt's work is the question, "Close to what?" Efforts to make students read closely have tended to do so by asking them to suppress their own feelings and ignore their own associations and memories, and that is likely to make the reading distant and falsely objective, rather than close.

A reading that really respects the integrity of the text must also pay attention, close attention, to the readers' responses, thoughts, feelings, and memories, because without that close attention to self readers have no way of knowing where anything comes from. They have to define themselves against the background of the text, and the text against the background they themselves provide. Similarly, they must learn to pay attention to the shaping influence of context on the meaning and significance of the literary work.

Rosenblatt's vision of literary experience suggests that we might appropriately broaden our conception of the literature curriculum so that it includes attention to more than just features of texts and information about writers, periods, and techniques. Until now, most literature curricula have been devised on the basis of information we have accumulated about texts. The typical twelfth-grade literature course, for instance, is British literature, organized historically. Moving chronologically from *Beowulf* to Virginia Woolf, it explores periods, influences, movements, developments—that is to say, it invites the students to learn the information we provide them about the history of British literature. The same observations may be made about the eleventh-grade course, where American literature is likely to be the topic. At other grade levels, other patterns dominate. Arrangement by genre is fairly common, with texts divided into sections on poetry, drama, essays, and so forth.

Courses such as these betray our tendency to look for organizing principles in the information *we* have acquired about texts, virtually ignoring the transactions students are likely to have with texts. And we do so for obvious reasons. Those transactions are harder to describe, to predict, to manage, to arrange. If we look to the history of literature for our organizing principles we find the year's instruction falling neatly into place. We know where we should begin, and where, if time allows, we will end. Furthermore, goals and objectives come quickly to mind, and we know how to find a huge reservoir of information to fill the days. Lessons, questions to ask for discussion, and essays to assign are all suggested by the historical arrangement. We can ask about the influences of Christianity evident in *Beowulf*, the characteristics of Elizabethan drama, the social circumstances that affected the development of the novel, the dissatisfactions of the Romantic poets with their immediate predecessors, and on, and on.

The problem, however, is that little of this curriculum, its goals, and the teaching that prevails within it, may attend much at all to the nature of the students' transactions with texts. It may encourage the students to acquire information about texts, but it may not entice them to read those texts. And yet it seems possible that we could reconceive literature instruction so that it would reflect the vision of literary experience as a coming-together of reader and text, as a significant event in a reader's intellectual and emotional life.

Rosenblatt's vision suggests that literary experience is a significant way of coming to know about more than texts. Consider, for example, the possibilities in such a text as "Sign for My Father, Who Stressed the Bunt" by David Bottoms (1985).

Literary Knowing

Knowing about Self

We could read "Sign for My Father," focusing upon the text itself, and learn something about metaphor and rhythm. We could see it as a representative of twentieth-century poetry and discuss its contemporary imagery. We could consider it an example of Southern poetry, and speculate about the significance of narrative and of the colloquial voice in poetry from this region. We could, perhaps, look at it as biographical critics might, and reflect upon, perhaps even conduct research into, the connections between this text and Bottoms's life.

But we might also, if inclination led us in this direction and if the classroom allowed, reflect upon aspects of our own lives evoked by the transaction with the text. The literary transaction is, first of all, a way of knowing something about the self. It is quite likely, for instance, that a reader of this text might find him- or herself recalling personal experiences that were somehow connected with the text. We might be able to predict some of the themes or patterns in those transactions, but we would be unable to predict the form they might take, or the details. Some may well have to do with the relationship of parent and child—that wouldn't surprise us—but in other readings other concerns may surface, some of them perhaps unexpected.

In one discussion, for instance, a reader (an adult—not a secondary school student) remarked about the decreasing political and intellectual distance she observed between her and her parents. She wondered aloud if that revealed a weakening of commitment on her part, an unconscious slide toward a more conservative view, or if, as had the speaker in Bottoms's text, she was beginning to get a grip on something her parents had understood. Was she moving forward—or backwards? There was at least the possibility that further reflection on her reading, on the questions it had awakened in her, might have led her to some sharpened insight into her own mind, and perhaps into her parents' attitudes. Here was an opportunity for the transaction with a text to lead to understanding of the self.

It could be objected, of course, that reflection on those matters departs from the text and is unlikely to lead to thorough and accurate interpretation. If we view literary readings as nothing more than the drawing of defensible inferences about authors' intentions, or the explicating of patterns within texts, or the unearthing of relationships among texts—nothing more, in other words, than the making and proving of propositions about the text—then the objection is well-founded. But if we see literary reading as something more complex, an experience in which our own memories, perceptions, values, and ideas may be explored and shaped, then the objection is less significant. We may grant that this reader was not focusing her thoughts upon the text, but she *was* reflecting upon her transaction with the text, and that transaction included the awakening of private memories and thoughts. If they mattered enough to her to pursue them further, reconsidering her own history, clarifying her understanding of herself, then the text will have served her well, even if she has not bothered to make demonstrable propositions about it.

That reading dealt with issues that many—probably most—of the readers thought clearly tied to the text. Another reading, however, surprised at least some members of the group. A second reader in that same group reported her annoyance at the masculinity of the poem. It was, she objected, a male poem, with male characters, about male experiences. Her transaction with the text had led to expressions of her attitudes, not about parent-child relationships, as many of us might have expected, but about the relationships of men and women, especially those relationships having to do with power. Again, as with the first reading, the transaction provided an opportunity for a reader to articulate perceptions and attitudes. Both readings, different as they were, allowed readers to sharpen their understanding of themselves.

It seems reasonable that learning about oneself might be a legitimate purpose for the study of literature. The significance of introspection and reflection on one's own values and beliefs, one's own place in the culture, should be recognized, and our teaching should invite and encourage such exploration. We might do so by beginning with such questions as these, phrased, of course, in language appropriate for the age and ability of the group:

> What feelings did this text evoke in you as you read?
>
> Did this text awaken any memories, recall for you any people, or places, or experiences?
>
> What are your first, uncensored, thoughts about this text?

Some teachers have found it useful to allow students five or ten minutes, immediately after reading a shorter text, to write their reactions to questions such as these, or simply to write freely whatever comes to mind, rather than asking them to begin the discussion immediately. The silent writing gives students time to crystallize their own reactions, to find some words, perhaps tentative and halting, for elusive thoughts and feelings, and thus enables them to offer something to subsequent discussion.

The brief paragraphs produced in these few minutes serve as material for talk about the literary experience. They may be handled in a wide variety of ways. The teacher might simply begin the discussion with a very open-ended question: "What are your thoughts?" Or he may ask four or five students to read aloud, or to summarize, what they have written, and try to identify, with the help of the class, several patterns or themes in the responses that might serve as the organizing issues for the talk. Students might be cast arbitrarily into small groups and given some time to share their notes and identify issues worth discussing when the entire class reconvenes. One teacher preferred, at least occasionally, to collect the written responses and ask students to reread the text while she quickly and intuitively sorted them into four or five stacks. She then placed students in the discussion groups that resulted and asked them to consider the similarities and differences in their readings.

These questions, the short written responses, and the discussions that emerge from them, are all intended to have students respect their own readings, and invite them to use the experience as a way to articulate and investigate their own emotions and thoughts. The goal is sharpened understanding of the self, exploration of diversity and commonality, not consensus on an interpretation.

With longer works, the same goal—coming to know oneself better—may be pursued through the use of journals or reading logs. Teachers have set up such journals in various ways, but most of them have students read and take notes, not just on what is transpiring in the text, but on the associations, emotions, and ideas, whatever they may be, that surface during the reading.[1] One form, for example, requires paired entries, with one column for notes about what is happening in the text and the other for the reader's comments about it (see figure 1).

Another requires three entries: the first, an immediate reaction; the second, later reflection; and the third, notes on possibilities for writing of one's own (see figure 2).

Drawing upon these journals, we might begin discussion by instructing students:

> Now that you've read the chapter (novel, essay, play) and recorded what happened as you read, read back over your notes and think back over the experience. What is your own sense of the text or of the experience it offered you—does it have any significance for you; does it recall memories, associations; does it affirm or contradict any of your own attitudes or perceptions?

We might hope that the outcome of discussions focused upon the readers' feelings and thoughts, upon their perceptions of both text and unique personal experience, would be further insight into themselves. That insight should be the first goal of the literature classroom.

Knowing about Others

One virtually inevitable result of concentrating upon individual responses to texts is that students will see similarities and differences within the classroom. They will notice that readers make sense of texts in different ways, that significance and meaning depend as much upon the reader as upon the text. Too often, unless they are encouraged to see it otherwise, the existence of these differences will be seen as

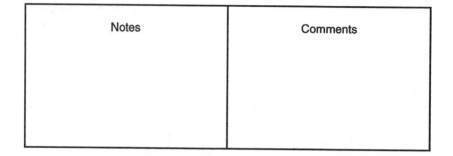

Notes	Comments

Fig. 1. A two-part note/response journal format.

evidence of a hierarchy of readings, some better than others, and attributed to differences in skill or intelligence or diligence. Students will likely have been encouraged for much of their schooling to judge their own statements in terms of correctness, assuming that the knowledge they are seeking—or avoiding—is something outside them, something that may be judged by externally imposed standards.

They might, however, be encouraged to see these differences as indications of the uniqueness of each reader, and as opportunities to learn something about others. The reader who had objected to the maleness of Bottoms's poem, for instance, was challenged by another reader, a woman, who argued that although the metaphor of baseball *was* male, the text was about any parent-child relationship, whether between father and son, mother and daughter, or any other combination. And that reader was then challenged by still another, who asserted that *she* had played a great deal of baseball as a child, and that the game was not exclusively for men. Each reader created a unique poem, a synthesis of text and personal experience, from the words Bottoms had provided.

The discussion of their various readings gave them an opportunity to learn something about one another. That sort of learning has seldom been an explicit goal of the literature curriculum. If, however, literary studies are to communicate the cultural heritage, to help with the assimilation of the individual into the society, then it seems reasonable to begin with efforts to acquaint the students with one another. Literature should socialize, humanize. It should offer us the chance to sharpen our insights into the human condition.

Those several students who traded comments on "Sign for My Father" may not have been expressing profound, eternal truths, but we may hope for some value in their exchange of perceptions. We

Immediate Reaction	Later Reflection	Reading/Writing Experiment

Fig. 2. A three-part reaction/reflection journal format.

may hope that they will gradually grow more accepting of the differences among people, better able to consider viewpoints other than their own, and perhaps more likely to grow intellectually.

Teachers interested in encouraging students to come to understand one another better may do so, in part, by acknowledging the validity of that kind of knowing, and by setting up discussion and writing designed to call attention to the similarities and differences among readers. Questions that focus upon readers, rather than upon texts, are appropriate. We may, for instance, pair students and offer the following instructions for a discussion.

> Please discuss your readings with your partner. Talk about the memories, the thoughts, and the feelings each of you had as you read. What similarities and differences do you notice in your experiences with the text? Was the reading more pleasant, or annoying, for one than for the other?

What accounts—or what might account—for those differences? For longer works, a reading log designed to initiate some exchanges between students may help. This one, requiring four entries, is laid out to cover two adjacent pages in a notebook (see figure 3).

It sets up a written exchange between students. Working on a novel, for example, students may be asked, after each chapter has been read, with notes on and responses to the text entered into the first two columns, to trade logs with another student. Students would then read through the notes and responses they now have in hand and write comments that come to mind. The journals would then be returned to their owners who would be asked to reply. Exchanges such as these suggest a great deal of material for the class discussions, and may lead students to see the text, themselves, and one another more clearly.

Other designs for the classroom make learning about another student

Notes on the text	Response	Comment (by another student)	Reply

Fig. 3. A four-part reading log/response journal format.

the explicit purpose of the activity. One, a structured interview, divides the class into pairs, each of which is given two short texts so that each student may serve once as the reader and once as the interviewer. Students are then asked to move through the following steps:

1. One student will be designated the interviewer; the other the reader. Interviewers should quickly read through the text, while the readers wait.

2. The readers should then read the text, talking about it as they go. They should make any comments that come to mind— about memories that arise, feelings that are evoked, problems or confusions with the text itself, or anything else. The interviewers should take notes, as thorough as possible, on everything the readers say.

3. The readers should then read it again, commenting further, trying to elaborate upon earlier remarks, catching any thoughts that they failed to mention on the first reading, noting anything new that comes to them.

4. After the second reading, the interviewers should ask for clarification of anything unclear the readers may have said, or for elaboration on any points. Again, they take notes.

5. The interviewers should then go through their notes, circling the 3–5 most interesting, problematic, or confusing points. They comment on or ask a question about each, again taking notes on the replies.

6. The interviewers should then discuss the reading, telling the readers anything interesting they observed, wondered or speculated about. It is a report, however, not an evaluation.

7. Readers and interviewers now trade roles and run through steps 1–5 again, using the other text.

8. Each student should now take the notes he/she has accumulated and use them to write a page or so about the partner's reading of the text. (An option at this point—one that places less emphasis upon learning about the other reader—is to turn all the notes over to the readers when the discussion is finished, so that they may use them in writing about their own readings of the text.)

There are several purposes for the pattern—one is simply to slow down the reading, encouraging productive pauses. A second is to provide helpful responses—prods, questions, reactions—that might stimulate further thought about the reading. A third is to encourage some collegiality among students, to cast them into the role of helper for one another, while giving them some guidance in that role. And the fourth is to invite them to come to know one another better.

Knowing about Texts

Traditionally, the emphasis in the classroom has fallen most heavily upon learning about texts. That's understandable—it is easier to organize information than it is to organize such unpredictable matter as transactions, and we have, furthermore, a great deal of information about texts. That information can both fill and structure our time, suggesting courses arranged historically in the upper grades, perhaps by genre in the junior high schools. Much of the information we offer students in these courses is of dubious value, but clearly it *is* important that they learn how texts work upon them, controlling and directing them, either intentionally or inadvertently.

It is worth noting, for instance, how the images in "Sign for My Father" conspire to evoke memories and to suggest significances beyond their obvious reference. The home run contrasted with the sacrifice bunt, for example, suggesting the contrast between grand dreams and necessary sacrifices; the association of the home run with youth and the sacrifice with maturity, suggesting that age brings with it wisdom— or is it just a loss of hope? What the individual reader will make of such images we cannot say, but we can notice the patterns, observe our reactions, speculate about the intent.

The last stanza, for example, presents some readers with the image of a young man growing wiser, finally realizing what his father has taught him; to others it has offered the image of a young man growing old and tired, accepting the despairing visions, the loss of hope, for which his father tried to prepare him. Observing patterns within the text and its effects upon various readers will enable students to take control of texts rather than to submit to them, to define their own perspectives against those offered by the text. The reader, for example, who rejected Bottoms's text because it dealt with male issues may perhaps, after discussion and reflection, decide that it could be read in another way, one in which the sex of the characters is irrelevant. The images, annoying as they may have been to her at first, could lead her to reflect on aspiration and sacrifice, or perhaps on other matters of personal significance. If so, she will have learned something about how texts work, and about how reader must work with texts.

A text such as "Sign for My Father" also provides an opportunity for taking some pleasure in the artistry of the writer. A student familiar with baseball may be able to point out the baseball terms that function metaphorically throughout the poem—the "tiresome pitch," "laying down," and of course "sacrifice" and "sign." And those observations may lead to speculation about the possible metaphoric significance of other words as well. The bunt, dropped "like a seed," may suggest to some readers that the father's teaching was itself a seed in the young man's mind, barely noticed at first, but blossoming years later.

Students invited to respond to texts will often observe and comment on aspects of the text as they explain their reactions, explore the problems they encounter, and attempt to deal with differences in the readings offered by classmates. We might occasionally encourage students to look more closely at texts from the outset by asking them to compare their perceptions:

> What did you see happening in the text? Paraphrase it—retell the event briefly. What image was called to mind by the text? Describe it briefly. Upon what, in the text, did you focus most intently as you read—what word, phrase, image, idea? What is the most important word in the text?

Often, simple paraphrase will reveal radically different readings that sustain discussion for quite awhile. The teacher's greatest problem when that happens is to make sure that the talk does not become a debate, that students do not fall back into the assumption that there is a right interpretation, that someone is correct and the others are wrong. The teacher needs to encourage students to consider other readings in building their own understanding of texts. It is occasionally appropriate to focus discussion on inferences about the intention and assumptions of the author, the beliefs or values of characters within stories, the influence of historical events upon writers, and the like.

When the talk deals with those matters, then distinctions can or should be made between stronger and less effective reasoning.

It is, of course, possible to be wrong, to be incorrect, in an assertion about a text, and students need to learn that some statements commit them to demonstration or argument. Students must learn to make the distinction between attributive statements: those that purport to describe objects or events in the world outside the reader's mind; and expressive statements: those that describe the state of the mind itself. A reader who asserts that this text is about football is flatly wrong; the reader who reports that the text calls to mind for him memories of football, if we assume that he is telling the truth, is flatly right. The reader who asserts that the speaker in the poem resents his father's instruction is perhaps less indisputably wrong, but he is likely to have a difficult time mustering the evidence for that assertion in the text. It may be that his thought arises not out of the text, but out of other experience, perhaps with his own father or his teachers, and so the statement may well be worth exploring. Demonstrably incorrect assertions about texts may lead to meaning if they are explored delicately. Looking within the text may reveal the importance of looking elsewhere.

Knowing about Contexts

Making meaning out of literary experience is not a simple matter of analyzing the text. That sort of inquiry may be valuable in determining the validity of some propositions about the text or its author, but meaning and significance are more complex. They depend not on text alone, nor on the reader alone, but on the context in which reader and text come together as well. It is important for students to understand that, and it is easy to demonstrate.

With "Sign for My Father," students should be able to speculate about, if they cannot actually observe within the class, the shaping effects of a reader's context. They may be asked, for instance, to consider how a reader might deal with the text

if he were very young, and felt badly confined and constrained by a dictatorial, tyrannical parent;

if he had just lost his father in an accident;

if he were a father with a son who had dreams of glory but no inclination to work for them.

They may be asked to consider how they themselves might have read the poem five years ago; how they might read it ten years from now; how their own parents might read it. They may be asked to consider how the context of the classroom affected what they could do with the text. Were there, for example, thoughts that they censored or ignored because the text was dealt with publicly, rather than in the privacy of a journal?

They may even be encouraged to take texts such as this one into other settings, with other groups, and observe the differences. A poem like "Sign for My Father," dealing as it does with parent-child relationships, might well be taken home and discussed with parents. "What was it like," you may ask them, "to talk about this text in your home with your parents?" Or it may be taken into an elementary school classroom where it might be responded to by younger children. They might then write about the question, "What effect did the discussion with younger children have on your reading of this text?"

Knowing about Processes (of Making Meaning)

Finally, students need to learn something about their own processes of making meaning from texts. This is a subtle and difficult matter, perhaps, but at the very least students can come to see that meaning is not magically achieved. They often have the impression that teachers simply know. They don't know how they know, they don't know where the insight originates, they don't know how teachers come to understand, but they know that teachers know and they don't. Students have too often been presented meanings and interpretations already made, finished, complete, and they have too seldom seen the stumbling, tentative, hesitating process of making meaning out of texts.

Possibly the single best way teachers may do this is to teach texts that they have never seen before. A colleague trusted not to sabotage the class can be asked to provide thirty copies of a suitable poem. Everyone begins then from the same position. The text is as new to the teacher as it is to the students, the burden of knowing what it means is lifted from the teacher, and he or she is allowed to muddle around in the text, making probing, tentative remarks, remembering other texts, other events, discarding some as irrelevant or uninteresting and focusing on others, hypothesizing, interpreting, reinterpreting, expressing personal feelings and telling stories called to mind—doing in public before the students, in other words, what they must do themselves to make sense of texts.

Students may observe that they attack texts in different ways. It is interesting, for example, to occasionally reformat a short text, perhaps a story, so that it occupies only the left half of pages, leaving a wide right margin in which students are asked to record, as they read, the thoughts, feelings, and responses that come to mind. With some groups, the differences are striking. In one class an irritated student reported that she was absolutely unable to interrupt the reading in order to make the notes. She said that she was sorry, but that she had given up on the activity, read through to the end of the story, and then gone back and tried to recall or recreate her responses and jot them down at the appropriate spot in the margin. In that same class another student reported that he had begun to write after reading a few paragraphs of the story, and had grown so interested in what he was writing that he failed to return to the story at all. He followed his thoughts so far afield that the text itself faded into insignificance for him.

Those two students may represent opposite ends of the spectrum, but differences are often apparent in the reactions of other readers, too. Some raise questions, some make interpretative statements, some express feelings, some are coldly analytical and intellectual, some tell stories or record memories. Some seem to have no preference or pattern, and do a little of everything.

Teachers can make the point that there are many ways of entering texts, and that we may profit by broadening our repertoire. The questions we present about literary works are, then, very important and have to be carefully considered. They should encourage students to learn something about themselves, about texts, about other readers, about contexts (the classroom setting, other literary works, and so on), and about the processes by which meaning is made from literary texts. For them to read closely, they have to be aware of all of those elements—they all contribute to meaning. Meaning does not reside in the text alone, as we have sometimes assumed. The problem, of course, is to find enough varied ways of asking those questions. And to find works that are provocative enough to sustain the labor implicit in the questions. But both those problems are solvable.

Toward Instructional Change

Implications for Instruction

This vision of literature instruction carries with it several implications for instruction. First of all, it suggests that we not overemphasize the expository, analytical essay. We need to teach it, but it is not the only genre suitable for the literature classroom. Of course, there should be sufficient attention to the interpretive, analytical essay, but students will write them more effectively if the works they deal with are significant to them, and if the essays are part of a real dialogue. Interpretive essays, for instance, might be most appropriate when there is some real disagreement about a text. The talk in the classroom could then lead into the writing of a more extended and carefully planned argument than oral discourse allows. Those papers themselves could then be the substance for further work; students could even be asked to write analyses of the arguments of their classmates.

Some of the writing we ask students to do, however, should be in other modes than the essay. If poetry and fiction are legitimate ways of making meaning, then we should have students try their hands at them. Students in music classes aren't asked just to listen and appreciate—they are invited to hum a tune or pound on a drum; literature students should similarly be asked to hum a poem once or twice during their schooling. Some writing might be very personal, perhaps the telling of one's own stories as they are called to mind by reading. Many of the invitations to write might suggest that students remember or invent incidents/situations/feelings suggested by a literary work, and develop them.

Students need to be taught that there are various possible ways of making meaning out of experience, either literary or otherwise, and that they have to exercise some responsibility in choosing. They need to know that telling their own stories is a perfectly legitimate, respectable act. They need to know, too, that setting a constraining question, perhaps "What did the writer intend in this work?" is also reasonable. And they need to learn that the writing these two different tasks might lead to would have to be judged by different criteria. The narrative cannot be evaluated as an argument, nor the argument judged as a story.

Implications for Curriculum

Although we have a great many ideas about how we might teach individual literature lessons, we still face the complex problem of devising a structure for the entire curriculum in literature. Most textbook series, I think, and most school curricula, follow designs that don't sustain the sort of teaching that we'd like to see, and, in fact, lure teachers away from it. The typical high school text, arranged by historical periods at one level, perhaps by genre at another, implicitly if not subtly encourages the teacher to emphasize history or genre. Most literature textbooks and curricula have found their organizing principles in the body of information we have about literature, the facts, the terms, the observable content, the testable data—knowledge, as compilers of dictionaries of cultural literacy conceive of it.

Some series have been arranged around themes, but those themes also seem to have arisen primarily from a consideration of the texts, rather than of the possible encounters with the texts. They have always reflected more time in the library than with adolescent readers. Still, we ought to be able to combine what we know about adolescent development, about the recurring issues and themes of our literature, about reading interests, about literary theory, and about learning to write, and find somewhere in all of it a structure that is not just logical, but also psychologically valid.

There ought to be some correlation between what students go through as they grow up and what great writers have written about. For instance, one of the great themes of western literature is romance and love; one of the great issues of adolescence is "the chase"; and clearly one of the reading interests of adolescents is sex and romance. The connection suggests that the literature curriculum could respect both the concerns of the students and the literary heritage.

Similarly, one of the themes is coming-of-age; one of the tasks of adolescent development is getting out from under parents' thumbs and acquiring some autonomy; and one of the reading interests of early adolescence is animal stories. Those are stories in which the child is *depended* upon—by Lassie or Black Beauty or another creature— rather than *dependent* upon. In other words, the central figure is a child coming-of-age, demonstrating some autonomy and self-reliance. It's possible that those stories satisfy students not so much because they are about animals but because they happen to address the human issue children begin to confront about the time they hit junior high school.

It may be possible, in other words, for us to look for organizing principles in the transactions between reader and text. That's a less precise, concrete, tangible basis for a textbook or a curriculum, but if we could come up with something workable, it might be a much more powerful and interesting program. Speculation about the correlations between literary themes and patterns of growth and interest might be fed both by studies of adolescent development and by studies of reading interest. Havighurst's (1972) work, out of date, and probably sex biased, suggests some of the possibilities. Among the ten or so "developmental tasks of adolescence" that he identified are several that sound like statements of the themes running through much of our literature:

Achieving new and more mature relations with age-mates of both
sexes.

Achieving a masculine or feminine social role.

Achieving emotional independence of parents and other adults.

Achieving assurance of economic independence.

Preparing for marriage and family life.

Desiring and achieving socially responsible behavior.

Acquiring a set of values and an ethical system as a guide to
behavior. (pp. 45–69)

It's conceivable that analysis of such studies as this one might guide
our choice and arrangement of literary selections. If one of the tasks
of adolescence is "achieving mature relations with age-mates of both
sexes" then the literature dealing with romance and awakening sex-
uality is surely relevant and likely to be of interest to the young reader.
Romeo and Juliet's place in the curriculum is then justified, not only
because it represents Shakespeare's art, but also because it speaks
directly about an issue of burning importance to the reader. Its
justification derives, then, from the transaction we might expect it to
promote, as well as from textual or historical features. If we could
learn enough about adolescent psychology, we might be able to develop
a literature curriculum that would promote reflection upon one's own
experiences, informed by the similar reflections of the great writers.
The great literature would be more in such a curriculum than mere
artifacts to be acquired, to be exposed to as if they were inoculations
of culture. Instead, they would be there because they invite students
into the ongoing dialogue of the culture about its most significant
issues. Literature would become, in Kenneth Burke's (1957) words,
"equipment for living." It might help students learn to assimilate the
literature into their intellectual and emotional lives, and convince them
that literature is more than just material with which to play critical or
interpretive games.

Rosenblatt and other critical theorists have suggested some directions
for us. We have devised a wide array of strategies for the classroom.
Our next step is redesigning the curriculum. Neither chronology nor
genre seems to give us appropriate principles, but it may be possible,
if we struggle with it long enough, to devise a structure that respects
the uniqueness and individuality of the reader. I suspect that such a
structure will recognize the potential in literary experience for learning
about ourselves, about those who surround us, about the myriad of
factors that contribute to the making of meaning, and about the rich
reservoir of strategies by which we might make sense of life and texts.

Notes

1. I'd like to be able to identify the original source for these several journal formats, but I've run into them over and over again in slightly different forms from Atlanta to Anchorage. I believe that I picked up the second of them—the journal with three entry columns—from Bill Corcoran when he visited the states several years ago. The other two seem, by virtue of their effectiveness, to have become public property.

References

Anderson, R., Hiebert, E., Scott, J., and Wilkinson, I. (1984). *Becoming a nation of readers: A report of the Commission on Reading.* Washington, DC: National Institute of Education.

Bottoms, D. (1985). Sign for my father, who stressed the bunt. In D. Smith and D. Bottoms (Eds.), *The Morrow anthology of younger American poets.* New York, NY: William Morrow and Company.

Burke, K. (1957). *The philosophy of literary form: Studies in symbolic action.* New York, NY: Vintage Books.

Dickey, J. (1965). *Babel to Byzantium: Poets and poetry now.* New York, NY: Farrar, Straus and Giroux.

Dickey, J. (1987). Interview with W. Packard (Ed.), *The poet's craft: Interviews from the New York Quarterly.* New York, NY: Paragon House Publishers.

Frost, R. (1949). *Complete poems of Robert Frost.* New York, NY: Holt, Rinehart, and Winston.

Havighurst, R. (1972). *Developmental tasks and education.* New York, NY: McKay.

Rosenblatt, L. (1978). *The reader, the text, the poem: The transactional theory of the literary work.* Carbondale, IL: Southern Illinois University Press.

Wellek, R., and Warren, A. (1956). *Theory of literature.* New York, NY: Harcourt, Brace and World.

5 Challenging Questions in the Teaching of Literature*

Susan Hynds
Syracuse University

Teacher: Okay. Do you have any questions on number three that says "a romance contains mysterious, magical, and supernatural events?" Does anyone have any questions about that?

Student: What do you mean by supernatural events?

Teacher: Let me just give you an example. There's one knight that we are going to read about in the section of tales that we have whose power wanes at twelve o'clock noon, which means that if you are a knight that wants to try to defeat him, at what time would you want to fight him?

Student: Twelve o'clock P.M.

Teacher: Right. Twelve o'clock. Yes, because his powers would not be as strong. That's what I mean by supernatural events.

The high school students in the preceding excerpt are talking about *The Tales of King Arthur.* If we take this small sample of talk as somehow representative of this teacher's approach to classroom questioning, we can make several different types of observations.

We might begin by looking at the *cognitive dimensions* of this teacher's questions. We could ask, for instance, what proportion of her questions are "higher level," and what proportion are "lower level," according to some taxonomy of thinking skills. We might look at whether this teacher's questions are focused on literal or implied ideas, content or form, and so on. We might then try to determine how the types of questions this teacher asks over a period of several classroom interactions relate to her students' overall understanding or achievement.

Beyond the cognitive dimensions, we might analyze this brief interchange as a *social interaction.* We could study the turn-taking

* The research on which this paper is based was sponsored in part by a grant from the Syracuse University Senate Research Committee. Sincere thanks are also due to Don Rubin and Mary McCrone.

episodes between teacher and students, noting how often the conversation shifts from teacher to student or from student to student. We might also study how the teacher, by evaluating (or failing to evaluate) students' responses positively or negatively, evokes the "acceptable" or "preferred" response.

Finally, we might look beneath and beyond the content and structure of this questioning episode, posing our own questions about the *cultural dimensions* of this teacher's classroom, as evidenced by the instructional choices she makes, the questions she poses, and the responses she rewards.

In this paper, I will argue that many treatments of teacher questioning in reading and literature have defined teacher questioning as a *cognitive process* (see Gall, 1970, and Gall, 1984, for reviews). Emanating from a "reading comprehension" perspective, this view of questioning argues that asking a variety of "higher level" questions will lead students from "literal" to more "inferential" levels of text understanding. However, approaches to literature teaching based solely on taxonomies of reading levels may not be entirely appropriate for explaining what happens when readers understand and interpret literary, as opposed to non-literary, texts.

From a sociolinguistic perspective, teachers' questions have also been envisioned as part of a *social interaction,* in which learning experiences evolve out of the mutual participation of teachers and students. From this viewpoint, for instance, teachers might analyze the proportion of talk belonging to them and to their students, or the degree to which they extend or close off conversation by the use of evaluative statements. However, this perspective can be somewhat limited when it deals only with the surface dimensions of classroom interactions—that is, the ways in which teachers and students use language. For there are, beneath and beyond what teachers and students say, implicit rules for acceptable behavior within the context of a particular classroom. Thus, in order to fully understand the dynamics of their questioning practices, teachers must learn to view these practices as part of a *cultural event,* where the very identities of each participant as student, teacher, learner, or interpreter are shaped and defined.

Understanding the cognitive, social, and cultural dimensions of the questions they ask, teachers can not only begin to ask more "challenging questions" of their students, they can begin to challenge the underlying assumptions behind the questions they ask, as well as the very predominance of questioning as an instructional technique.

Questioning as a Thinking Process

> *Julie:* [Teachers] usually ask questions that need specific answers and don't require a lot of deep thought, probably because it is easier for them to tell us whether the answer is right or wrong.
>
> *Nekia:* I think [a teacher's questions] are helpful because if he or she asks a question and you can't answer it someone else can remember both the question and answer and put them in your notes.
>
> *Ben:* Usually English teachers ask questions that have no meaning and can be answered without any thought.

The Types of Questions Teachers Ask

Beneath the words of Julie, Nekia, and Ben lie powerful messages about how these eighth graders think they are *supposed* to think about literature: as a task of rote memory, requiring little or no divergent thought. For many years, literature teachers have been encouraged to look at their questions in terms of whether they elicit "higher" or "lower" levels of thought, according to a hierarchy of cognitive skills, such as Bloom's (1956) taxonomy. Presumably, higher level questions require students to synthesize, apply, analyze, and/or evaluate information; lower level questions focus on recall of factual information (Pearson and Johnson, 1978).

Hierarchical models of reading are based on the premise that readers can be led through questioning techniques or comprehension guides to think about texts on "literal," "inferential," or "applied" levels (Herber, 1967). Over the years, a variety of question-based activities have been created for the reading classroom, including "QAR" (Raphael and Pearson, 1982), "Re-Quest" (Manzo, 1970), and DR-TA (Directed Reading-Thinking Activity) (Stauffer, 1959, 1969). A look at most classroom literary anthologies reveals this hierarchical model of reading in the structure and sequence of the study questions at the end of each selection.

However, Tierney and Cunningham (1984), in their review of instructional practices in reading, reported that "the effect of teacher-questioning behavior upon students is not clear" (p. 620). In addition, Dias (1990) has criticized instructional approaches based upon direct applications of such hierarchies by saying that these hierarchically organized comprehension activities may be appropriate for expository texts, but not for use in the literature classroom. The questions teachers and textbooks pose within these hierarchies tend to produce passive readers and to reduce the act of reading literature "to one of finding answers to questions which are not one's own—even if they are eventually appropriated by the reader" (Dias, 1990, 292).

Thus, although much literature and reading instruction centers on asking questions about texts, we are not sure if questioning has any more effect than other instructional strategies in getting students to think about what they read. Looking beyond the *types* of questions that teachers pose, we might begin to explore the *questioning practices* of teachers and the influence of these practices on student achievement and understanding.

How Teachers Ask Questions

Perhaps not surprisingly, studies of questioning practices in a variety of content areas have revealed that teachers place a strong emphasis on literal levels of questions, largely to the exclusion of questions which ask students to think in more abstract ways. In her review of research on questioning, Gall (1984) reported that even today "about 60 percent of teachers' questions require students to recall facts; about 20 percent require students to think; and the remaining 20 percent are procedural" (p. 42). She goes on to state that "it appears that teachers emphasize fact questions, whereas research indicates that an emphasis on higher cognitive questions would be more effective" (p. 42).

Current information about the reading classroom is no more encouraging. One study, for instance, demonstrated that approximately 75% of elementary reading teachers' questions about texts were literal, 10% were inferential, and 15% were evaluative (Chou, Hare, and Pullinan; 1980). The researchers concluded that "Teachers have not significantly changed their questioning habits in the last decade. Even after 12 years' time, inferential questions still are found to represent a small percentage of total teacher questions asked" (p. 72).

Most of what we know about teacher questioning practices in the *literature* classroom focuses on the instructional effects of teachers' questions and the congruence between teachers' stated preference for certain types of questions and their actual questioning behaviors. We have discovered, for instance, that teachers ask more questions about the content of a literary work than about form (McGreal, 1976). Furthermore, teachers' questions often direct students to remembering details about the literary work, rather than exploring their own imaginative responses (Folta, 1981). In many cases, it appears that literature teachers concentrate on meaning-making processes, rather than more "reader-centered" processes such as engagement or personal evaluation.

Finally, there is often little congruence between teachers' stated philosophies and their actual questioning patterns in classroom discussions (Purves, Foshay, and Hansson, 1973; Walker, 1979). Teachers may claim to value creative, interpretive responses, for instance, but concentrate mainly on literal responses in the discussions they actually conduct.

Questioning and Student Achievement

There is evidence in some selected cases that student achievement is related to the use of higher level questions in class discussions (see Redfield and Rousseau, 1981). From a reading comprehension perspective, for instance, there has been mixed support for the notion that asking questions before, during, or after reading relates to students' text comprehension and/or recall (Anderson and Biddle, 1975; Graves and Clark, 1981; Levin and Pressley, 1981; White, 1981; Willson and Putnam, 1982). However, in general, clear-cut relationships are difficult to draw (see Gall, Ward, Berliner, Canen, Winne, Elashoff, and Stanton, 1978; Mills and Rice, 1979/80). Perhaps the lack of clear distinctions is due to the fact that classroom questions cannot be clearly labeled as "higher" or "lower" level in isolation, but must be studied within the context of other instructional strategies and events.

Not surprisingly, teachers and parents model acceptable ways of reading and responding through the questions they ask (Heil, 1974; Michalak, 1977; Roser and Martinez, 1985). However, it has been shown that students produce more sophisticated responses when their teachers are not present than when class discussions are tightly controlled (Hammond, 1980), and when teachers' questioning styles are "open" rather than "closed" (Hackett, Brown and Michael, 1968).

Similarly, the writing that students do in response to literature shapes the quality of their response. Restricted writing (responding to short-answer questions) has been found to be very unsuccessful as a way of eliciting sophisticated responses (Colvin Murphy, 1987; Marshall, 1987). Such questions tend to fragment the reading experience rather than leading students to sophisticated or complex understandings of texts (Marshall, 1987).

Perhaps the most important issue, then, is not what types of questions teachers employ, or even what effect teacher questions have on student achievement, but whether questioning ought to be the predominant mode of literary instruction at all. In his recent study of classroom discussions about literature, Marshall (1989) found that teachers dominated most of the large-group discussions, generating two to five times more talk per turn than did students. He concluded that:

> The students' role was to help develop an interpretation, rarely to construct or defend an interpretation of their own. While the goal expressed by teachers was to help students toward a point where they could individually develop a reasoned response to the text, we saw in the classrooms we observed few occasions where students could practice such interpretive skills—at least during large-group discussions. (p. 42)

Thus, despite the evidence for the superiority of student-generated responses as opposed to teacher questions, it is clear that teacher questions are a predominant aspect of literature instruction and have a powerful influence on student responses. By and large, teachers who confine student responses to short-answer questions about literary works, as opposed to more open-ended student-centered instructional methods, inevitably limit and restrict what their students learn about literature. We will begin in the following section by challenging *how* questions are used in the literature classroom, and then consider *whether* teachers' questions should be the primary mode of instruction.

Questioning as a Cognitive Process in the Literature Classroom

Let's begin by looking at what happens as the students and their teacher in the opening excerpt continue their discussion of "King Arthur":

> *Teacher:* Okay. Number four is really a repeat of the characteristics of the romantic hero. He is graver, nobler, and more honorable than any ordinary human. Often the hero or heroine has the use of magic or other extraordinary powers. Can someone give me an example of what I mean by magic or extraordinary powers? Think about Arthur.
>
> *Student:* Can talk to the animals.
>
> *Teacher:* Right. He talks to the animals in the churchyard and is able to pull the sword from the stone and no one else can. Okay. The fifth characteristic that you need to have is what?
>
> *Student:* They put on a disguise.
>
> *Teacher:* Okay, often the romantic hero will put on a disguise to conceal his true identity. Anyone remember why Gareth does that? Wendy?
>
> *Student:* To find out who his true friends are.

Teacher: Right, to find out who his real friends are. Okay. Good.

This teacher focuses on straightforward recollections of factual information from the textbook, rather than "higher level" thinking processes (i.e., "Anyone remember why Gareth does that?"). The majority of questions are procedural ("Does anyone have any questions about that?") or literal ("The fifth characteristic that you need to have is what?"). The teacher is focused on some very specific information, presumably to help her students understand the characteristics of a particular literary genre. None of her questions encourage the students to explore their own personal hunches, feelings, or evaluations. Overall, the questions are very closed-ended, eliciting, in each case, no more than one-sentence responses from the students. In fact, student comments constitute a very small proportion of the classroom talk.

The problem of teacher questioning in the literature classroom, however, is not as simple as merely instructing teachers in using more higher level questions in their class discussions. There is a danger of oversimplification inherent in Gall's assumption that a larger proportion of higher level cognitive questions in the literature classroom would be more effective.

From a reading-as-comprehension view, this teacher's questions are appropriate for determining whether the students have understood the characteristics of a particular literary genre. However, in terms of the multidimensional understandings necessary for the reading of literature, the content and conduct of the questions fall short. Readers are not encouraged to develop an understanding of how the text relates to them personally, the cultural and social dimensions of the text, its aesthetic dimensions, or even *why* romance novels were written as they were. Furthermore, we might wonder whether these readers, in talking *about* the text, were ever encouraged to *read* it as both artifact and meaning source.

Considering the diversity of possible responses to any literary text, it is problematic to speak in terms of higher or lower order responses if thinking only about literature. Recently, Dias (1990) has argued that cognitively oriented instructional materials may undercut the very meaning-making processes they seek to foster:

> Such procedures—previews, study-guides, and the like—interfere in vital ways with the processes of literary reading. Although they direct reading to meet teacher-determined objectives and are often quite effective for dealing with unfamiliar text in the social studies or science, they are not necessarily compatible with, and quite likely subvert, the reader's own strategies for making sense of

literary text. They are likely to cultivate a passive, receptive attitude
to text at the expense of an active effort after meaning. (p. 286)

Thus, viewing teacher questioning in terms only of higher- or lower-
level cognitive processes places the emphasis on cognition and ignores
other essential elements of readers' responses, including affect, engagement, and empathy. Further, focusing on *text understanding* to the
exclusion of other important sources of understanding limits the literary
experiences of readers. Finally, teacher-controlled activities, including
study questions, often undercut the reader's creative meaning-making
processes.

As Judith Langer (1985) has argued, distinctions between literal and
inferential questions in the reading process ignore the constructivist
notion that meanings are arrived at gradually through a process of
forming local and global envisionments. Thus, assessments of the effect
of questions on reading comprehension formulated at only one point
in the reading process fail to capture readers' developing responses
over a period of time. Readers need, for example, to proceed through
a series of local "envisionments" in order to arrive at more global
interpretations.

In addition to ignoring the total range of readers' responses, viewing
teacher questioning only in terms of its cognitive dimensions fragments
the questioning process, isolating classroom questions from their linguistic and social context. Percentages of "higher-level" questions paint
a very incomplete picture of the role of questioning practices in the
literature classroom. A teacher, for instance, may use literal-level
questions as a way of leading students to discover nuances of meaning
and authorial intention.

The students in this eighth-grade classroom, as an example, are
disappointed because a poem they are reading does not rhyme. Through
a series of literal, fact-oriented questions, the teacher brings them to
an insight about the appropriateness of the author's technique:

> *Teacher:* Okay. Compare [the lack of rhyme scheme] to the theme
> of the poem itself. What happens to the people in the poem?
>
> *Student:* They get old.
>
> *Teacher:* They get old, but what do they *think* is going to happen
> to them?
>
> *Student:* Oh! They're gonna get money and be successful and that.
>
> *Teacher:* I know. What happens?
>
> *Student:* But they, but they . . .
>
> *Student:* But they die!
>
> *Teacher:* They either die or . . .

Student: They get old and can't do anything!

Teacher: So, to the people in the poem, they think they know what's gonna happen. They work all their lives, they save their money, they have paid vacations, they have good jobs, and then it doesn't happen to them. You think the poem is gonna rhyme, and it doesn't! You see the parallel?

Students: Oh!

While one may argue that this teacher was subtly leading students to her own "preferred response," it is important to note that she asked literal-level questions, not to test students' recall of minute details, but to encourage them to explore why the writer did what he did. A straightforward categorization of her questions into higher and lower levels would fail to capture the underlying purposes behind her questioning technique.

Studies which isolate teacher questions from their social context and focus only on their cognitive dimensions ignore the aims and purposes of questioning within the overall goals of a particular literature lesson. There are occasions, for instance, where literal-level questions are necessary to establish agreement on what basically happened in a complex literary work. There are other occasions when teacher responses which validate, paraphrase, or add to student responses are far more appropriate than "higher-level" questions. Recently, Gall (1984) has argued that "most research on teacher questions over the past two decades has investigated the effectiveness of recitations in which questions vary in cognitive level. A more basic issue, however, is whether recitations, irrespective of cognitive level, are effective" (p. 44).

A look at teacher questioning as a social interaction in the following section will allow us to consider the aims and purposes of classroom questioning, as well as the social roles and academic norms implicit in the language of classroom questioning.

Questioning as Social Interaction

Chiquinia: Sometimes [teachers' questions] are boring and they make you answer. I guess that is how you learn things because you really don't want to hear it.

Sara: I think it might depend on the teacher who's asking the question, but mainly [teachers ask questions] so we don't just sit there and do nothing, and so we pay attention.

Leslie: I have never really studied literature but a lot of times when teachers ask questions it seems they really want you to

> write a lot—not just answer it but they always ask "why?"
> and that sorta bugs me. But I guess there is really nothing I
> can do because that's the way the teacher finds out if you
> know what you read.

As the responses of these three students demonstrate, teachers'
questions do as much to reveal the ways in which students should *act*
in the classroom, as they do to guide students toward an understanding
of the text-at-hand. One subtle way in which teachers direct classroom
interactions is in the language they use to reward or reshape student
responses.

Information-Seeking Versus Known-Information Questioning

If we analyze the following excerpt from the "King Arthur" discussion,
we see an example of what sociolinguists call an "Initiation-Reply-
Evaluation" sequence (Mehan, 1979a, 1979b; Shuy and Griffin, 1978):

(INITIATION)	Teacher:	Everybody look on page 447. What is the code of chivalry? According to the code, what is the first thing a knight should do?
(REPLY)	Student:	Correct wrongs.
(EVALUATION)	Teacher:	Right, correct wrongs.
(INITIATION)	Teacher:	Can somebody give me an example?
(REPLY)	Student:	A damsel in distress is rescued.
(EVALUATION)	Teacher:	Right, a damsel in distress, and the knight takes off and rescues her from the big bad knight.

In this questioning episode, the teacher initiates the question, waits
for a reply, and, by her positive response, signals an end to the
conversational sequence. Further, the turn-taking pattern in this excerpt
moves from teacher to student and back again. Never does the
conversation move back and forth from student to student.

Not surprisingly, studies of the interactive nature of question and
response patterns have revealed that questions asked in schools are
distinctly different from the questions asked outside of schools (Mishler,
1975a, 1975b; Shuy and Griffin, 1978; Sinclair and Coulthand, 1975).
Mehan (1979b) and others (Labov and Franshel, 1977) have distinguished between *information seeking* questioning sequences (i.e., "What
time is it, Denise? . . . Thank you, Denise") and *known-information*
questioning sequences (i.e., "What time is it, Denise? . . . Very good,
Denise" (Mehan, 1979b, 285).

The "King Arthur" discussion is an excellent example of "known-information" questioning. It is obvious that this teacher has a definite idea of the only acceptable answer. Her request for the "first thing" a knight should do is an additional sign to the students that acceptable answers also follow a predetermined order of some sort. Further, this teacher's positive and negative evaluations are powerful tools for setting the rules and limits of acceptable classroom discourse.

Often, when students fail to give the desired response to "known-information questions," teachers will withhold positive evaluations and employ several conversational strategies, including prompting, repeating elicitations, and reducing the complexity of the question (Mehan, 1979b). In pursuing the preferred response, teachers of literature often give messages about what it takes to "succeed" in English. Notice, for example, the underlying messages this eighth-grade teacher sends to her students in the following discussion of Bill Cosby's book, *Fatherhood*:

> *Teacher:* So basically if you had to say one thing about the book what would it be?
>
> *Student:* Good! (laughter)
>
> *Teacher:* Good! (laughter) What makes a book good, Brock?
>
> *Student:* Like he's telling the truth, you know? It's like he talks about how his kids do stupid things like that, or how to discipline them, like he is not the boss of his own house . . .
>
> *Teacher:* Oh, if you were to, uhm, watch a comedian like Bill Cosby—what is the difference between a good comedian and a poor comedian? Jeremy?
>
> *Student:* I think the difference is facial expression. If you look like at Bill Cosby, his face is uhm, his face moves . . .
>
> *Teacher:* That's true. Okay. Good point. Charlotte?
>
> *Student:* There's this guy who like talks in a monotone, and everything he says is in this monotone . . .
>
> *Student:* Yeah, I know him! (several voices)
>
> *Teacher:* (over the voices) Okay. Let's get going. 'Cause there's something—these are all very good, and there's something that I'm looking for to make my point here. . . . Brock, do you know what I'm trying to get at?
>
> *Student:* Yeah. I know what you're talking about 'cause Bill Cosby, right? He's tellin' the truth. He just makes it funny, that's all. 'Cause a lot of things that kids do, teenagers do, he just writes it and, I mean to an adult, this book is full of laughs, and kids, like "Man, I'll get you for this!"
>
> *Teacher:* Adrienne? . . .
>
> *Student:* Basically, what a comedian should do is turn something ordinary into something funny.
>
> *Teacher:* Isn't she wonderful? She's *so* wonderful! But Brock started it. Hands down and listen to me for a second . . .

There are several interesting aspects of this conversation as a social interaction. In the beginning of the discussion, the teacher appears to be inviting a variety of student responses ("That's true. Okay. Good"). As the discussion proceeds, however, it becomes apparent that, rather than exploring a variety of interpretations, the students must seek the teacher's preferred response ("These are all very good, and there's something that I'm looking for to make my point"). Her question to Brock ("Do you know what I'm trying to get at?") continues to establish that the floor is still open for the "right response."

The search continues as the teacher seems to ignore Brock's statement about the book's "truthfulness" and invites a response from another student ("Adrienne?"). It is immediately apparent that Adrienne has hit the interpretive "jackpot" ("Isn't she wonderful? She's *so* wonderful!"). Mehan (1979b) calls such conversational sequences "extended elicitations." By holding off on a positive evaluation and prompting students, the teacher in this excerpt extended the discussion until she received the "preferred response." Once she received Adrienne's reply, her positive evaluation ("Isn't she wonderful?") was followed quickly by a move to take control of the remaining discussion ("Hands down and listen to me for a second").

Thus, positive and negative evaluations of readers' responses in literature discussions not only reinforce the notion of "correct" interpretation, they create a pervasive social climate with hidden rules and agendas for succeeding in English. According to Mehan (1979b), the evaluation act "seldom appears in everyday discourse" (p. 290), yet is a fundamental feature of classroom interaction where "it contributes information to students about the teacher's intentions, and contributes to the negotiation of a mutually acceptable reply" (p. 290).

While viewing teacher questioning as part of a social interaction recognizes students' and teachers' roles in a social process, such a view often assumes that merely changing the interactional "language of the classroom" will somehow change the classroom culture. Mehan, for instance, says:

> The interaction and accomplishment of social facts like answers to questions has implications for the way we view students' competence in educational environments. . . . Since each educational arrangement imposes constraints on learning, educators can examine the interactional demands of various educational and evaluative arrangements to determine if any particular arrangement is consistent with their educational goals and the child's previous experience. (1979b, p. 294)

While this is undoubtedly true, it is important to remember that classroom cultures emerge not only out of the instructional decisions of teachers and the responses of students, but out of the attitudinal frameworks of all participants. That is, behaviors of teachers and students subtly reveal their attitudes toward schooling, toward reading, toward interpretation, and toward each other. The underlying social roles and interpersonal dynamics of a particular classroom cannot be understood apart from an understanding of the attitudes and beliefs that shape and influence the classroom climate.

Thus, analyses of the *language* of classroom discourse give us valuable cues to social dimensions, as well as to power relationships and academic equity issues in classrooms. However, without some attention to student and teacher *attitudes and goals*, such analyses give us only part of the picture. Recent approaches to literature teaching from an anthropological or socio-psycholinguistic framework have begun to investigate teacher questioning as it functions in and creates the total classroom community.

Questioning as Cultural Event

> *Amy:* Mrs. [X] asked stupid questions that you could look into the book and find. I like questions that you have to look into yourself to find, go beyond the words in the story.
>
> *Becky:* I think [teachers' questions are] kind of boring for real. I wish there was a little more life in literature.

If we view teacher questioning as part of a cultural event, we see that as hidden agendas and curricular assumptions are subtly revealed in classroom discussions and assignments, students learn to fit their responses within the accepted conventions of a particular classroom interpretive community (Fish, 1976; Culler, 1975). In Mrs. X's classroom, success was measured by how adeptly students could answer study questions at the end of each selection. Students like Amy and Becky have learned to view reading in schools as reading devoid of personal relevance. In every classroom, readers like Amy and Becky must quickly develop the pragmatic skills to "read" and respond not only to the literary text before them, but to the hidden rules of "acceptable" interpretation in their particular classroom (Hynds, 1985, 1989, 1990). As Bloome (1986) has argued,

> In schools, students learn to use reading and writing in ways consistent with the classroom community. In part, this may mean learning how to do worksheets, fill-in-the-blanks, and copy from books on the blackboard. In part, learning to use reading and

writing in school may mean learning how to appropriately behave
and respond to the teacher during literacy activities. (p. 74)

Given the pervasiveness of these accepted interpretive norms, the
idea of the "unique" or "individual" response is problematic. As
students listen and respond to each other in class discussions, their
responses are ideally formulated through a collective process of "in-
tersubjectivity" (Bleich, 1986). Sometimes, though, student responses
are stifled rather than enriched through participation in class discussion.
The ways in which students are reinforced for responding to teachers'
questions and to each other constitute powerful messages about their
status in the classroom community.

In the following sections, I will explore some fundamental issues
that teachers might consider in understanding the classroom culture
created by their questioning practices. In considering how teacher
questioning can be used to facilitate rather than frustrate student
response and interpretation, we might begin by considering the goals,
purposes, and overall character of classroom interactions.

Questioning and Stances Toward Texts

> *Nat:* I think [teachers] ask (*no offense, Mrs. [Y]) dumb questions.* I
> mean I really don't like English that much. And I find reading
> and then answering questions worthless! *But I love just plain
> old reading.* Especially the Vietnam War!

As Nat's response reveals, the way in which we pose questions in
class discussion and in written activities greatly influences readers'
stances and orientations toward literary texts. Louise Rosenblatt (1978)
has distinguished between "efferent" reading (reading that is focused
on what will happen after the literary experience, such as a test) and
"aesthetic" reading (reading characterized by near total absorption in
the momentary reading experience). Despite the fact that most of us
have become lifetime readers on the basis of our ability to become
totally immersed in the reading act, our students often become inor-
dinately focused on the study or test questions immediately before or
after the reading experience.

Hunt and Vipond (1985, 1986; Vipond and Hunt, 1984) have
distinguished among three basic orientations in reading: story driven,
information driven, and point driven. Although the authors do not
posit one reading stance as "superior" to another, they note that few
readers approach literature from a "point-driven" orientation. But, not
surprisingly, readers' stances in school contexts are strongly influenced

by the questions asked by teachers in examinations and study guides. As Vipond, Hunt, Jewett, and Reither (in press) observe:

> A reader's stance towards text depends in part on the task he or she expects to perform. For instance, a student who anticipates questions of the type, "What color was the heroine's coat?", is likely to read in an information-driven way. Questions about texts that imply there is one right answer or that require students to identify "the" theme, also invite information-driven reading—not to mention the more disturbing fact that they tend to alienate students from reading itself. . . . Simplistic, *ex cathedra* statements about "what the author meant" often function in classrooms to end discussion rather than to promote dialogue, and are therefore effectively information-driven. (p. 36)

Thus, teachers' questions not only affect students' literary responses and interpretation processes; they effect the stances students take toward texts and toward reading in general.

Recitation Versus Discussion

> *Tom:* Most questions only describe the topsoil of stories, because most teachers, it seems to me, don't care about what students feel about stories, only about what they know.

Sadly, as Tom so eloquently argues, in many classrooms, literature is treated as a means to an end: discovering what students can memorize and repeat. In light of this disturbing fact, Dillon (1984) has argued that many classroom "discussions" are really thinly disguised "recitations." Discussion, according to Dillon, is characterized by student–student interaction, an emphasis on complex thinking processes, and higher levels of student talk (at least 40% of the total classroom discourse). Recitation, on the other hand, is characterized by teacher–student interaction, rote recall of factual information, and a low percentage of student talk. Citing Bridges (1979), Dillon proposes that "openness" is the fundamental characteristic of discussion. He sets forth the following prerequisites for distinguishing discussion from recitation. In discussion, he says: (a) the matter is open for discussion; (b) the discussants are open-minded; (c) the discussion is open to all arguments; (d) the discussion is open to any person; (e) the time limit is open; (f) the learning outcomes are open, not predictable; (g) the purposes and practices of the discussion are out in the open, not covert; and (h) the discussion is open-ended, not required to come to a *single* conclusion (p. 52).

The "King Arthur" excerpt in the beginning of this paper is an illustration of *recitation*. There is no openness to multiple responses.

Students are engaged in a single task: recalling specific facts about the characteristics of the romantic hero. Turn-taking proceeds from teacher to student and back again, with only a very small proportion of the classroom talk emanating from the students. What little students *do* say is in direct response to the teacher's prompts and bears little evidence of thinking "beyond the information given."

By contrast, the following excerpt is an example of students and their teacher engaged in *discussion*. A high school class is exploring the theme of love in *The Pigman* by Paul Zindel:

> *Teacher:* Somebody else over here said something about the love aspect of the story.
>
> *Student:* Oh, love has many meanings in this book, 'cause uh, you know, uh, love expressed in many ways by John and Lorraine in the, uh, love chapter, and the companionship, and the way Mr. Pignati and John and Lorraine got, get along together. And uh, they never hardly argue with each other. They're always trusting each other; they're always affectionate and caring.
>
> *Teacher:* Uh huh.
>
> *Student:* John and Lorraine showed they liked him 'cause when the store clerk asked Mr. Pigman where they were (garbled) she said they (garbled).
>
> *Student:* They also told the hospital that they were his children.
>
> *Student:* In a way, it was like they had a love for Mr. Pignati, too. Because when he died, they were very much upset. And he cared about them. You know, because, well, mainly it was because they became happy to talk to him or because it got them things. But still, I mean, they showed they cared about each other.
>
> *Teacher:* Yes they did. They definitely showed that. Definitely true. All right. Yes?
>
> *Student:* Uhm, and their parents, uh, Lorraine's mother wasn't like too much, like she tried to protect Lorraine by telling her she was fat and everything, but you know, the reason [her mother] was telling [Lorraine] this was 'cause she wouldn't go out with men. Uh, I think Lorraine's mother was kinda lonely. She didn't want Lorraine to be off all the time, so she wouldn't go anywhere. She made her stay at home, and she didn't want her to do anything without Lorraine having to go behind her back. But she was protecting Lorraine, but she was really overprotecting her.
>
> *Teacher:* Uh huh.
>
> *Student:* And John's family, his father didn't act like he loved him, but he just, he didn't know much really to help John be a man, you know, uh . . . if he really loved John . . .

Teacher: You made a good point. If you really love somebody, you
don't go to the extreme of overprotecting them nor do you
appear to be uncaring. All right. I've got a big question. How
do you know when you are loved? April? . . .

Student: You support . . .

Student: Sometimes you don't. That's what causes problems . . .

Student: I think if you love somebody, you love everything about
'em. And uh, I mean, there were things they didn't like about,
about that person, yet they just accepted them because they
were part of them.

Teacher: You've used three important terms: "love," "like," and
"accept." Are "like" and "love" always the same? Can you
love someone without liking some of the things they do?

The preceding discussion is different in several ways from *recitation.*
The floor is open for a variety of student opinions, the learning
outcomes are not predictable, and the largest proportion of talk comes
from students. Students' responses build on each other and are not
constrained or overly directed by the teacher's evaluations. There is
no single "preferred response" that the teacher appears to be moving
toward.

Interestingly, only very few of this teacher's utterances are in the
form of questions. She begins by turning the discussion over to the
students with a statement ("Somebody over here said something about
the love aspect of the story"). Her next few statements seem to function
only to let students know that she has heard what they have to say
("Uh huh"). She continues to validate student responses ("They
definitely showed that"), without leading the discussion in any pre-
defined direction.

At two points she briefly interrupts a student to paraphrase an
important point ("You made a good point. If you really love somebody,
you don't go to the extreme of overprotecting them . . ." "You've used
three important terms . . .").

The last three questions she asks are both global and personal. They
deal with larger issues of literary meaning, yet relate to the students'
own personal experience ("How do you know when you are loved?"
"Are 'like' and 'love' always the same?" "Can you love someone
without liking some of the things they do?").

Interestingly, then, the teacher in this classroom achieved a high
degree of student interaction and involvement by asking relatively few
questions. This suggests, as Dillon (1984) argues, that perhaps alternative responses to students are more effective in fostering discussion
than a constant barrage of teacher-created questions. According to
Dillon, "An invariant rule of thumb is to ask questions only when

perplexed and genuinely needing to know. One or two perplexed questions in the midst of many alternatives is likely to have a positive effect on discussion" (p. 55).

As alternatives to teacher questions, Dillon suggests: declarative statements (i.e., opinions), reflective restatements, descriptions of our state of mind, invitations to elaborate, encouragement of student questions, encouragement of students to ask questions of other students, and "deliberate, appreciative silence" (1984, 55). Such alternatives might do much to promote an inviting climate for reading, understanding, and responding to literature.

Challenging Questions or Challenging *Questions*?

> *Shayna:* Well I don't really [know what to think about teachers' questions] because my last-year teacher didn't ask questions, we just did questions in the book but if they did [ask questions] I might be interested.
>
> *Eric:* I like [teachers' questions] because I learn from my answers.
>
> *Heidi:* Some [questions] cause you to think. That's a pretty good challenge.

Recently, Bloome (1986) has argued that often, "from the perspectives of at least some students, what reading and writing in the classroom are about is *getting through*" (p. 73). Regrettably, "in classrooms literacy may not necessarily be a tool for gaining knowledge or for communication but rather a series of events that must be endured" (p. 73).

As a way of "enduring" or "getting through" classroom literacy events, teachers and students often engage in what he calls "mock participation" or "procedural display." In mock participation, students go through the motions of engaging in classroom interactions (raising hands, looking attentive), but are totally unaware of what is actually taking place. In procedural display, students and their teachers are participating in the academic lesson without really engaging in any of the academic substance. In Bloome's words, procedural display "can be compared to a group of actors who know their lines, say them at the appropriate times, but who have little sense about what their lines or the play in general mean" (p. 73). In Bloome's view:

> If building literacy is to move beyond procedural display and mock participation, it must be viewed within the context of building or rebuilding the classroom community. Educators must consider the inherent and implied goals, social structures, and histories that move beyond procedural display. (p. 75)

If we look at the *cognitive* dimensions of teachers' questions, we can see the importance of moving beyond the literal and into more interpretive dimensions of literary response and understanding. Unfortunately, however, a heavy emphasis on reading as a cognitive skill has fragmented our notions of literary reading, just as the typical short-answer questions about literature have fragmented our students' understandings of texts. When what students *know* becomes more important than what they think or feel, teachers' questions exist for the sole purpose of determining whether the students have actually read the text, and what they can recall from the experience. The result is that the aesthetic dimensions of literary reading are often lost entirely. Thus, parsing the text and passing the test can become more important than participating in an engaging encounter with literature.

It is important, then, to look at teachers' questioning practices as a *social interaction*. In becoming more aware of the proportion of student and teacher talk, of student responses directed to the teacher rather than to each other, and of teacher evaluations that close off rather than extend class discussions, teachers can enhance the quality and substance of classroom interactions. By understanding their choices of questions, and seeing how they reward or fail to reward particular student responses, teachers can loosen the reins of students' interpretation and response. Underneath and within the language patterns of classroom talk, then, lie many valuable insights about the social aspects of teachers' questioning.

Beyond these social dimensions, however, teachers must become aware of the ways in which their classroom conversations, study guides, and evaluation measures signal students to conform to preferred modes of behavior and response within the classroom interpretive community. Thus, learning to pose questions that challenge rather than constrain demands not only an understanding of the cognitive and social dimensions of literature teaching; it demands an understanding of the *cultural climate* that simultaneously emerges from and influences the language, thinking, teaching, and learning within the literature classroom.

As Shayna, Eric, and Heidi seem to argue, *challenging* questions are those that ask students to move beyond mock participation and procedural display, to a near-total immersion in the wonder and potential of literary interpretation and response. Posing questions that invite students to "learn from their answers," however, involves some element of risk. It means moving beyond study guides and comprehension quizzes, beyond the words in a story to the richness, possibility, and idiosyncrasy of each student's own experience.

Challenging questions are those that lead students to direct their responses to each other, rather than to the teacher alone—questions that encourage variety, diversity, and even idiosyncrasy, rather than conformity of response. Such questions allow literary themes and ideas to interact and coalesce, rather than to fragment and disintegrate; they nurture self-assured interpretation, rather than blind dependence on teachers or study guides.

But beyond learning to pose challenging questions lies an even bigger challenge: the creation of an environment where questions derive only from a genuine need to know. In such a classroom, students and teachers might begin to embrace, rather than to avoid, the essential complexity and uncertainty that makes literary reading truly *literary*. Perhaps, rather than trying to ask better (i.e., "higher order") questions of their students, teachers might simply stop, listen, and learn. And in the "deliberate appreciative silence" that follows, compelling answers about understanding and learning in the literature classroom may emerge.

References

Anderson, R.C. and Biddle, W.B. (1975). On asking people questions about what they are reading. In G.H. Bower (Ed.), *The psychology of learning and motivation* (Vol.9). New York, NY: Academic Press. GO–132.

Bleich, D. (1986). Intersubjective reading. *New literary history, 27*(3), 401–421.

Bloom, B.S. (Ed.) (1956). *Taxonomy of educational objectives: The classifications of educational goals, Handbook I: Cognitive domain.* New York, NY: David McKay.

Bloome, D. (1986). Building literacy and the classroom community. *Theory into Practice, 25,* 71–76.

Bridges, D. (1979). *Education, democracy, and discussion.* Windsor, England: NFER.

Chou, H.V., and Pullinan, C.A. (1980). Teacher questioning: A verification and an extension. *Journal of Reading Behavior, 12,* 69–72.

Colvin Murphy, C. (1988). Eleventh graders' critical comprehension of poetry through written response. (Doctoral Dissertation, University of Nebraska–Lincoln, 1987). *Dissertation Abstract International, 48,* 17–18A.

Culler, J. (1975). *Structuralist poetics: Structuralism, linguistics, and the study of literature.* Ithaca, NY: Cornell University Press.

Dias, P. (1990). A literary response perspective on teaching reading comprehension. In S. Straw and D. Bogdan (Eds.), *Beyond communication: Comprehension and criticism.* Upper Montclair, NJ: Heinemann/Boynton/Cook.

Dillon, J.T. (1984). Research on questioning and discussion. *Educational Leadership, 42,* 50–56.

Fish, S. (1976). Interpreting the variorum. *Critical Inquiry, 2,* 465–485.

Folta, B.C. (1981). Effects of three approaches to teaching poetry to sixth grade students. *Research in the Teaching of English, 15,* 149–161.

Gall, M.D. (1970). The use of questions in teaching. *Review of Educational Research, 40,* 707–721.

Gall, M.D. (1984). Synthesis of research on teachers' questioning. *Educational Leadership, 42,* 40–47.

Gall, M.D., Ward, B.A., Berliner, D.C., Canen, L.S., Winne, P.H., Elashoff, J.D., and Stanton, G.C. (1978). Effects of questioning techniques and recitation on student learning. *American Educational Research Journal, 15,* 175–199.

Graves, M.F., and Clark, D.L. (1981). The effect of adjunct questions on high school low achievers' reading comprehension. *Reading Improvement, 18,* 8–13.

Hackett, M.G., Brown, G.I., and Michael, W.B. (1968). A study of two strategies in the teaching of literature in the secondary school. *School Review, 76,* 67–83.

Hammond, M.J. (1980). *Poetry with teacher and without.* Unpublished Master's thesis, University of Melbourne.

Heil, C. (1974). A description and analysis of the role of the teacher's response while teaching a short-story. (Doctoral dissertation, University of Pittsburgh, 1975). *Dissertation Abstracts International, 35,* 77–71–A.

Herber, H.L. (1967). *Teaching reading in content areas.* Englewood Cliffs, NJ: Prentice-Hall.

Hunt, R.A. and Vipond, D. (1985). Crash-testing a transactional model of literary reading. *Reader: Essays in Reader-Oriented Theory, Criticism, and Pedagogy, 14,* 23–39.

Hunt, R.A. and Vipond, D. (1986). Evaluations in literary reading. *Text, 6,* 53–71.

Hynds, S.D. (1985). Interpersonal cognitive complexity and the literary response processes of adolescent readers. *Research in the Teaching of English, 19,* 386–402.

Hynds, S.D. (1989). Bringing life to literature and literature to life: Social constructs and contexts of four adolescent readers. *Research in the Teaching of English, 23*(1), 30–61.

Hynds, S.D. (1990). Reading as a social event: Comprehension and response in the text, classroom, and world. In D. Bogdan and S. Straw (Eds.), *Beyond communication: Comprehension and criticism.* Upper Montclair, NJ: Heinemann/Boynton/Cook.

Labov, W., and Franshel, D. (1977). *Therapeutic discourse: Psychotherapy as conversation.* New York, NY: Academic Press.

Langer, J.A. (1985). Levels of questioning: An alternative view. *Reading Research Quarterly, 10,* 586–602.

Levin, J.R., and Pressley, M. (1981). Improving children's prose comprehension: Selected strategies that seem to succeed. In C.M. Santa and B.L. Hayes (Eds.), *Children's prose comprehension: Research and practice.* Newark, DE: International Reading Association.

Manzo, A.V. (1970). Reading and questioning: The re-quest procedure. *Reading Improvement, 7,* 80–83.

Marshall, J.D. (1987). The effects of writing on students' understanding of literary texts. *Research in the Teaching of English, 21,* 30–63.

Marshall, J.D. (1989). *Patterns of discourse in classroom discussions of literature* (Report No. 2.9). Albany, NY: Center for the Learning and Teaching of Literature.

McGreal, S. (1976). Teacher questioning behavior during classroom discussion of short stories. (Doctoral dissertation, University of Illinois, 1976). *Dissertation Abstracts International, 37,* 2798A–2799A.

Mehan, H. (1979a). *Learning lessons.* Cambridge, MA: Harvard University Press.

Mehan, H. (1979b). What time is it Denise?: Asking known information questions in classroom discourse. *Theory into Practice, 28,* 285–294.

Michalak, P.A. (1977). The effect of instruction in literature on high school students' preferred way of responding to literature. (Doctoral dissertation, State University of New York at Buffalo, 1976). *Dissertation Abstracts International, 37,* 4829A.

Mills, S.R. and Rice, C.T. (1979/80). The correspondence between teacher questions and student answers in classroom discourse. *Journal of Experimental Education, 48,* 202–204.

Mishler, E.C. (1975a). Studies in dialogue and discourse: An exponential law of successive questioning. *Language in Society, 4,* 31–52.

Mishler, E.C. (1975b). Studies in dialogue and discourse II: Types of discourse initiated by and sustained through questioning. *Psycholinguistics Research Journal, 4,* 99–121.

Pearson, P.D., and Johnson, D. (1978). *Teaching reading comprehension.* New York, NY: Holt, Rinehart and Winston.

Purves, A., Foshay, A., and Hansson, G. (1973). *Literature education in ten countries.* New York, NY: John Wiley.

Raphael, T.E., and Pearson, P.D. (1982). *The effects of metacognitive strategy awareness training on students' question answering behavior.* Urbana, IL: University of Illinois, Center for the Study of Reading.

Redfield, D.L., and Rousseau, E.W. (1981). A meta-analysis of experimental research on teacher questioning behavior. *Review of Educational Research, 51,* 237–245.

Rosenblatt, L. (1978). *The Reader, the Text, the Poem: The transactional theory of the literary work.* Carbondale: Southern Illinois University Press.

Roser, N. and Martinez, M. (1985). Roles adults play in preschoolers' response to literature. *Language Arts, 62,* 485–490.

Shuy, R. and Griffin, P. (1978). *The study of children's functional language and education in the early years.* Final report to the Carnegie Corporation of New York. Arlington, VA: Center for Applied Linguistics.

Sinclair, J., and Coulthard, R.M. (1975). *Towards an analysis of discourse: The English used by teachers and pupils.* London: Oxford University Press.

Stauffer, R.G. (1959). A directed reading-thinking plan. *Education, 79,* 527–532.

Stauffer, R.G. (1969). *Directing reading maturity as a cognitive process.* New York, NY: Harper and Row.

Tierney, R.J. and Cunningham, J.W. (1984). Research on teaching reading comprehension. In P.D. Pearson (Ed.), *Handbook of Reading Research*, New York, NY: Longman.

Vipond, D. and Hunt, R.A. (1984). Point-driven understanding: Pragmatic and cognitive dimensions of literary reading. *Poetics, 13,* 261–277.

Vipond, D., Hunt, R.A., Jewett, J. and Reither, J.A. (1990). Making sense of reading. In R. Beach and S. Hynds (Eds.), *Becoming readers and writers in adolescence and adulthood.* Norwood, NJ: Ablex.

Walker, R.K. (1979). Variables related to the literary response style preferences of high school English teachers. Doctoral dissertation, Peabody College for Teachers.

White, R.E. (1981). The effects of organizational themes and adjunct placements on children's prose learning: A developmental perspective. (Doctoral dissertation, Northwestern University, 1981). *Dissertation Abstracts International, 42,* 2042A–2043A.

Willson, V.L. and Putnam, R.R. (1982). A meta-analysis of pretest sensitization effects in experimental design. *American Educational Research Journal, 19,* 249–258.

6 Teaching Literature: From Clerk to Explorer

Jayne DeLawter
Sonoma State University

> I was surprised at how long they kept going on the dialogue; they just kept writing to each other. In reading their conversations and reflection notes, I learned that some kids were really making personal connections with literature; others just touched on it here and there. The ones who seemed to make those connections were kids who had difficult things going on in their lives. The literature was really speaking to them.
>
> Doing the written conversation, especially, convinced me to go ahead with the character interpretation. I probably would have stopped with that if I hadn't seen their response to those two experiences. It was sort of like sitting on this gold mine and thinking, "Where do we go from here?"
>
> At this point, I'm still learning about these strategies. I still don't know all the possibilities. I'm finding out—still exploring. If I tried to limit things at this point, I'd be losing something. I'm really eager to try both of them again because, you know, you always find out something, something different when you do it. Both of the experiences turned out so much better than I'd imagined they would. I want to find out what can be done.

The quotation above captures the excitement and commitment of a teacher who regularly leads her students in explorations of literary texts. The teacher's concerns contrast sharply with current practices and beliefs about teaching and prompt the question: what are appropriate metaphors for teaching literature?

Prevalent metaphors for education tend to be atheoretical composites borrowed from industry, medicine, business, the military, and computer science, and have been attacked as being both inappropriate and constraining to professional educators (Smith, 1988). Acting on the beliefs implied by such metaphors, many schools expect teachers to act as curriculum clerks, carrying out other people's decisions about subject matter and classroom management. Management "systems" are established which require teachers to follow prescribed procedures and maintain lists and records of student scores; in this role, teachers become clerks. Rarely are they encouraged to express their own professional voices or to implement their own views of teaching and learning. Nowhere is this lack of voice more obvious than in the teaching of literature.

A promising new metaphor for professional educators is that of teacher as explorer, the leader of an expedition into unfamiliar territory. The image of explorer changes our perspective on teaching goals and roles and frees us to consider new alternatives and traditions which promote exciting practices in the classroom.

The Prevalent View: Teacher as Curriculum Clerk

In response to recent educational reform mandates and restructuring proposals, and to trends in the field of literacy instruction, many elementary teachers are attempting to integrate literature into their curricula. They most often start with the teaching of reading by substituting trade books and literature anthologies for stories from the basal readers. Although their materials have changed, their teaching methods continue to reflect recommendations in teacher's guides which accompany each basal series and techniques learned through socialization into teaching. The teachers introduce "new vocabulary words"— words they believe will be difficult for their students—prior to the children's reading these words in the context of the story. They read aloud to small groups to guarantee that the children don't miss any of the words in the story. They conscientiously devise "comprehension questions" for children to answer after each section of the book in order to check for understanding. For individual titles they seek units or kits that have been commercially published or developed by a school district to ensure that their students get enough practice on word analysis skills, dictionary skills, and other conventional components of reading programs. They (and their administrators) look to standardized test results to determine whether or not the use of literature is succeeding in making their students "readers." These teachers are eager to do well by their students; they want to keep up with the profession without "throwing out the baby" (McCallum, 1988). Although some believe that the focus on literature is simply another pendulum swing that will eventually fade into another fad, they welcome new ideas that will make their teaching more effective.

Most of these teachers are implementing effectively what the profession and the public have come to accept as reading instruction. The teachers reflect the prevailing culture of the reading establishment for the past twenty-five years in their understanding of reading as a set of skills. From this perspective, fluent reading results from mastery of specific skills which must be taught sequentially using controlled materials. Success in reading is equated with high standardized test scores. The substitution of trade books and anthologies for basal stories seems to answer adequately the reform mandates for teaching literature, although some teachers express concern about how the skills will be "covered" without the use of hierarchical materials. They do not realize that research and theory support a view of reading which is not skills-based, but rather meaning-centered.

Further, these teachers rarely differentiate between teaching reading through literature, teaching reading along with literature, and teaching literature itself. They rely on materials, rather than on themselves, as the key to effective instruction. As Freeman (1988) asserts, teachers have used basal reading packages for so long that many of them have "lost confidence in themselves as professionals able to help children make choices about what they read and write" (p. 242). As teachers have sought to be accountable for literacy skill development, they have accepted a metaphor which reduces teaching to assigning and assessing. They have become curriculum clerks.

What is the problem with this metaphor for teaching literature? Aren't these methods acceptable as first steps in the transition from skills-based programs to literature-based ones? Maybe. Maybe not.

The Basalization of Literature Teaching

A major problem with the teacher-as-clerk metaphor and the practices it entails is that literature teaching becomes "basalized" (Goodman, 1988; Babbitt, 1990). The potential literary experience (Rosenblatt, 1938, 1978) for the students disappears as literature is treated as a vehicle for teaching skills rather than as an opportunity to experience literature as a unique journey into the worlds of text (Rosenblatt, 1988).

When instructional materials are designed to ensure introduction and practice of isolated skills, the consequence of reading a story is changed from exploring the ideas triggered by the story to completing training exercises on those skills. Consider an activity book developed to accompany *Roll of Thunder, Hear My Cry* (Taylor, 1976), a children's novel set in a southern community in the 1930s. This workbook, *Reading Skills through Literature: Roll of Thunder, Hear My Cry* (Tillman, 1985), presents a set of lessons related to chapters in the novel. Although the author asserts that "activities have been designed to encourage the student to read the original text" (p. 1), the worksheets clearly illustrate a view of reading as skill mastery.

The first exercise, "Changing Short Vowels" (p. 7), is identified with chapter 1 of the novel. The drill requires students to change the vowels in words which follow each sentence and then to fill in the sentence blank with the newly formed word:

> 1. Little Man wore shiny _____ shoes. *block*
> 11. Miss Crocker had _____ yet talked to Mama. *nut*
> 14. Books were piled high on the teacher's _____. *dusk*

A later lesson, "Discovering Meaning through Context" (p. 27), associated with chapter 6, asks children to use the sentence context to figure out which of three word meanings is the correct meaning for an italicized word:

> 1. Big Ma did not answer, but nodded her head *mutely.*
>   silently   slowly   quickly
> 5. Slaves were taught to obey because their owners feared they would *revolt.*
>   rebel   listen   recover

The last lesson in the workbook, "Explaining Feelings" (pp. 51–52), requires students to describe the feelings they had as they read the book. They are directed to "write [their] response on the lines provided" and to "be sure to use complete sentences":

> 1. How did you feel when Cassie saw the car headlights coming toward her house?
> 2. How did you feel when Mr. Barnett refused to wait on the children at the store?
> 3. How did you feel when Big Ma made Cassie apologize to Lillian Jean?

Activities such as these define clearly the underlying goals—use of "a classic title in children's literature to teach reading skills" (Tillman, 1985). Such worksheets ignore the readers' literary experience. Instead, they focus on small bits of textual material, right answers, and rigid response formats. Children who are asked to do such assignments on a regular basis are taught that the purpose of reading literature is to learn to produce acceptable answers in the workbook. Discussions of right answers to the assignments simply emphasize the importance of the prescribed task. The answer key becomes the authority on literature. In the context of such activities, discussion of the story itself—the impact of the events on the student readers, their notions about the characters, why they think the author wrote the story—too often becomes peripheral.

The use of stories to teach reading skills often leads to another compromise in the teaching of literature—mutilated texts. Literary selections are often abridged or rewritten when they are chosen for instructional purposes (Goodman, Shannon, Freeman, and Murphey, 1988). Publishers of anthologies at all levels adapt texts. They attempt to satisfy grade-level expectations and special-interest group challenges. They change specific words in order to meet traditional readability requirements or to satisfy demands of vocabulary control. Whole sentences may be altered to "simplify" language structures, and entire sections may be omitted to conform to space constraints; even illustrations are modified or eliminated to reduce costs or to meet other market pressures. All of these changes affect the author/reader transaction (Goodman, 1984). Reading an altered work is not reading the author's work.

Finally, the basalization of literature contributes to the image and practice of teacher as curriculum clerk. Packaged as vehicles for skill development, these "teacher proof" literature programs supply questions and other assignments for students as well as patterned and scripted instructional sequences for teachers. These extensive guides embody a prescribed scope and sequence of activities. Although the guide may suggest open-ended projects and reading of trade books as enrichment or extension activities, the series' tests and other support materials are designed to assess and promote skill acquisition.

In these programs, teachers find little help in developing text-specific teaching strategies that boost student strengths and keep reading and writing processes functional and whole. Discussions of alternative strategies that focus on strengths of second-language learners and other children who are traditionally at risk are rare. Although the use of literary texts may provide more interesting and well-written stories for students, the recommended pattern of instruction remains conventional and teacher-centered in most prepackaged literature units.

Beyond Basalized Teaching

With occasional exceptions, teachers who view reading not as skill acquisition but as constructing meaning with written language find that they cannot use such programs productively. Often identified as whole language teachers, they want to plan a more personal literature curriculum based on what they know about the specific group of children they are teaching and how they learn. They want to use instructional strategies that suit the particular piece of literature. They treat literature as a new universe to explore and believe they can enter with their students into an author's world—each bringing personal strengths, interests, and intentions on the journey.

As exploration leaders, these teachers acknowledge their professional responsibility to "teach reading." Further, they respect the author's work and their students' minds and know that they cannot—and should not—try to control all the potential experiences. They expect to build on students' responses to the text as well as their own, and to adapt their teaching strategies to promote reading, rereading, and shared discussion by all their students. Their goal is to entice, excite, include, and involve students in the study of literature through authentic language experiences in the classroom.

An Example from the Classroom

A classroom illustration demonstrates the theoretical underpinnings and practical possibilities of the explorer metaphor. The social and personal nature of written language use—both reading and writing (Goodman, 1968, 1984; Langer, 1989; Nelms, 1988), the significance of literary evocation (Rosenblatt, 1938, 1978; Smith, 1953; Hazard, 1960; Sayers, 1965), and the generative nature of language (Lindfors, 1987; Harste, Woodward, and Burke, 1984): all are apparent in the work of twenty-nine fourth-graders in a suburban, ethnically diverse elementary school classroom in California. The class was entering its third week of literature study on *Dear Mr. Henshaw* (Cleary, 1983). The book had been read in its entirety, and the children had participated in a variety of oral and written experiences to extend their initial evocations.

Ms. Dakin, the teacher, designed a morning session to highlight the character of the recently divorced mother of Leigh Botts, the twelve-year-old protagonist. She chose two primary strategies for that day: written conversation (Harste, Short, and Burke, 1988, 375–379; King, 1983) and reflection notes. First, students were to write with a partner about Mrs. Botts—to describe what they thought she was like and to jot down questions they had about her. Following that activity, students were to reflect independently on the written conversation process, noting what they had learned, questions they still had, and their general reactions to the experience. In the following sections, student responses to these two experiences are analyzed.

Written Conversation

Written conversation provides an informal communication experience in which partners write and read each others' messages. Like oral conversations, each dialogue has a life of its own, prompted by the interests and intentions of its participants. Students often engage in spontaneous written conversations as they pass notes about personal concerns; this silent dialogue builds on their natural desire to respond and comment on shared experiences.

Matthew and Russell focused their written conversation on characteristics of Mrs. Botts and on her relationship with Leigh (see figure 1a). They asked each other questions, stated opinions, and noted their areas of agreement and disagreement. They also negotiated a way to conduct the conversation. In his second turn, Matthew suggested a format for Russell's next comment. Later on, Russell expressed some frustration with Matthew's apparent interrogation. Both boys were fully engaged during the half-hour exchange. While one wrote, the other sat quietly with pencil in hand, looking thoughtfully into space or around the room at other partner groups. Their reflection notes revealed both boys' enthusiasm about the written conversation process (see figures 1b and 1c).

All Ms. Dakin's students were active in exchanges with their self-selected partners. No one was excluded; students who traditionally might be isolated for special reading and writing instruction because of low test scores or because their family language was not English participated fully. The personal nature of reading transactions was evident in the students' written visions of Leigh's mother, in the diversity of their written conversations, and in the range of content and emotional tone of their exchanges. For example, while Matthew and Russell stuck to story specifics about the day at the beach and the TV controversy, students Lisa and Maidie's exchange shows quite a different focus, the issue of divorce (see figure 2).

Lisa immediately personalized the conversation by revealing her own parents' divorce. Maidie sensitively affirmed Lisa's feelings by relating them to the story as well as to her own family situation. This explicit identification with the story continued as Lisa expressed concern that the personality change she and Maidie noticed in Mrs. Botts wouldn't happen with her own mother. Within the context of their personal experiences with divorce, Lisa and Maidie's written conversation focused on Leigh's mother's character evolution. They frequently referred to the text ("at the beginning," "but then she changed," "I'm glad the story finally got her in the picture," "in the ending part"), but they did not address specific story events as did Matthew and Russell.

The contrast between these two pairs of partners highlights the diversity of responses that teachers can expect and encourage when literature engages readers in a lived-through experience. Both conversations presented Ms. Dakin with opportunities for expansion through subsequent classroom activities.

The written conversations also generated ideas that likely had not surfaced during a reader's own reading. For example, several children raised questions of each other. Matthew asked Russell four questions; he had time to answer only one (see figure 1a). Another partner group wrote about Mrs. Botts:

> *Jonathon:* Why does she keep bugging him about Mr. Henshaw?
>
> *Bay:* What do you mean she's bugging Leigh?
>
> *Jonathon:* About Mr. Henshaw! Don't you pay any attention to the book!

Students also expressed differences of opinion with their partners. Although they did not pursue it further, Angela and Lindsay discovered that they held differing views about the closeness of the relationship between Leigh and his mother:

> *Angela:* You know Leigh and his mother are not that close.
>
> *Lindsay:* Are you sure they aren't? I thought they were pretty close.

In another conversation, Chrissy and Molly's views about life on welfare emerged:

> *Chrissy:* I think that she is mean because she didn't fix the TV. Even if she doesn't have a lot of money, she should get it fixed.
>
> *Molly:* Chrissy, would you rather have enough to eat or watch TV?
>
> *Chrissy:* It is only two people on welfare. You can feed two people and get your TV fixed and still have some money left.
>
> *Molly:* They don't have enough money as it is.

Variations in interpretation were spontaneous and natural in the conversational context. These variations, unlike prepackaged questions, guided students back to the text to justify or modify discrepant views. Through subsequent focused rereadings, Ms. Dakin could help the children discover how the author led them to conclusions. Through discussions, she could validate their prior knowledge as a basis for their personal versions of the story. The written conversation data provided Ms. Dakin many leads for future extension and critique.

Because written conversation acknowledges the social nature of language as well as its generativity, partner writing expands and deepens students' literary experience. It provides a structure through which students can explore their initial experience with literature. It gives the teacher unobtrusive access to students' developing insights and questions. Because written conversation is a face-to-face, albeit silent, dialogue, the purpose of writing and the impact of a specific audience is quickly realized by the children. Ideas not risked aloud often flow freely on paper. Written conversation allows for airing honest reactions and sharing concerns without whole class response. Because the focus is on content rather than form or correctness, thoughts find expression in an activity which feels safe. Written conversation allows students to work through their understanding of an aspect of literature and to consider their partner's alternative interpretations.

For young children and students of any age whose second language is English, written conversation demonstrates relationships between oral and written language. It shows reading and writing in process as partners take turns making marks on paper that are intended to trigger meaning for the other person. The activity provides a social setting for writing with immediate response and emotional connections. It can be used to generate ideas for later discussion or further individual writing.

Teachers can use written conversation data for further planning—a prompt for making decisions about future literature study or additional instruction in language arts. When collected periodically, students' written conversations complement other writing samples as documentation of reading choices, growth in linguistic sophistication and style, and knowledge of language conventions.

Reflection Notes

The reflection notes invited children to think about their written conversations by writing and drawing about them. They were to respond briefly to each of four prompts: *What We Did, What I Learned, Questions I Have,* and *My General Reactions/Responses.* Just as in the written conversations, these papers demonstrated the individuality of children's understandings of *Dear Mr. Henshaw* and of the classroom tasks themselves.

The *What We Did* section showed the children's understanding of the instructions for the written conversation. About half of them wrote slight variations of "We did a silent dialogue," the teacher's terminology for written conversation (see figure 3).

Some students elaborated on the process, thereby showing clearly that they understood it (see figure 4).

In *What I Learned,* most of the children commented about story details. They also acknowledged that their peers held different views of the story. Frequent references to story elements and events were made. Several children focused on what they had learned about Leigh's mother as a person:

> *Didem:* I learned that Leigh's mother can be very loving.
>
> *Nicole:* I learned how Leigh's mother felt towards the TV.

Other children acknowledged the variety of views held by classmates:

> *Dustin:* I learned that Erik thinks Leigh's mom should get remarried.
>
> *Angela:* I learned that everybody had pretty much different things and had a lot of background to what they said.
>
> *Jonathon:* Not everyone thinks Ms. Botts is mean.

Several children devoted their *What I Learned* section to reflections on the *process* of the written conversation itself rather than the story:

> *Matthew:* I learned to be silent longer.
>
> *Jamie:* Me and Tosh are a good pair, I think.
>
> *Antony:* I learned it wasn't that fun because I'm a big mouth and I wanted to talk.

Students' comments occasionally acknowledged traditional school values as well as the children's developing ability to distance themselves from an activity and to reflect on it (see figures 5 and 6). A few children acknowledged learning personal information about their partner (see figure 7).

While the third section invited *questions* from the children, well over half of them submitted none, not a surprising response from self-assured fourth-graders (see figure 8).

The questions that were raised referred primarily to the story plot:

> *Dustin:* Why will the mommy not get married?
>
> *Erik:* Why doesn't Leigh's mother get the TV fixed?
>
> *Sarah:* Why do kids steal Leigh's lunches?
>
> *Russell:* Does Leigh's mom have a close friend?

A few children addressed larger issues. Josh, for example, asked,

"What kind of person is Leigh's mother?" Armondo noted, "I still want to know more."

Other students posed questions that went beyond plot. Vanessa wondered about the faithfulness to the text in her partner's comments (see figure 9). Jenny, her partner, seemed more concerned with Vanessa's use of language conventions than story line (see figure 6).

In the final section of the reflection notes, *Responses and Reactions*, children were asked to think more generally about the entire literature study experience and to write and show their overall impression of the session. Most stated that they liked doing the written conversations. Several asked to do it again. Others were more specific:

> *Angela:* I thought it was very fun and enjoyable.
>
> *Russell:* The whole thing was educational, and we should do it again.
>
> *Lindsay:* Doing this really gave me a better idea of what the mother was like.

One boy expressed both enjoyment of the experience and anxiety about the optional sharing (which he did not do) which followed the partner writing (see figure 10).

On the whole, the children clearly expressed their views of the written conversation experience in their reflection notes. Their references to the text showed attention to literary elements and issues. Active involvement with the story was illustrated in drawings and comments. Many children demonstrated an awareness of the social and psycholinguistic dimensions of the written conversation experience.

The reflection notes suggest instructional possibilities just as did the written conversations. Future class discussions and small group activities could be planned to expand and clarify students' understanding of the story. Close readings and issue-focused dialogues could be scheduled. Students might use the reflection notes as prompts for more writing. Teachers might pair students in different combinations for further partner work and in other ways modify the classroom social climate. They might also use reflection notes to encourage self-evaluation of other classroom experiences.

Classroom Context

Ms. Dakin's classroom provided a context for extension and elaboration of an aesthetic experience with a literary text. The generative and recursive nature of language was apparent in all of Ms. Dakin's activities. Language—both oral and written—permeated the setting, and invitations to use language were varied and carefully orchestrated. During the hour-and-a-half period, time was available for reading to self, to small groups, and to the whole class. Children were involved in writing with a partner and individually. They talked in groups of four and most of them contributed to whole-group discussion; they listened in large and small groups to classmates and to the teacher.

Nearly all of the classroom language was directed toward the children's literary experiences and their responses to the story. Children were asked if and how the characters related to their own experiences. They were reminded by peers as well as the teacher to check the text when incongruities between interpretations appeared, to see what in the text made them think that way. Although sustained reading of the novel was not a part of this day's plan, the children had obviously read the text to themselves and were aware of the story as a whole, not simply as a series of segments and assignments.

Teaching and Learning Literature: Becoming an Explorer

Recently, teacher groups have become more political and vocal in their efforts to foster authority and responsibility for both teachers and learners. They have insisted on participation in curriculum and evaluation decisions because they know that their first-hand knowledge of their students must take precedence over external curricular mandates when the two realities conflict. They have worked to restore their role in decision-making and to extend professional options and prerogatives in the schooling hierarchy.

The proposed metaphor of teacher-as-explorer fits into this professional movement. As the leader of an expedition into territory both known and unknown, the teacher sets the course and decides on means and methods for moving ahead. In the teaching of literature, the teacher selects and develops curricular goals in literature, based on responsible assessment of the conditions, resources, and constraints in the educational environment, and on knowledge of students' characteristics. Once the expedition has commenced, the teacher bears the responsibility to adjust the direction and timing of daily events and to use resources based on the actual conditions faced by the group. In this role, the teacher of literature makes decisions about specific texts for exploration, organizes the classroom environment to foster and expand lived-through experiences of the literary texts, documents on a regular and frequent schedule both group and individual progress (as well as detours), provides encouragement and support to all, and offers specific assistance to those who need it.

To initiate and maintain this philosophical change from the role of curriculum clerk to that of educational explorer, teachers will need to involve themselves in several tasks: selecting texts, organizing the classroom for lived-through experiences, documenting student progress, and expanding their own professional knowledge.

Selecting Texts

One of the first changes made by "explorer" teachers in teaching literature is to provide students with authentic whole texts rather than abbreviated, mutilated, or contrived ones. They place their pedagogical emphasis on lived-through experiences with literature and language use in context, rather than language and comprehension exercises with a text controlled to teach specific skills. In this atmosphere, students are trusted to handle increasingly difficult linguistic structures and a variety of genres. With real texts (both literary and others), teachers encourage students to apply their linguistic and experiential strengths as they make sense of their reading. When students encounter or select texts that are inappropriate because of complex linguistic structures and dense or unfamiliar conceptual content, teacher/explorers assist them over the new literary terrain by using a variety of supportive instructional strategies. These strategies grow from the teacher's knowledge of the reading process and of language learning as well as from a broader background of literary texts. Occasionally, they may even encourage deferment of a particular text in favor of another more accessible one—thereby providing a temporary detour or an alternate route which keeps with the expedition.

Teachers-as-explorers do not assign texts designed to teach skills nor do they create situations in which students need to exclude aspects of themselves from meaning-making with the texts they encounter. Rather, students read and learn to read selections which expand their worlds by acknowledging and building upon their present understandings and attitudes. Through work with peers and teachers, they discover elements in the texts that extend beyond the particular book to larger contexts and issues of significance. Teachers highlight connections among different titles and help students make explicit linkages with previous readings. Teachers make available a wide spectrum of texts and encourage students to make frequent choices about their own reading. The "Mine, Yours, and Ours" notion (Goodman and Watson, 1977) structures teacher input for ongoing student reading and conferencing. In this way students read concurrently at least three titles: one they themselves choose, the second selected by the teacher (perhaps a text in common with other classmates—a core text such as *Dear Mr. Henshaw*), and a third text they agree on together, one which might extend classroom themes or earlier reading.

Organizing the Classroom for Lived-Through Experiences

Ms. Dakin's classroom, presented earlier, provides *one* view of a classroom atmosphere and organization supported by the metaphor of teacher-as-explorer. All of the students were included in the exploration of *Dear Mr. Henshaw*; no one was tracked out. This use of one text as a core selection meant an intensive study of a book in common, one of several selections throughout the school year. Designating a common title did not mean limiting the entire class to an easy book. Rather, for each core text, many opportunities for entering the text world were afforded to all students over an extended period of time. Ms. Dakin's students, for example, were engaged with *Dear Mr. Henshaw* for approximately six weeks. The explicit and overriding focus was on collaborative meaning-making involving all students in the exploration.

Ms. Dakin's classroom focus was teaching literature, not teaching reading skills by using literature. Because she knew that language is learned through use in authentic and engaging situations, she was confident that her students were becoming more proficient readers as they read, wrote about, and discussed the story world of *Dear Mr. Henshaw*. Ms. Dakin believed that students learn to read in the process of reading literature and hearing it read aloud, but her purpose for using literature was to foster a literary experience, not to provide practice on selected subskills.

She also acknowledged that she was teaching, implicitly, conventions of written language. For example, although the students were not overly concerned about correctness in their written conversations, they did have to make sure that their messages were understandable to their partners. They were faced with immediate reasons for using familiar spelling patterns; unconventional spellings were of concern only when communication was interrupted. In her role as explorer, Ms. Dakin used expressive writing as a source of information about her students' use of language conventions just as a trekker uses information found along the route as a guide for planning and possible rethinking of the route. In both situations, the relevance of the information and urgency for action are evaluated with respect to larger goals and knowledge of individual participants.

All children were expected to participate fully and contribute actively, with the assumption that each would experience the text in a personal and significant way. As in any life situation, different personal histories foster individual understandings of the story, and individual strengths and interests compel participants to pursue different paths. Ms. Dakin planned instructional tasks which assumed and valued different student abilities, strengths, interests, and outcomes; in fact, she viewed the variety of student experiences evolving from study of the core work as highly desirable. Each student's unique reading of the text contributed and enlarged the meaning potential for all classroom participants. The frequent use of informal writing for the purpose of stimulating thinking and communication exemplified the value she placed on the exploration of ideas.

Organizing classrooms where students feel comfortable to evoke and explore responses to literature requires a shift in notions about curriculum development. In such settings, teachers draw on their own responses to a text and their knowledge of the larger context of literature and language learning, as well as information they gain from careful ongoing observation of students' responses to the selection and to other planned classroom experiences. The locus of control shifts as teachers take responsibility for using student response and class interaction as primary sources of curriculum planning. Published teacher's editions for basal anthologies and other source books take their place as references rather than directives. No single or external source is assumed to "contain" the essential elements of an ideal literature curriculum. Such a view requires trust and professional commitment from teachers, and support beyond the classroom. It is, however, an exciting and legitimate curriculum alternative which embodies the "teacher-as-explorer" metaphor.

Documenting Student Progress

Teachers who view their role as explorers change their purposes and procedures for documenting and evaluating student growth. Teachers become astute "kid watchers" (Goodman, 1978). Because they recognize the social nature of learning, they audio- and videotape group sessions for analysis and evaluation. Because they expect diverse, personal interpretations to arise from their students' readings, they seek measures which capture individual responses to literature without distorting them. Because they value the aesthetic experience literature can provide, they encourage alternate modes of response. Because they acknowledge that reading and writing are processes and not sets of skills, they employ techniques which keep language whole and purposeful. They use student products to inform their curriculum development, to assess student strengths and interests, to evaluate their teaching effectiveness, and to demonstrate to students and others the nature of growth in language and literature.

As explorers, teachers search for evaluative evidence that emerges from classroom projects, daily routines, and uninterrupted samples of reading and writing, rather than from contrived assessments and formal tests (Barrs, 1989). Student work is chosen by students and teachers and collected over time to chronicle tasks and provide samples of current competence. Portfolios containing works-in-progress, first drafts, sketches, notes about potential projects, peer responses, photographs of projects, and out-takes from completed tasks provide other cues to student strengths and interests. Completed work is shared with peers and often published outside the classroom. Projects frequently are displayed around the school as well as in community settings and public agencies.

In addition to samples of student work, these teachers keep brief informal written records about students' individual work patterns and their involvement in classroom activities (Barrs, 1989). These classroom observations provide anecdotal records which, over time, add perspective as teachers periodically decide on the letter grades most schools require to summarize and report student progress. To augment the single-letter quantitative assessment, copies of representative student work are included to illustrate the quality of learning.

Expanding Professional Knowledge

Leading students on successful expeditions into literature requires pedagogical and literary knowledge as well as the confidence that accompanies such knowledge. Teachers who adopt the explorer role recognize the power of classroom observations (i.e., kid watching) as one important source of their competence. However, many desire additional support as they reconsider and reconstruct life in their classrooms. These teachers need to know current research and theory about literacy learning and evaluation, and to be readers of literature themselves. They need to know experientially the power of writing, drawing, enacting, and talking, as ways to make meaning. They need access to available cross-cultural literature. They need to develop criteria for selecting texts both for and with their students. In order to move toward a meaning-centered, literature-based curriculum, teachers need to engage in ongoing professional development (Barr, 1988).

Teachers of literature must *experience* the power of strategies which reflect the principles of literacy development and reader-response theory. In order to realize (or to be reminded of) the power of literature, they must *read* artful texts which inspire and captivate them. While working through their new understandings, they need to confer with other teachers already using meaning-centered literature study and to *observe* their classrooms. They must *try* the new ideas and strategies in their own classrooms and *reflect* on their students' as well as their own reactions to the changes. Knowing that revision is as vital in teaching as in composing, they must take risks and *accept* themselves as learners as well as teachers.

Finally, in order to change the metaphor for teaching literature, teachers who wish to lead their students into explorations of text worlds need time and support. Designing new literature curricula, revaluing student work, reading unfamiliar trade books, consulting professional references, and discussing plans and results with peers and experts are time-consuming tasks. Rather than hurriedly instituting across-the-board changes, comfortable adjustments to existing teaching patterns are recommended, even when they seem minor. As confidence in an evolving philosophy and changing teacher role grows, theoretically consistent activities will begin to occur intuitively. "Good" activities will crowd out less productive tasks. Reflection on the new practices provides critical guidance, especially as it is shared with colleagues.

In addition to support from peers, teachers moving toward the explorer role need clear sanction from administrators. When teachers are trusted with the content and pacing of changes in their classrooms, they take responsibility for the results. Administrators can create a supportive context which enables teachers to "own" the philosophy they are implementing. Assurances that success will be based on more than just conventional measures of student growth, such as standardized test scores, contribute to teachers' willingness to try new ideas. Deferment of external judgments during early months of implementation builds further confidence. Administrators who take time for conversations with teachers about their curriculum changes provide important opportunities for the growth of mutual respect and professional commitment.

Summary

The notion of teacher-as-explorer, although not new, is not yet a dominant metaphor for the teaching of literature. Still, evidence from classrooms and implications of current research and theory suggest the metaphor is strong and apt. Teachers can be explorers who lead students beyond themselves into text worlds. It is only when literature provides a context for exploration that the aesthetic experience described by Rosenblatt (1938) a half century ago occurs: as teachers lead students "toward a fuller participation in what the text offers" (p. 78), they enable the readers to "participate in another's vision— to reap knowledge of the world, to fathom the resources of the human spirit, to gain insights that will make their own lives more comprehensible" (p. 7).

Exploring literature requires revision of prevalent beliefs about the teaching and learning of literature and of literacy. It calls upon different traditions of research and theory. It demands the replacement of methods and materials commonly assumed to be necessary to teach literature and reading. It requires thoughtful and responsible planning and active decision-making as students progress into, through, and beyond the author's world. In the same manner that teachers become exploration leaders, students become explorers. As student responses are validated and extended, their sophistication with language and literature grows, and the journey into literature becomes an exploration of life itself.

References

Babbitt, N. (1990). Protecting children's literature. *The Horn Book Magazine,* 696–703.

Barr, M.A. (1988, March). *Implementing a research-based curriculum in English-language arts, K–12.* California Staff Development and Curriculum Conference. Sierra Madre, CA: KAW Co.

Barrs, M. (1989). Primary language record. Portsmouth, NH: Boynton/Cook, Heinemann.

Cleary, B. (1983). *Dear Mr. Henshaw.* New York, NY: Dell.

Freeman, Y.S. (1988). The California reading initiative: Revolution or merely revision? *The New Advocate, 1*(4), 241–249.

Goodman, K.S. (1968). The psycholinguistic nature of the reading process. In K.S. Goodman (Ed.), *The psycholinguistic nature of the reading process.* Detroit, MI: Wayne State Press.

Goodman, K.S. (1984). Unity in reading. In A.C. Purves and O. Niles (Eds.), *Becoming readers in a complex society: 83rd yearbook of the National Society for the Study of Education, part 1* (pp. 79–114). Chicago, IL: University of Chicago Press.

Goodman, K.S. (1988). Look what they've done to Judy Blume!: The "basalization" of children's literature. *The New Advocate, 1*(2), 29–41.

Goodman, K.S., Shannon, P., Freeman, Y.S., and Murphey, S. (1988). *Report card on basal readers.* Katonah, NY: Richard C. Owen.

Goodman, Y. (1978). Kid watching: An alternative to testing. *Journal of National Elementary Principals, 57*(4), 41–45.

Goodman, Y., and Watson, D.J. (1977). A reading program to live with: Focus on comprehension. *Language Arts, 54*(8), 868–879.

Harste, J.C., Short, K.G., with C.L. Burke. (1988). *Creating classrooms for authors.* Portsmouth, NH: Boynton/Cook, Heinemann.

Harste, J.C., Woodward, V.A., and Burke, C.L. (1984). *Language stories and literacy lessons.* Portsmouth, NH: Boynton/Cook, Heinemann.

Hazard, P. (1960). *Books, children, and men* (4th ed., M. Mitchell, Trans.). Boston, MA: The Horn Book. (Original work published 1944)

King, D.F. (1983). Written conversation. In J.L. Collins (Ed.), *Teaching all the children to write* (pp. 65–74). New York, NY: State English Council Monograph.

Langer, J. (1989). *The process of understanding literature* (Report Series 2.1). Albany, NY: Center for the Learning and Teaching of Literature, SUNY at Albany.

Lindfors, J.W. (1987). *Children's language and learning.* Englewood Cliffs, NJ: Prentice Hall.

McCallum, R.D. (1988). Don't throw the basals out with the bath water. *Reading Teacher, 42*(3), 204–207.

Nelms, B.F. (1988). Sowing the dragon's teeth: An introduction in the first person. In B.F. Nelms (Ed.), *Literature in the classroom: Readers, texts, and contexts* (pp. 1–16). Urbana, IL: National Council of Teachers of English.

Rosenblatt, L.M. (1938). *Literature as exploration* (4th ed.). New York, NY: Modern Language Association.

Rosenblatt, L.M. (1978). *The reader, the text, the poem: The transactional theory of the literary work.* Carbondale, IL: Southern Illinois University Press.

Rosenblatt, L.M. (1988, October). *Literature as experience.* Presentation at the Academy of the California Literature Project, Long Beach, CA.

Sayers, F.C. (1965). *Summoned by books.* New York, NY: Viking Press. (Original work published in 1937)

Smith, F. (1983). The choice between teachers and programs. In F. Smith (Ed.), *Essays into literacy* (pp. 107–116). Exeter, NH: Heinemann.

Smith, F. (1988). Misleading metaphors of education. In F. Smith (Ed.), *Joining the literacy club* (pp. 93–108). Portsmouth, NH: Heinemann.

Smith, L.H. (1953). *The unreluctant years.* New York, NY: Viking Press.

Taylor, M. (1976). *Roll of thunder, hear my cry.* New York, NY: Bantam Books.

Tillman, C.D. (1985). *Reading skills through literature: Roll of thunder, hear my cry.* Portals to Reading Series. Logan, IA: Perfection Form.

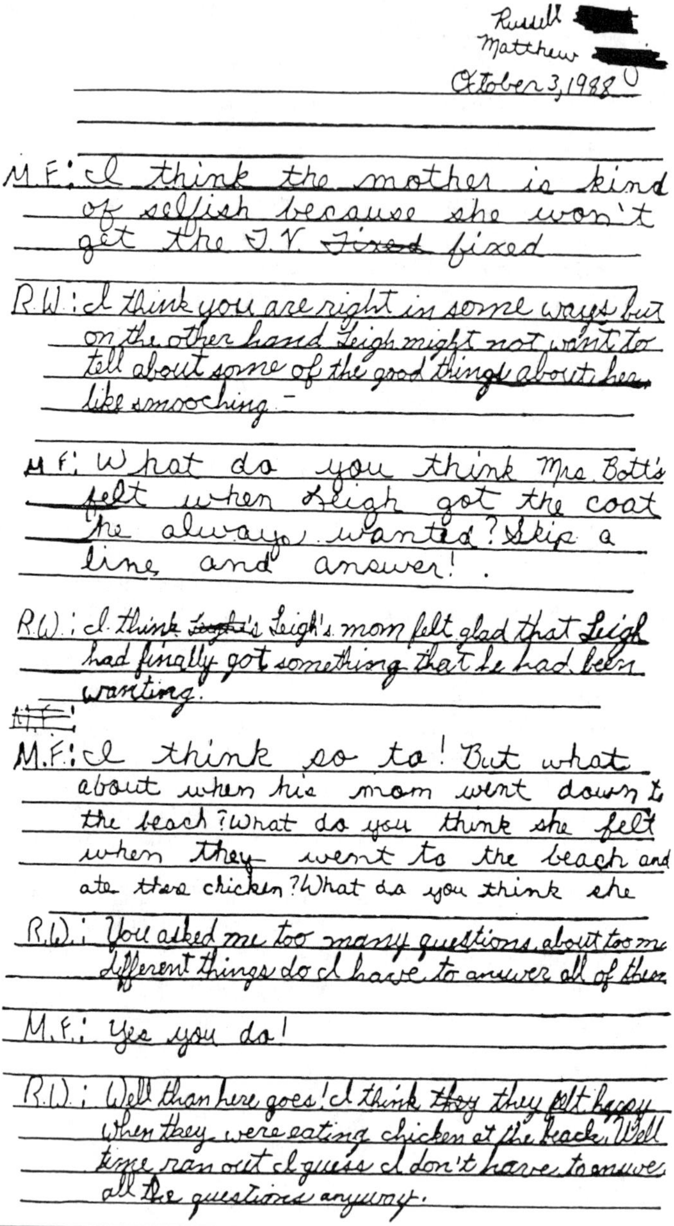

Russell ▮
Matthew ▮
October 3, 1988

M.F: I think the mother is kind
of selfish because she won't
get the T.V. ~~fixed~~ fixed

R.W: I think you are right in some ways but
on the other hand Leigh might not want to
tell about some of the good things about her
like smooching —

M.F: What do you think Mrs. Bott's
felt when Leigh got the coat
he always wanted? Skip a
line and answer!

R.W: I think ~~Leigh's~~ Leigh's mom felt glad that Leigh
had finally got something that he had been
wanting.

~~M.F:~~

M.F: I think so to! But what
about when his mom went down to
the beach? What do you think she felt
when they went to the beach and
ate there chicken? What do you think she

R.W: You asked me too many questions about too m
different things do I have to answer all of them

M.F: Yes you do!

R.W: Well than here goes! I think ~~they~~ they felt happy
when they were eating chicken at the beach. Well
time ran out I guess I don't have to answer
all the questions anyway.

Fig. 1a. Written conversation (Matthew and Russell).

Fig. 1b. Reflection notes (Matthew).

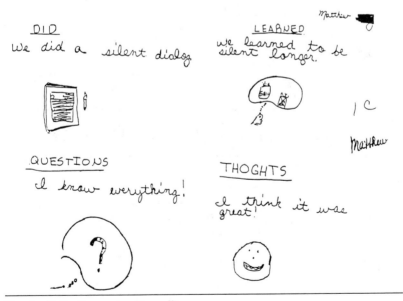

Fig. 1c. Reflection notes (Russell).

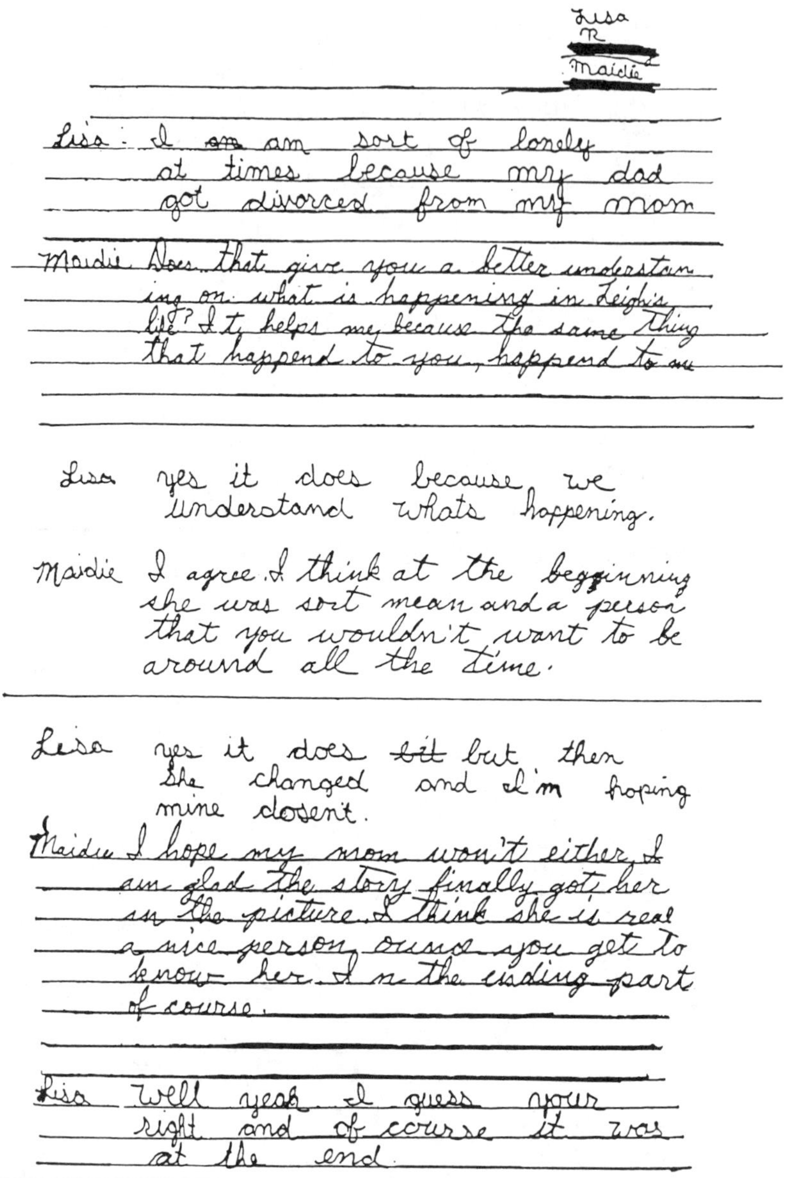

Lisa ~~am~~ am sort of lonely
at times because my dad
got divorced from my mom

Maidie Does that give you a better understanding on what is happening in Leigh's life? It helps me because the same thing that happend to you, happend to me

Lisa yes it does because we understand whats happening.

Maidie I agree. I think at the beginning she was sort mean and a person that you wouldn't want to be around all the time.

Lisa yes it does ~~bit~~ but then she changed and I'm hoping mine dosen't.

Maidie I hope my mom won't either, I am glad the story finally got her in the picture. I think she is real a nice person, once you get to know her. I n the ending part of course.

Lisa Well yeah I guess your right and of course it was at the end.

Fig. 2. Written conversation (Lisa and Maidie).

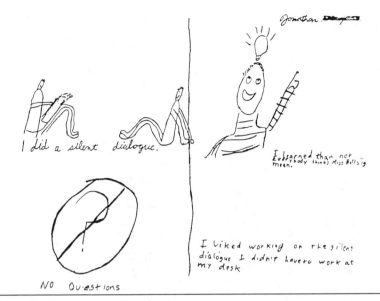

Fig. 3. Reflection notes (Jonathon).

Fig. 4. Reflection notes (Tate).

Fig. 5. Reflection notes (Lindsay).

Fig. 6. Reflection notes (Jenny).

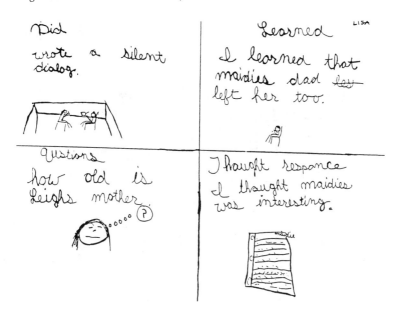

Fig. 7. Reflection notes (Lisa).

Antony

We did silent dialogue that I learned it wasn't fun because I'm a big mouth and I wanted to talk.

I don't have any questions.

I think that if we ever do it again we should be talking

Fig. 8. Reflection notes (Antony).

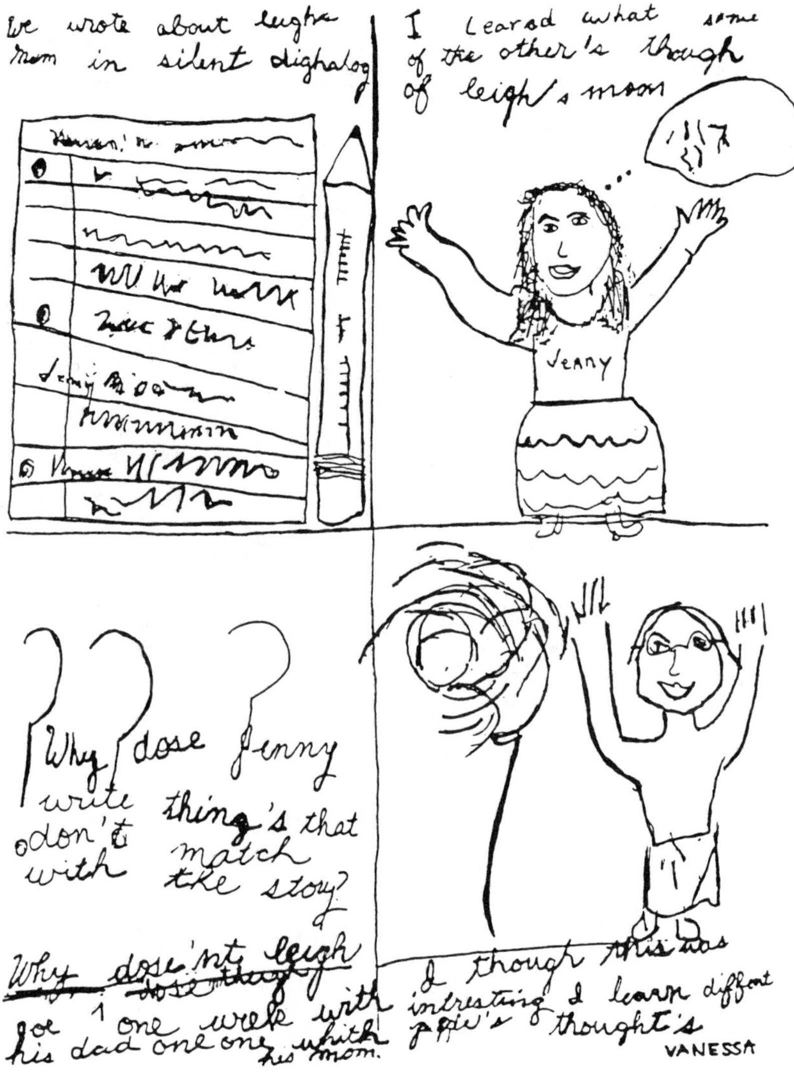

Fig. 9. Reflection notes (Vanessa).

DID
WE DID O silent
DIALOG ON LEIGH'S MOTHER

LEARN
I LEARNED THAT THE MOTHER
WAS really a nice person.

questions?
I still don't Know why
Leighs mother does'nt get the TV.
FIXED

WHAT you ~~DID~~ THOUGHT
I thought everything was
FUN but I was nervous because I
did'nt want to go up in front of the class

Erik

Fig. 10. Reflection notes (Erik).

7 Literary Reading and Classroom Constraints: Aligning Practice with Theory*

Patrick X. Dias
McGill University

Over the past two decades, theory and research in the fields of reading and reader response have converged toward some central understandings with respect to what occurs in literary reading, that is, what occurs in the transactions between readers and literary texts. Mike Hayhoe and I have argued elsewhere at some length (Dias and Hayhoe, 1988) that such understandings are remarkably consistent with developments in literary critical theory, accommodating as well some of the basic and less flamboyant arguments in post-structuralist literary criticism. At the core of these developments is the view of the reader as actively engaged in making meaning and of meaning as residing neither in the reader nor in the text, but constantly renewed in the transactions that occur between reader and text. A strong proponent of such a position has been Louise Rosenblatt, who introduced such notions in 1938 and developed them more fully in 1978. It is only recently that several related fields of inquiry have converged to confirm the theoretical and practical validity of her views.

This chapter proposes a reorientation of classroom practices in the teaching of literature, a reorientation proceeding from these new understandings of literary reading. The argument supporting it falls into four sections. The first section, "Literary Reading: New Understandings," reviews those particular convergences in current theory and research on literary reading that teachers ought to consider when rethinking classroom practice. The second section, "Reader Response

* This paper is based on research funded by the Social Sciences and Humanities Research Council of Canada (grant no. 410-86-0237). I am deeply grateful to Mrs. Linda Fernandes for implementing the procedure in her classrooms and providing very useful feedback over the last fourteen years. I thank her Secondary 2 class at St. Pius X Comprehensive High School, Montreal, for making it so easy to work with them. I own much to Alayne Sullivan, who was a reliable and hardworking research assistant on this project. For their careful reading and helpful suggestions, I thank my colleagues Ann Beer and Anthony Pare, as well as the two anonymous reviewers of this paper.

Theory and the Teaching of Literature," considers to what extent current classroom situations and practices in the teaching of literature are hospitable to our new understandings of literary reading. The third section, "Response-centered Practice: Overcoming Classroom Constraints," suggests how classroom situations and practices might be more properly aligned with what we know about acts of reading literature. The fourth and closing section points up some of the key issues teachers ought to consider in developing agendas for reader-centered classrooms.

Literary Reading: New Understandings

The Literary Transaction

Rosenblatt's (1978) use of the term "transaction" to describe the literary experience reminds us that a literary work does not have its existence apart from a reader and the particular occasion of its reading. Each act of reading a particular literary text is a re-creation of that work; as Terry Eagleton suggests, one never really reads the same poem twice (1983).

Such a view of literary reading represents a current concern in critical thought. Other movements have seen the "poem," on the one hand, as an autonomous object, an entity residing largely or entirely in the text, apart from the contexts of its creation or its readers—views expressed by New Critics such as Brooks (1947), Wellek and Warren (1949), and Wimsatt (1958). On the other hand, in reaction to such a position, a subjectivist view has been advanced by critics such as Holland (1973, 1975) and Bleich (1975, 1978), who argue, in the words of Bleich, "that reading is a wholly subjective process and that the nature of what is perceived is determined by the rules of the personality of the perceiver" (1975, p. 3). The view of Rosenblatt and like-minded critics, including current post-structuralist critics, is not necessarily a compromise between these two rather deterministic positions; rather, it takes account of the reading situation, the continually altering contexts that should affect how and what one reads, and the consequent instability of meaning. Quite obviously, reading a story to answer some comprehension questions set by a teacher is not the same as reading for one's own pleasure or to search for occurrences of a particular word or image.

The importance of the reader's stance in determining how and what one reads is illustrated by Rosenblatts's notions of aesthetic and efferent reading:

In nonaesthetic reading, the reader's attention is focused primarily on what will remain as the residue *after* the reading—the information to be acquired, the logical solution to a problem, the actions to be carried out. . . . As the reader responds to the printed words or symbols, his attention is directed outward, so to speak, toward concepts to be retained, ideas to be tested, actions to be performed after the reading.

To designate this type of reading, in which the primary concern of the reader is with what he will carry away from the reading, I have chosen the term "efferent," derived from the Latin "efferre," "to carry away." . . .

In aesthetic reading, in contrast, the reader's primary concern is with what happens *during* the actual reading event. Though, like the efferent reader of a law text, say, the reader of Frost's "Birches" must decipher the images or concepts or assertions that the words point to, he also pays attention to associations, feelings, attitudes, and ideas that these words and their referents arouse within him. "Listening to" himself, he synthesizes these elements into a meaningful structure. *In aesthetic reading, the reader's attention is centered directly on what he is living through during his relationship with that particular text.* (1978, pp. 23–25)

If we are considering, then, how best we might align classroom practice with current understandings of the act of reading, we need to begin by asking how and to what extent classroom contexts predetermine an efferent stance on the part of readers.

The Literary Work

The literary text is often defined as a blueprint (Iser, 1978), a potentiality of meaning to be activated or realized by the reader. One of the more productive aspects of post-structuralist criticism is that it regards literary text as a dynamic entity and welcomes considerations of alternative meanings: a dwelling in uncertainty rather than an effort to close in on the one right meaning. Literary texts afford possibilities of meaning rather than merely concealing meanings that can only be realized by close analysis. Notions of the literary text and of meaning as unstable are congruent with a view of literary reading as a transaction. At the same time, such a view of literary reading *does not* accommodate a position that a literary work means whatever one wants it to mean. The reader must work within the constraints imposed by the lexical, semantic, and formal components of the text. This brings into question the roles of teachers as authorized readers, as those who mediate between canonized texts and apprentice readers, and how they can guide their students to become skilled meaning-makers.

The Reader's Role

When literary reading is considered transactional, readers are viewed as active performers of text rather than as passive receivers. Activity goes much beyond decoding meaning; it involves ascribing intentions, considering analogical situations, and attending to the feelings and associations called up during the reading, including memories of other texts. It is an act of analysis as well as an act of composing, of "writing" the text. And like writing, it is recursive; that is, it has both a forward and backward movement, and does not necessarily proceed serially.

Individual Strategies in Reading Literature

Given the individuality of readers and their active involvement in the making of meaning, it should not be surprising that readers differ in their strategies for making sense of literature. Readers are particularly individualistic in their past histories as readers, in how they believe they must proceed in making sense of literature. I have observed in a small number of cases that those readers who have grown used to reading in order to answer quizzes on their reading are often quite easily put off reading long fiction, simply because they have learned to become more attentive to minor details at the expense of the larger events and themes in the story. In my research on how adolescent readers go about making sense of poetry (Dias, 1987), I have noticed patterns of reading that reflect classroom practices. There are readers who read a poem only to paraphrase it because they have somehow internalized the notion that their task as readers is to translate the complex language of poetry into simple prose. Other readers see their task as puzzling out the theme of the poem and announcing from time to time in their reading a generalization (about nature or humanity, for instance) in the hope that they will somehow hit the mark. This notion of the poem as a puzzle is engendered in the ways questions are asked and answers entertained in some classrooms. Without opportunities for pupils to reflect and analyze before answering, a trial-and-error strategy seems the most practical strategy they can adopt.

There are other patterns of reading, but those two examples should suffice to make my point: readers' strategies, more often than not, develop from classroom practices. Instructional activities make some strategies more productive than others. As a consequence, readers' expectations as to what they must read for are powerful determiners of how they will approach other texts in the same genre. Reading in the expectation that one's comprehension will be tested by the teacher is unlikely to promote either enjoyment of reading or the likelihood that an individual will voluntarily read such texts in the future.

Reader-Response Theory and the Teaching of Literature

If we agree that one of our main aims in the teaching of literature is the development of independent readers, readers who work from their own responses yet are open to newer possibilities of meaning, we need to ask to what extent such an aim is realizable within the situations that prevail in most English classrooms. There are several aspects of typical classroom practice that work against the development of autonomous readers and subvert the processes that support aesthetic reading, cultivating instead reading that is largely efferent.

The Literary Work as an Event in Time

The typical relationship between teacher and taught, particularly where the teacher functions as guide to and arbiter of meaning, is inconsistent with the notion of reading as transaction where meaning is continually recreated in each act of meaning. Moreover, the organization of reading and discussion in set blocks of time assumes that all readers can be expected to realize the literary work in the same way and at the same pace. There is little time for reflection and reversal and too urgent a demand for the immediate right answer. Part of the difficulty is, of course, that the teacher is not usually an equal partner in the conversation, having read the work several times and, more often than not, being armed with an arsenal of questions. Such a situation can only lead to students' believing that the correct version of the work is locked in the mind of the teacher and that it is their job to ferret it out—most likely by attending to the signals the teacher transmits.

As teachers, we are often unaware of the extent to which our authority directs and eventually subverts student inquiry. A project involving a group of sixteen year olds who met informally with their teachers once a week after school in reading discussion groups might serve as an example. The teachers understood, as a condition of their involvement in the project, that they would not function as authority figures, but participate with their students as curious and equal readers. At a meeting with the groups toward the end of the year, I asked the students whether their teachers behaved any differently during the discussion sessions than they did in the regular classroom format. After the students agreed that they felt much more comfortable within the discussion format, they hesitantly went on to point out some important differences. If and when the teachers asked questions in the discussion sessions, the students felt their opinions were genuinely sought, quite unlike how they felt when these teachers asked questions in the regular classroom. The questions during the discussion sessions were real inquiries; the teachers wished to be informed, and the students were sure there were no correct answers against which they were being measured. That the questions were genuine was easily apparent since the teachers were not impatient for answers, providing time for everyone to reflect and reconsider. By contrast, in the regular classrooms, the teachers hardly paused to allow for reflection; students were expected to have ready-made answers. If they did not answer, or, more likely, guess correctly, they were provided the teachers' versions.

Overall, however, the students were unanimous in supporting their teachers' restrictive approaches in their regular classroom. They felt (1) the teachers could not afford the leisurely pace that was allowed in the discussion sessions—they had a program to cover; (2) the students had to be prepared for examinations and for what was expected of them in postsecondary studies, and certainly, however much they enjoyed it, informal discussion was impractical preparation for such a world. In a sense, the students had accepted arguments that justified a particular kind of teaching, even if they wondered what they were really learning.

Typical classroom settings also promote the notion that class sessions must move toward consensus on central issues raised by the set reading. Students are not expected or even encouraged to differ with each other, or to entertain ambiguity. It is not expected that some issues will resolve themselves only over time, will raise new questions, will emerge anew in other readings. It is accepted that tests and examinations demand definitive, final answers. One can defend and account for the popularity of crib notes, like Coles's or Cliffs notes, simply on the basis that such notes, unchanged it seems for years, provide *the* answers, and, of course, perpetuate a belief that the answers as well as the questions will always be the same. If literary reading is truly an event in time, we must find ways of consistently demonstrating this belief in practice.

The Literary Work as "Evoked"

Rosenblatt uses the term "evocation" to refer to "the lived-through process of building up the work under the guidance of the text" (1978,

69). She distinguishes between the reader's evocation of a poem and that reader's interpretation of that evocation. I have argued above that the typical classroom allows little time for a developing response, and by that I mean little time for the reader's evocation of a literary work, what Rosenblatt has also described as the "lived-through current of ideas, sensations, images, tensions . . ." (1985, 103), as well as for the response to that evocation, which develops, if called for, into interpretation as well. The point to keep in mind is that the large-group format with the teacher up front is inhospitable to those deeply personal engagements, the recalling of personal experience, that the term "evocation" implies. Those evocations need to be worked out, filtered through, within the supportive confines of a small group rather than held back and denied within the large group. In interviews with adolescent readers, I was particularly aware of some students who felt (and had demonstrated by their teacher's failure to call on them) that their personal experiences were largely irrelevant to their understanding of a literary work and its discussion in the classroom. Even where students had been asked to keep reading logs, teachers rarely had legitimized the value of personal experiences either by specific instruction or by commenting favorably on what students had written in their logs.

Readers' Expectations

Readers' expectations are powerful determiners of how and what they understand of literary text. The expectation that a text will not make sense is quite likely to ensure that it doesn't. Such expectations seem to disengage one's sense-making efforts, efforts which would normally work around the difficulties of the text, unfamiliar vocabulary, etc. For instance, I do not expect to understand the fine print in my insurance policy, and therefore, I do not put forth the initial effort that would allow me to make even minimal sense of it, or later, with growing familiarization, to develop some degree of competence in the reading of such texts. Expectations regarding literary text are engendered largely in the classroom from previous encounters with literature. Too large a proportion of students believe, for instance, that they cannot make sense of a poem on their own. Such an expectation could easily have grown from the classroom practice of teachers asking questions about poems before their students have had sufficient time to attend to and recognize what the poem has evoked in them. Over ten years ago, I asked eighty English teachers how many readings of a poem they allowed for before they asked their students the first question on that poem. The mean number of readings turned out to be 1.6. Whatever the nature of that first question, such a practice transmits a message that students should have, with one or two readings, come to some understanding of the poem. Because students quite obviously can't, they must conclude that they are not really capable of understanding poetry on their own. Teachers—at all levels—ought to remind themselves how often they themselves read a poem before they decide to use it in their classroom; they should also recall how uncertain they might have felt in their first encounters with that poem.

Another expectation generated by classroom practice is the notion of literary text as a static entity. Such a notion is particularly apparent in some teachers' efforts to wrap up and put the final seal on the literary work. It is apparent as well in some hierarchical sequences of questioning that point to a predestined conclusion. As I said earlier, students are quick to read the signs which cue them in the approved direction. They soon learn to clamor for the right answer: "Aren't you going to tell us what it really means?" The notion of literary texts as dynamic entities that grow or shrink with each rereading, with the reading of other texts, and, in general, with one's growing experiences of life, is a notion certainly worth cultivating. In addition, students need to learn to live with and value ambiguity rather than to seek and demand fixed and final versions of the literary texts they read.

It is worth recalling here Lakoff and Johnson's *Metaphors We Live By* (1980) and their discussion of the *problem as puzzle* and *problem in solution* metaphors. I suggest that problems regarded as puzzles have closed answers: once answered, the puzzle no longer intrigues one into another effort at answering it. Problems regarded as being in solution suggest temporary resolution: the problem may precipitate out whenever an appropriate catalyst is introduced. Many classrooms treat the poem as puzzle; once one is done with it, there is nothing left to return to. In contrast, poems treated as problems in solution continually intrigue and involve because their resolution is held in tension; new ideas, new experiences, the passage of time can bring the poem out of solution again.

I have described two constraining expectations which are supported by typical classroom practices: the expectation that a literary work, particularly a poem, will not make sense without the directive intervention of the teacher, and the expectation that literary texts are static, unchanging entities. Such expectations are not easily dislodged. In the first instance, students need to experience success in reading and understanding several poems on their own. In the second instance, they need to come to value postponing closure, not settling too early and easily on meaning.

Readers' Roles in the Making of Meaning

In my research on individual patterns in making sense of poetry (Dias, 1987), I describe a pattern of reading I call *problem solving*. Readers in this pattern entertain several possibilities of meaning, delay closure, consider their feelings, and do not ignore information from the text that seems to be inconsistent with the meaning they are constructing. Peter, whom I described as reading in a problem-solving pattern, reported that he was considered disruptive in his English classroom, simply because his initial approach as a reader was to recognize several possibilities of meaning, some of which might be characterized as remote, on the ground that poems do not always mean what they seem to at first glance. When he announced such possibilities in response to his teacher's questioning, he was told that he should shelve such far-fetched notions and pay more attention to the text. On the other hand, those who read in the paraphrasing pattern I described earlier never felt they were out of line with the teacher's agenda. Seeing their task as mainly one of translating the poem into simpler language, they were able to fit well into a line of questioning whose primary purpose was to establish what the poem stated literally before launching into what it might mean.

We need to ensure that teaching procedures are hospitable to individual ways of making sense and that they do not frustrate ways of reading that allow readers to assume fuller responsibility for the meanings they make.

Demystifying Reading

If we consider our own experience of reading for pleasure, we know that we seldom question the validity of our own reading and understanding: "I have read what I have read!" We respect the rights of critics to differ, and may advert to their opinions without, of course, feeling deflated and inadequate as readers. I believe students who have not yet abandoned reading fiction for themselves do not consider themselves accountable to anyone else for what they read at home. They do not have to read with much of their attention and enjoyment diverted by wondering what a teacher might want them to realize from their reading. When they feel the need, as most readers do, to share their enjoyment or their displeasure, to confirm their observations or their puzzlement, they turn to other readers—not to authorities such as teachers or critics, but to fallible readers like themselves. I would argue that this is one, if not the only, reason we lend books; we wish to confirm we are not idiosyncratic in how we read books and, for that matter, how we read the world. *Classroom practice needs to change in ways that reduce and even eliminate the gap between school reading and real-world reading.* We may begin by demystifying literature, making it a familiar object, a subject of common parlance, about which one can venture opinions without having prepared an elaborate defense, and to which one can pay attention and trust one's intuitions. It should not be long before students recognize that the mere fact that they have shared a reading in common (an assigned text) is an occasion to be taken advantage of—for the richness of opinion it promises— in extended discussion and shared inquiry. Such moves must emanate from the students and their felt need to do so.

Reading Collaboratively

Often in discussions of response to literature, response is referred to in the abstract, with no reference to whether that response has been spoken or written or felt and thought. While we can conceive of a full and satisfying response that remains unarticulated, for all practical purposes we need to consider response as it is expressed in talk or in writing. I wish to press here for the importance of talk in articulating and developing one's response, talk that is tentative, shaping, recursive, and attentive to the responses of others. It is the recursiveness of talk, by which I mean both a forward and backward flow, a recovering and revising of earlier observations, which makes it such a vital instrument for coming to understand one's transaction with a literary work. It is a living through the work again but with the added benefit of other supporting memories to confirm or to reject, to collaboratively recreate the literary work. As well, talk allows for immediate expression of a developing response; it is tolerant of uncertainty and approximation, of detours and diversions; it seems particularly to invite analogy ("It's like . . .," "You know what I mean?") and calling on personal experience ("I remember when . . .") in the effort to find a name and a shape for one's experience of that work.

I am thinking of talk in small groups, which, as opposed to whole-class discussion, multiplies the opportunities for individuals to try out and formulate their ideas. Such an insistence on the value of talk is not to deny the value of writing. There *are* ways of using writing to help students work from their initial responses toward a fuller and more organized statement. But more often than not, I believe, especially for the reluctant readers and writers I have in mind, writing interposes a barrier between a reader's response and his or her articulation of that response. Talk can stay more immediately in touch with one's response, can capture fleeting impressions; it does not censor as much as writing often does or encourage one to come to closure as quickly. The linear, sequential nature of writing forces the writer to jettison so much in a response which does not seem immediately relevant and which may not be recalled when it comes to matter. I have compared protocols obtained from individual students asked to think aloud during their efforts to make sense of a poem, with these students' written stream-of-consciousness responses to another poem of a similar level of difficulty. The transcripts of their think-aloud responses average nine pages of double-spaced text, while their written responses are generally fairly short, about a page of handwritten text, despite considerable urging to reread and write on. D. M. Travers's study (1982) of a fourteen-year-old boy responding both orally and in writing to a poem is particularly telling on this point. His oral response shows how without training he is able to "explore most of the aspects of a poem which teachers would hope for, including the demand for evidence to support his views" (p. 57); however, what he is able to write or chooses to write falls far short of representing the fullness of his response to the poem.

Response-Centered Practice: Overcoming Classroom Constraints

Aligning Practice with Theory

In the past several pages I have tried to relate certain key understandings about readers' transactions with literary text to the kinds of classroom practice they point to. I have suggested that some aspects of institutionalized classroom practice are inhospitable to the kinds of teaching that take account of these understandings and the goals they imply. Thus, for instance, the notion of a literary work as a dynamic entity continually recreated with each new reading, and varying with each reader and the contexts of that reading, is utterly denied by teachers who proceed as though their students, having all read the same text, have also read the same "poem" and experienced the poem in more or less the same way. In the following pages I outline a procedure for the teaching of poetry to demonstrate one way in which classroom practice can be consistent with and support a transactional view of literary reading.

Why poetry? For one thing, it allows me to provide a model that fits conveniently within a typical classroom period. More important, I am aware of a strong degree of antipathy to poetry among many junior high school and most high school students and a consequent reluctance among teachers to teach poetry or include more than a token number of poems in their programs. Such attitudes toward poetry prevail in schools in most English-speaking countries (Dias and Hayhoe, 1988). It was a question about the source of this antipathy that led me to the approach.

I hypothesized that the source lay in the conviction among most students that they could not make sense of a poem on their own and an accompanying willingness of teachers to function as guardians of the poem's meaning. What if students were to read poetry with the understanding that they were expected to understand poems for themselves? What if teachers were to shed their roles as final arbiters of the poem's meaning? My intention in following up these questions was to discover the full extent of the students' resources as readers of poetry in the hope that once these were demonstrated, teachers might cease to control and direct students' responses.

With the aim of finding out the real capabilities of students as readers of poetry, I devised a procedure for small-group discussion of poems and for reporting back in a plenary session. Tape recordings of these sessions provided the evidence of what students could do on their own. I shall not detail the results of this experiment (Dias, 1979) except to say that over ten days of reading and discussing poems in this undirected fashion, the students (they were sixteen-year-old comprehensive school students of average ability) demonstrated an unexpectedly high degree of competence as readers of poetry. I also realized that these competencies were not merely latent abilities which had not been exercised and were just waiting to emerge. The process of undirected discussion itself was a means of helping students become autonomous readers. In the search for answers to a question about the real abilities of students as readers of poetry, I had stumbled on an approach that would help students, within a period of two weeks, develop an enthusiasm for poetry and a confidence in their ability to read and make sense of poems for themselves.

I detail the procedure below as it has been revised over years of using it with classes of varying ability at several grade levels in junior and secondary schools. My account has gained as well from demonstrating the procedure in workshops to hundreds of teachers over the past ten years and from hearing their accounts of their experiments with the approach (Bryant, 1984; Engbrecht, 1986). Specifically, the procedure recognizes:

- that talk is a valuable means of articulating and developing one's response.

- that collaborative exchange within a small group helps individuals refine and clarify their responses and at once obtain the confirmations they need to develop trust in their intuitions and the relevance of their experience.

- that the teacher ought to withdraw from the forefront of classroom activity and assign students full responsibility for the meanings they make.

- that meaning is a dynamic entity that shifts with newer readings and the contributions of other readers.

Procedures

Students ought to know that they will be involved in a class activity in which they will be expected to read and understand a poem for themselves without direction from the teacher, and that they have among themselves, within their groups and as a class, the resources to do so. The teacher will provide any help they require without directing them towards one interpretation or another. They should understand that they will work in groups to arrive at an account of their experience of the poem which they will share with the other groups. The teacher demonstrates the steps listed below, initially with the class as a whole and later with members in groups, using several short poems so that the procedure becomes familiar and does not distract later from their real task of coming to terms with a poem under discussion.

1. Groups are formed. I have found that six groups of about five students each work best in a class of thirty or so students. Because the procedure makes students very much aware of the value of working in groups, it is quite likely and desirable that small-group work become the standard procedure for future classroom activities. As the makeup of the groups will change as students shift to other activities, it does not really matter how the groups are constituted initially—as long as group members are compatible and some effort is made, without drawing attention to it, to keep the groups equally varied in terms of their ability as readers.

2. Each group chooses a reporter, whose responsibility it is to chair the discussion and report back to the large group in the plenary session. Members of the group take turns reporting from one day to the next.

3. The teacher distributes copies of the poem and reads it aloud. Students are invited to ask for the meanings of unfamiliar words and allusions. The teacher provides literal meanings, encouraging the students to determine the specific meaning from the context. The poems, mostly contemporary, should be of sufficient interest and complexity to challenge and justify group effort and sustain discussion.

4. A member of the class reads the poem aloud to the whole class. From this reading the teacher recognizes and clears up likely stumbling points that might cause unnecessary difficulty (e.g., the misreading of particular words or difficulties with unusual syntax or punctuation). If need be, the teacher asks another student to volunteer a reading.

5. Within each group, one member reads the poem aloud.

6. Following this reading, each member of the group *in turn* reports an initial impression: a feeling, an observation, puzzlement, an association. Members of the group are not to react to these initial statements until all of them have spoken. It is important that students come to recognize that they are not expected to have understood the poem even after this third or fourth reading, and that their initial impressions often provide important clues to how the poem speaks to them. At the same time, they can say that they remain untouched by the poem.

   The teacher needs to insist that students register their initial impressions, particularly in the early sessions before they have come to recognize the value of this stage. Speaking without fear of interruption allows individuals to register their impressions without having them dissipate because someone else has presented an articulate and convincing account. Such is often the case in the regular classroom, where confident readers provide explanations that override nagging doubts and often leave uncertain readers wondering why their own thinking is so often off the mark. It is not long before such readers learn to shelve their responses and wait for appropriate cues that will direct them to the "right" interpretation.

   Because all members of the group have had an opportunity to say something this early in the process, the passage to further contributions has been eased, especially for reticent speakers. Moreover, quite often such contributions are seen to matter in the developing discussion and provide a necessary boost to the confidence of these students. Uncertain readers also take on decisive roles when it is their turn to report for their group.

7. Having reported their initial impressions, the students are now free to proceed to pick up on these responses or to take a careful look at the poem by reading and discussing it a stanza or several lines at a time. The latter procedure allows them to establish the text of the poem, particularly in light of the various impressions they have heard. It is through this slow rereading of the text that they begin to confirm certain observations and set aside or dismiss others. Their discussion is also driven by the need to prepare a report for the large group.

8. Students are encouraged to reread the poem, particularly when discussion has stalled and also just prior to assembling their final report, so that last-minute insights might be recorded.

9. About twenty minutes into the discussion, the teacher alerts class members that they have another five minutes to get their reports ready. It is an important feature of this procedure that students are not permitted to take notes in preparation for presenting their group report. Such notes often record where they've been rather than where they've arrived. Further, notes may freeze out newer insights; group members may settle too easily for what has already been written and discourage further tampering with meaning. Although students feel insecure at first without notes to guide them, they soon realize that they can function effectively without them. They also recognize that, at least in poetry, one can and should not settle too early on meaning, and that their final reports are open to revision in the light of what other reporters say. Because of the injunction that reporters must *build on* what previous reporters have said, the reports bear little resemblance to what the group may have rehearsed. Alert to new possibilities of meaning, reporters recall, and place as relevant, aspects of the discussion that had not figured in their earlier versions.

10. The groups report in turn, but the order of reporting shifts from day to day so that, over the ten days, any one group has reported first or last only twice. Initially groups are happy to report first, believing the last group will have little to say after the other groups have reported. From the fifth or sixth session on, however,

the groups begin to value hearing other versions of the poem against which they can set their own account. In building on earlier reports, those reporting can acknowledge common understandings but must attempt to add to the growing account of the poem as well. Reporters are also encouraged to report minority opinions from their groups, as well as to seek help from other members if they have lost track of what they wished to say. The teacher assists such a process after each reporter has spoken by asking other members of the group if they wish to add anything to the report. Often they do.

11. In a fifty-minute class, there are usually five to ten minutes for a final rereading of the poem and a consideration of what new meanings may have emerged in the light of all they have heard. The teacher invites questions and redirects them to groups or individuals who may have addressed those particular questions. *At no time must the teacher function as someone who has the right answers but is unwilling to share them.* I am suggesting that teachers aver a genuine curiosity about the students' responses, so that questions are always deflected back to the students—not simply in the manner, "Well, what do you think?" but more in the spirit of, "Well, I wondered about that as well. Did some of you discuss this point and have an opinion on it?" Riding crucially on this point is whether the students will finally accept full responsibility for the meanings they make and therefore willingly continue to engage in the kind of effort that makes such taking on of responsibility possible. I can assure teachers that it will not be long before students begin to resent directive interventions from the teacher, preferring to work things out for themselves. It is at such a stage that I am willing to risk, "Do you want to know what I think?" and confidently expect a disapproving collective "No!"

But the teacher does have a role: one of providing information students need, of urging and encouraging, of generally managing the process. At this stage the teacher has also selected the texts they will read and discuss, though eventually, as their confidence as readers grows, they can be assigned responsibility for negotiating in groups the particular texts they wish the class to study.

One such instance might involve individuals in each group contributing two poems to the group's pool from among the anthologies with which the teacher has flooded the classroom. There is no telling the number of poems an individual might read to settle on just the two which will fit the criteria that the class may have agreed to in advance, be they poems on a theme or from a particular period or author. What is more, each member of the group will now have to consider at least ten poems to decide on the two which now must be presented for inclusion in the class pool. The reading and negotiating involve a comparative valuing of each poem, an exercise in criticism not easily justified in most classrooms. Whether explicitly or implicitly, students are considering what makes a poem worth reading and worth the collective inquiring of a group. But the teacher is not excluded from responding to the poem. Students also keep daily journals in which they write their responses to a later rereading of the poem they have discussed during the day. Their understanding, one promoting the notion of a poem as an event in time, is that their responses may have altered in the light of the discussion and with the passage of time and the other experiences and associations that have impinged on their consciousness since discussion's end. The teacher can now respond as another reader, sharing, confirming, being informed, and quite often pushing class members to reexamine and reflect. The one right answer is no longer an issue.

I have set out the details of this procedure in order to illustrate the careful defining of roles and tasks necessary to promote teaching and learning consistent with our knowledge of the reading process and the kinds of relationships that promote authentic responses and authorize readers. While I have listed steps, their delineation is largely arbitrary, only a means of keeping activities in sequence. Much also depends on the students' familiarity with group process and their attitudes toward poetry. I have worked generally with classes considered hostile or at least indifferent to poetry and not used to participating in groups. My experience is that these procedures are effective in a variety of situations and with other genres of literature as well. When they are not, most likely they have been used mechanically and/or are incongruent with the attitudes to literature and literary study promoted by the teacher and the institution.

I will illustrate these procedures by examining extracts from the discussions of one class. The students are thirteen year olds of average to above-average ability in a large, comprehensive secondary school in Montreal attended mainly by children of first-generation Italian immigrants. The students had been discussing poetry in the manner I have described over ten days with their regular teacher in charge. I conducted the session under conditions not so congenial to easy and unrestrained discussion: a large room, video-cameras, lights, tape-recorders and microphones at each table, and the presence of four unfamiliar adults. (Some teachers, who probably subscribe to the pressure-cooker theory of accomplishment, have discounted the performance of these students as somehow enhanced by these adverse conditions.) The poem I had chosen was Ted Hughes's "The Thought-Fox," a poem I consider challenging and difficult, particularly for thirteen year olds. Several hundred teachers with whom I have shared this discussion agree it is a fairly complex poem and normally one they would not consider assigning to thirteen-year-old readers. On the other hand, its very difficulty instigates and justifies a concerted collaborative effort after meaning. The discussion that follows represents a high level of achievement, which to my mind directly resulted from the students' involvement in undirected discussion of poetry over the previous ten days.

The Poem

The Thought-Fox**
I imagine this midnight moment's forest:
Something else is alive
Beside the clock's loneliness
And this blank page where my fingers move.

Through the window I see no star:
Something more near
Though deeper within darkness
Is entering loneliness:

Cold, delicately as the dark snow,
A fox's nose touches twig, leaf;
Two eyes serve a movement, that now
And again now, and now, and now

Sets neat prints into the snow,
Between trees, and warily a lame
Shadow lags by stump and in hollow
Of a body that is bold to come

Across clearings, an eye,
A widening deepening greenness,
Brilliantly, concentratedly,
Coming about its own business

Till, with a sudden sharp hot stink of fox
It enters the dark hole of the head.

The window is starless still; the clock ticks,
The page is printed.

Ted Hughes

The Discussion

There are six groups of five to six students in the classroom. The students have heard the poem read three times. One of them has asked for and been given the literal meaning of "lags" (i. 15). What follows is an abridged version of the discussion, sampling students' talk in various groups and their progress through the poem with just those segments that illustrate the process and the quality of the effort toward meaning.

Group A's initial comments focus on what happened to the fox in the end, mainly questioning several puzzling aspects of the poem:

> *Sandra:* You guys, what do you think happened at the end? That's what I'm wondering. . . . Did anybody else think that the fox died at the end? 'Cause you know the way he ends it, it's sort of dramatic, you know: "The window is starless still; the clock ticks,/The page is printed." You know?
>
> *Lina:* But it says, "Till, with a sudden sharp hot stink of fox . . ." What does that mean? "Hot stink"?
>
> *Rose:* But it says, "It enters the dark hole of the head" . . . what does that mean?

In Group C, Toni's initial comments are worth noting:

> *Toni:* When I read this poem, I thought about . . . OK, let's say you're writing a composition, you're stumped, you don't know what to write about. So maybe he's doing his homework and he doesn't know what to write about, so he imagines it. . . . Maybe he looks out through the window, through his window, and he imagines the fox. And he imagines all these things. And he writes . . . the page. That's what I think.

Toni draws on an experience they can all relate to in order to explain what might be happening in the poem. When we look at Group D, they have already shared their initial impressions and are now looking more closely at the poem, wondering what's going on:

> *Diane:* Is he thinking about the fox or is he really seeing?
>
> *Joanne:* I think he's thinking. . . . The first line gives you a hint. It's "The Thought-Fox"—thought about the fox.
>
> *Gina:* He's imagining like the . . .
>
> *Barbara:* He sees the two eyes . . . I think; because "across clearings

an eye." But in the fifth stanza: "A widening deepening greenness"—maybe the eyes of the fox were green.

Joanne: I guess they were brilliant.

Diane: And like they were nice. . . .

Barbara: "Coming about its own business."

Diane: Just walking around.

Joanne: Yeah, searching for food.

Diane: It's not bothering anyone.

Gina: And, like, it's quiet.

Diane: He's minding his own business.

Joanne: And the fox is probably going into a cave or something.

Gina: "And enters the dark hole of the head."

Barbara: The head might be the cave.

Diane: But then it says, "The page is printed."

What is interesting here is the constant attendance to the text in the effort to establish what is happening. Diane's question is central: Is he thinking about the fox or is he really seeing? As they pick up on that question, they remain in touch with what they themselves imagine. But then Diane wonders what this all has to do with "The page is printed."

Group E is going through the stage of establishing the text of the poem.

Pat: But then "something more near . . ."

Paula: The fox, "though deeper within darkness . . ."

Nadia: And he also can see no stars because it's winter. Like he says about the snow, and in winter there's no stars.

Phil: Well, in the winter there could be some stars . . .

Nadia: But they're rare. Very rare. You don't usually see . . .

Paula: But here, this might mean something: "Across clearings, an eye . . ."

Nadia: He's imagining the deepening greenness of the eye . . . coming about its own business.

Pat: Could this mean something: "Sets neat prints into the snow . . ."? Like he's talking, like in the fourth stanza . . .

Nadia: Like he's writing it down; he's setting the story down: "Sets neat prints into the snow" . . .

Paula: Like the fox and him writing it down. Like he's thinking of the fox making prints in the snow and him, he's printing . . .

What one might note about this segment is how members of the group pick up from one another and confirm, differ, or elaborate. Also interesting is their alertness to the possibilities of meaning: "Could this mean something?" When we return to Group C, we notice that they also are reading sections of the poem and talking about them:

Anthony: He's always moving around, seeing what's happening.

Debbie: I agree with Anthony because . . . ah, and "now, and now, and now," like he was probably thinking what he was going to say next. He's continuing with the plot of his poem. I agree with Anthony.

Marilyn: Because he's imagining these things.

Raphael: (reading) "Sets neat prints into the snow,/ Between trees, and warily a lame/ Shadow lags by stump and in hollow/ Of a body that is bold to come . . ." In this stanza I think he's still imagining about the fox; he's trying to write about it; he's trying to put a picture of the fox inside his mind. So he's seeing it go between trees; it's probably looking for food; and he sees the shadow.

Debbie: He's comparing what he's like with what a fox would be like . . .

Marilyn: I think, ah OK, the fox is walking, all right? And it's following close to him, so close you can imagine, so close that you could smell the fox.

Debbie: So he's imagining it, and he feels it coming towards him.

Marilyn: And then it enters the dark hole of the head.

Debbie: So that he's entering his head is the imagery.

Anthony: It's not really that; maybe it's a figure of speech or something else but it can't be that . . . he's thinking . . . maybe a skunk stinking or something, but not a fox. Maybe it's . . . an expression.

Marilyn: I think you could smell something coming except for a cat.

Debbie: You don't smell my cat!

Marilyn: You could smell it coming; you could see it coming . . . like he's probably saying it that way. Like he's saying it's coming but he's putting it in these kind of words. Like he's saying "with a hot stink of [the] fox," it's saying it's coming . . .

I have chosen this segment because it particularly illustrates an essential aspect of the collaborative process: the merging of closely parallel individual commentaries so that one takes on aspects of the other. Note Debbie's moving in tandem, first with a key comment on Raphael's reading, equating the fox's movement with the movement of the poet's mind, and then with her accompaniment to Marilyn's observations. We note also Anthony has somehow come to terms with accommodating "smell of the fox" with his belief that foxes don't "stink," and allowing that it might be "a figure of speech or something," an explanation which for him probably allows for all sorts of inaccuracies in poetry.

As we move forward to the close of the discussion, about twenty-five minutes since the first reading, we find Group D planning what their reporter might say:

> *Barbara:* "It enters the dark hole of the head . . ." probably means he's going into a cave.
> Joanne: (rehearsing Diane, who will be reporting for the group) And don't forget to say that we think it's good that the poet is remaining himself.
> *Diane:* This poem is comparing the poet to himself . . .
> *Joanne:* Say it over . . . all in your own words.
> *Diane:* OK, the title of this poem, "The Thought-Fox," is a very good title because it suits the poem very much, because . . .

Quite casually, Diane puts forward a complex recognition: the poem represents the poet's own process of creation. The poet is like the fox, but yet "remains himself."

While an abbreviated run-through of the discussion phase can never fully represent the concertedness of the inquiring, the attention to text, the overall tentativeness, the high level of collaboration and involvement that occurs across several real-life discussions, it does illustrate the active questioning and meaning-making in which the students engaged. What follows reproduces most of the reporting-back phase. One must recall that the reporters are speaking extemporaneously, with the assurance that other members of the group can pitch in when needed. One should look particularly for evidence that reporters are taking account of the reports of previous reporters, that there is a cumulative building up of meaning.

Reporting Back

Slightly diffident, because she has to report first, Lina speaks for Group A:

> *Lina:* OK, my group thought there was this poet, and he's getting ready to write a poem. He has this blank page in front of him, and, ah . . . and he has a pen in his hand, because it says, "And this blank page where my fingers move." So he's starting to write. And he has, there's a window near him and he sees outside this window. And it's all dark because it's midnight. And outside he sees a, it's a forest, and he sees a fox and like it's nervous; and it's in the night. And he's going through forest and, it's um . . . While it's walking, there's another shadow

in the night and it's like, tired. This shadow's a hunter because . . . He's walking halfway through the forest; and then it says, "Across the clearing, an eye/ A widening deepening greenness." We think that he sees the fox and he's interested. You know, he's a hunter and he wants to kill him. So near the end, like, he shoots the fox and the bullet enters the hole, the bullet enters the head . . .

And in the end the poet wrote his poem because he wrote what he saw. The poem doesn't rhyme and . . . that's about it. Oh, we didn't know at the beginning whether the poet was imagining this or he saw it for real because the title is "The Thought-Fox," and it could be that he's imagining. And the first line says, "I imagine this midnight moment's forest" . . .

Group A has established that someone is writing a poem. The fox is the subject of the poem; "enters the head" and "a lame shadow" have suggested "bullet" and "hunter" respectively. Quite likely, an expectation that the teacher values technical information makes the reporter throw in the gratuitous, "The poem doesn't rhyme." The procedure allows students to report their uncertainties as well, so that they do not feel obliged to stake out and defend positions that may or may not be tenable. Group B's report follows immediately:

Albert: We thought that this poem is about a man; he's writing a poem and he feels like his surroundings are dead. He sees the dark forest and the clock is just ticking. And he feels . . . there's something else was alive near him. So he looks through the window and he sees a fox. Like, minding his business; like, it was in the dark—he felt the fox was so confident walking. And like, the man if he would be there, it would be like startled. And so the fox is walking, and then [in] the shadow he sees something bold. So like, the fox even though he's in that circumstance that there's a shadow, he's still like concentrating, unlike the man who can't. . . . And as the man is seeing this, he writes the poem. It's like an experience for him. It's everything is dead, and suddenly he sees this fox in a shadow. And he sees how the fox manages to do things in the dark. So, as he sees the fox, he does it himself. At the end, before he knew it, the poem was finished. . . .

And, ah, there's a, it's a comparison. He's comparing himself writing the poem to the fox escaping the hunter. There's a simile in the third stanza: "Cold, delicately as the dark snow." This setting is in the winter. . . .

We think it's a uh . . . we thought it was like a man in the country, but then a couple of guys in the group were disagreeing, and they said that it's a man in the city because he saw through the window and he didn't see any stars; and in the city you can't see stars because there's too much light.

Michael: (another member of the group supplements the report)—

In the first line of the stanza, it says, "I imagine this midnight moment's forest"; after that stanza, I think he imagines the whole poem. He's letting his imagination run loose. And after that, he wrote a poem about it.

This report moves from an awareness of the bleak mood of the poem/poet (darkness, dead surroundings, the clock just ticking) to contrasting the uncertainty of the writer with the confident movement of the fox. Again, this reporter believes it is necessary to establish group members' technical credentials: there's a comparison, a simile, and a winter setting. He also reports their disagreement about where the poem is actually set. Michael's contribution to the report points to the group's awareness of the poem's structure, an awareness that is more fully developed in Group C's report below:

> *Anthony:* There's this poet who's trying to find a topic to write about, and too, he tried to look out of his window to see if there's something of a start that could start his thinking. There's nothing. So then he thinks about a fox and a hunter. He tries to put it in words; he's thinking about it, and as he is thinking, he doesn't know, but he's writing about the fox trying to avoid the hunter. And finally the hunter gets him. And we also found that in the first paragraph the last sentence has a period. That was a . . . we thought that paragraph was in the present. Then all of a sudden in the next four paragraphs there's no periods, and that we thought that was only imagination, until the last paragraph, the second stanza, where is the period. . . . Then after that "the window is starless still, the clock ticks, the page is printed." After the period, he goes back to the present like in the beginning. We thought that he was comparing himself, that he was looking for something to write about, and he finally gets the fox.
>
> *Debbie:* (adds) The group said that this person must have been very creative, because at the beginning he had nothing to write about, but as time went by, he made up a poem; he didn't even [know?] what he was doing. Like, he was imagining but he wasn't . . . he didn't even notice he was really writing the poem. I also think that maybe, at the beginning, because the poet is stumped, because he didn't know what to write about; maybe he was nervous because he had a deadline to meet, and after when he looked out the window and everything was calm, then everything came to him.
>
> *Marilyn:* (adds) The sentence on the last stanza, first one [sentence], it says, "Till, with the sudden sharp hot stink of fox/ It enters the dark hole of the head." I think it means that the fox is coming closer and closer towards him, and when it says "the hot stink of fox," it's like he's smelling it. But it's not that. . . . Instead of saying, "The fox is coming," it's more creative to say "the hot stink of fox." It's more better. . . . It

shows that he's saying the fox is coming closer . . . it's a figure of speech.

What is noticeable about this report is Anthony's linking the scheme of the poem's meaning with the structure of the poem. The earlier reports have allowed the reporter to skim through the larger outline of the poem to concentrate on finer details. Other members of the group now seem to feel freer to supplement the report, again to draw attention to and clarify key details. Marilyn, for instance, picks up on her concern in the earlier group discussion to deal with the problematical "hot stink of fox" image. Again, like earlier reporters, she seems to believe that finding a school-valued label ("it's a figure of speech") for what she is trying to understand must matter in some way.

As we look at the contribution of Group D below, we might ask if they can possibly make some observations that earlier groups haven't reported.

> *Diane:* The title, "The Thought-Fox," we thought it was a good title for the poem because the poet is imagining that he's seeing the fox; he's really imagining. And while he's sitting down— we think he's sitting down at his typewriter—and, uh, he's trying what he's going to write about. And then he starts imagining the fox and the forest, the darkness, and it's so dark and lonely . . . He's lonely; he's very lonely. He's just sitting there and then all of a sudden, he starts imagining these things. And then at the end, he's . . . the page is printed . . . it means like all of a sudden, he stops imagining, comes out of his imagination, and the page is printed. Everything is done. And, oh, yeah, the poet of the poem is comparing the poet to the fox. Because the fox was lonely in the forest—he had nobody with him—and the poet neither had anybody with him because he's sitting down all by himself. And it's so dark and lonely he's just sitting . . . [??] The last stanza, second line, "It enters the dark hole of the head," we think it means that the fox, he's entering the cave and that's where the poet's imagination stops.
>
> *Gina:* (adds) When it says, "Till, with a sudden sharp hot stink of fox," like, the smell of the fox [is] what the poet is thinking of to write, like, his ideas . . .
>
> *Diane:* The poet is saying the story, "I imagine the [this] midnight moment's forest," so he's saying the poem and he was thinking about it. . . . he looks through the window and he sees no stars, that it's so dark, he sees nothing; so he imagines the imagery of the fox.

Group D's report again falls into the pattern of a cumulative building up of meaning. Diane relates the title to what occurs in the poem.

Her account of the poem is closely interwoven with what she feels and senses: "it's so dark and lonely," he's lonely; he's very lonely." "just sitting there," "all of a sudden." She also makes a nice distinction, "the poet of the poem [Hughes]" as opposed to the poet in the poem. Gina adds a further gloss to what had intrigued earlier groups, equating the smell of the fox with the poet's thoughts. Diane answers the question she raised earlier in her own group: "Is he thinking about the fox, or is he really seeing?" It is too dark for the poet to have seen anything; so he must have imagined "the imagery of the fox." What seems to be apparent here and in Group E's report that follows is an increasingly confident sense of the poem's integral meaning and form:

> *Nadia:* The whole . . . what he's writing in the poem, he's imag-
> ining it for sure. We know, the title tells us—"The Thought-
> Fox"—like, he's thinking of a fox; and the first line, "I imagine
> this midnight moment's forest: . . . " There's also the colon; so
> he starts imagining what he imagines. And he's saying the
> story; he's writing down his story he's saying. . . . We think
> that the fox is the author 'cause where he said, "Cold, delicately
> as the dark snow," it could be cold like a vague thoughts. Like,
> at the beginning he had very vague thoughts like about what
> to write about. We know it's been thought up, 'cause usually
> when you just for reality, when you just . . . you don't really
> count the fox's steps, but he did. Like, when he goes: "Two
> eyes . . . And again now, and now, and now/ Set neat prints
> into the snow," so he's like counting. He's kind of saying how
> many times he set the prints into the snow, the fox, and those
> prints we think he's saying of himself; he's printing the
> poem. . . . As the fox is [moving] (??), he is writing or he is
> thinking of him. We see, uh, dynamism [hesitantly] of character.
> Like a story, like, at the beginning they go through obstacles
> and then they overcome their obstacles, and at the end, like
> they've overcome them. The speaker in the poem, he overcame
> his obstacles, and then he wrote the poem.

[Nadia's reporting has been interrupted by several fits of coughing. She seems to have trouble speaking; so the teacher uses this opportunity to suggest that they should come back later to some of the interesting points her group has raised. BUT . . .]

> *Nadia:* I am still not finished. So then the first and last stanza,
> they're opposites. 'Cause at the end, the clock's loneliness, and
> at the end it's ticking; and here the blank page and at the end
> it's printed; so it's the opposite. "Till, with a sudden sharp hot
> stink of fox," like, he imagined it and it's like the thought is
> going away, but the smell is still staying, like, the thoughts are
> still in the air. And when it enters the dark hole, like the

thoughts are still in his head and he's writing them down. The window is starless at the beginning, and it is also starless at the end. That's the reality. It was always starless. No matter what he thought, the window was always starless. And we also know that he imagined it where it says "an eye,/ A widening deepening greenness,/ Brilliantly, concentratedly," like usually in the darkness, you don't see the fox's eye very clearly. So he's imagining, the eye, a widening, deepening greenness, and it's also him that . . . it's his eyes deepening "coming about him that . . . it's his eyes deepening "coming about his own business" of writing the poem. And here "Between trees, and warily a lame/ Shadow lags by stump and in hollow/ Of a body that is bold to come"—that's the obstacle. He's very weak at the beginning of the poem; he doesn't know what to write. But later, it's "of a body that is bold to come." He knows that he's thought of this, and his writing will be stronger. Like, he's gonna write down what he thought of.

Nadia's report is undeniably fuller and more articulate than the earlier reports; however, its debt to the earlier reports is clear. Nadia builds on a firmer base of what had so far been advanced tentatively. She is in a position to argue with some sureness how several aspects of the poem might fit in: the title, the structure, the author/fox identity enhanced by her association of "snow" and "cold" with vague thoughts, and later the brilliant, concentrated realization of the poem, her association of footprints in the snow with printing the poem. Again, like others, she makes a customary bow to teacher concerns by speaking of "dynamism of character," a term she has borrowed from teacher discussions of characterization in short stories. What is brilliant about Nadia's or the group's apprehension of the poem (it is hard to say what is now being realized on the instant) is the fleshing out of the parallels between the poet's realization of the poem and the wary, lagging movement of the fox and its growing sureness in "coming about its own business."

I should also comment about my interruption halfway through Nadia's reporting. I had interviewed Nadia earlier that morning, collecting data for the larger project of which this discussion is a part. That interview had been interrupted by several fits of coughing. At the first sign of a recurrence of her cough in this session, I broke in because I knew further talk would exacerbate her coughing; I was also painfully aware of the camera focused intently on her face. I am struck therefore by Nadia's insistence on going on. She knew she was not finished, and that if she did not continue to speak, she would not have found expression for (and therefore come to know) the powerful ideas impinging on her consciousness. It is unlikely that others might have picked up on her report and carried on. I doubt they would, simply because Nadia's thoughts had gathered a kind of momentum that often in our best moments inspires a rush of perceiving and connecting. The notions she advances following the interruption clearly justify her insistence on continuing to speak, particularly her working out the differences between the settings at the beginning and end of the poem.

It is also important to note that the other students are traveling alongside rather than being left behind by her report. Their small group discussions and the reports of each group have primed them for the recognitions Nadia advances. I make this reference to traveling because I have in mind Douglas Barnes' (1976) notion that students in most classrooms arrive at destinations without having traveled. Often, the teacher, like an overly conscientious tour guide, has done the traveling for them.

When we consider the whole reporting-back sequence, what stands out is the developing account of the poem. Each report gets longer, the confirmations come through, new recognitions emerge. For me, the proof of the effectiveness of this procedure does not lie in Nadia's articulate account, an account made possible because of the groundwork clearly apparent in the earlier reports. It seems necessary that Group A brings clearly to light possible understandings that do not appear to hold under further discussion. All earlier reports have steadily built up a sense of what is actually going on in the poem and have thus afforded Nadia the opportunity to make the finer discriminations. I would venture to say that Group E might not have reported in this manner if they had spoken earlier in this sequence; there was just too much to be got out of the way.

I had said earlier in describing the procedure that groups initially would not relish reporting last. It turned out that over the ten days, those reporting last had learned to attend to the reports of other groups and exploit their particular advantage. As an aside, I might point out that those who advocate the specific teaching of "listening skills" should look to such naturalistic learning situations for instruction. Readers may also have noticed how the reporter speaks for the group: *we felt, the group felt.* There is also a clear sense that the class as a whole is defining its own agenda. In fact, the least productive parts of the reporting occur where students feel the need to attend to a teacherish agenda, a concern for technical know-how. The kind of technical know-how that does matter is organic to their account of what is happening in the poem. I have in mind their reporting on how the formal structure of the poem parallels the account of the poem's "events." I should also point out that through all these reports, we see that the groups have appropriated the text; it is embedded in their thinking and talking about the poem. Readers may have also noticed how the procedure enables and motivates talk, talk as the seedbed (to borrow James Britton's use of the word) of reflective thought. But talk here is not only a means but a clearly desirable product, as the extemporaneous reports of these thirteen year olds show.

Conclusions

This discussion of the "The Thought-Fox" was meant to demonstrate that maintaining a high degree of congruence between our understandings of the process of literary reading and classroom practice can actually be quite productive. The procedure described respects the transactional nature of literary reading, the notion of the "poem" as evoked, an event in time. It also respects the individuality of readers and affords them opportunity to negotiate their own understandings. It allows the teacher to shed the mantle of the expert, the role of final mediator between the reader and the text, a role which I believe is the most powerful inhibitor of students' taking ownership of their own reading and thereby becoming more responsive and responsible readers.

There are other criteria, other recognitions to keep in mind, and these are listed because they should enable teachers to extend the procedure to other genres, to adapt the procedure to elementary-level readers of literature as well as to postsecondary students, and to experiment with applications outside the study of literature.[1]

- classrooms must be organized in ways that allow students to trust and rely on their own resources as readers.
- working in small groups allows students to test their initial responses, take account of the responses of others, and recognize the several possibilities of meaning a work affords. In addition, the teacher no longer occupies the center.
- personal experiences evoked by the text are more likely to be shared within the secure confines of the small group.
- classroom procedures ought to allow students to live with and become tolerant of ambiguity, a condition of meaning that allows further exploration and rereading.

- familiarization in itself is a major step towards understanding, enjoyment, and discrimination in the reading of poetry (Britton, 1954; Harding, 1968). Poetry ought to be treated as and become a familiar object.

- collaborative exchange within and among groups stimulates exploration, responsible reading, and a genuine curiosity about the interpretations of other groups.

- tasks assigned for group work ought to be presented in ways which make collaborative exchange the most productive way of achieving their ends. Tasks should, in and of themselves, invite collaboration. (I am suggesting here that tasks that can be achieved just as well by individual effort do not usually justify the time and effort given to working in groups and inevitably fail as collaborative tasks.)

I have said little here about writing. My experience is that talk in small-group discussion and the reporting back helps develop articulateness in writing as well. As students come to be more in touch with their own thinking about what they have read, they find fuller expression for it. But until students have developed greater independence as readers, writing ought to remain secondary and incidental to the collaborative exchange of small groups.

A major concern remains, and it has to do with the role of teacher as evaluator. Teachers ought to find ways to make assessment a collaborative enterprise in a partnership among teacher, the group, and the individual student. Teachers must also be aware that while classroom procedures might assign power and authority to student readers, our role as evaluators of their performance can, in effect, subvert the very autonomy we wish to promote—ultimately, most of our evaluation practices assert that we still remain in charge of their reading. I would also be alert to maintaining a consistency in attitude and practice across the variety of literary reading activities that go on in any classroom. Teachers cannot flit in and out of roles, assuming at one time a stance that authorizes readers and asserting an authoritative guardianship at another. While there is no middle road, one can be assured that as student readers take on a fuller responsibility for the meanings they make, they will be less likely to surrender their rights as readers to speak and write from their own responses. Such gains will be consolidated if and as we shift the focus of assessment from final products to the processes students are engaged in both as individual readers and as readers in groups. Above all, we need to ensure both by policy and in practice that readers are not once more relegated to the sidelines, denying the validity of their own readings and wondering how they might approximate teacher-authorized versions.

Notes

1. I have used this procedure successfully with eleven year olds and with college-level students; and have had enthusiastic reports from teachers who have adapted the procedure in reading and discussing stories and poems with even younger children. If students have been won over to the process with poetry, they are eager to read novels in the same way; however, what they need to negotiate in their groups and report on will depend on the particular novel and how it is segmented for discussion.

References

Barnes, D. (1976). *From communication to curriculum.* Harmondsworth, Middlesex: Penguin Books.

Bleich, D. (1975). *Readings and feelings: An introduction to subjective criticism.* Urbana, IL: National Council of Teachers of English.

Bleich, D. (1978). *Subjective criticism.* Baltimore, MD: Johns Hopkins University Press.

Brooks, C. (1947). *The well wrought urn: Studies in the structure of poetry.* New York, NY: Harcourt, Brace and Co.

Britton, J. (1954). Evidence of improvement in poetic judgment. *British Journal of Educational Psychology, 45,* 196–208.

Bryant, C. (1984). Teaching students to read poetry independently: An experiment in bringing together research and the teacher. *English Quarterly, 17*(4), 48–57.

Dias, P. (1979). Developing independent readers of poetry: An approach in the high school. *McGill Journal of Education, 14,* 199–214.

Dias, P. (1987). *Making sense of poetry: Patterns in the process.* Ottawa: Canadian Council of Teachers of English.

Dias, P. and Hayhoe, M. (1988). *Developing response to poetry.* Milton Keynes, England: The Open University Press.

Eagleton, T. (1983). *Literary theory: An introduction.* Oxford: Blackwell.

Engbrecht, R. (1986). Individualizing approaches to poetry. In S. Tchudi (Ed.), *English teachers at work; Strategies from five countries.* Upper Montclair, NJ: Boynton/Cook Publishers, Inc.

Harding, D.W. (1968). Practice at liking: A study in experimental aesthetics. *Bulletin of the British Psychological Society, 21*(70), 3–10.

Holland, N. (1973). *Poems in persons: An introduction to the psychoanalysis of literature.* New York, NY: W.W. Norton.

Holland, N. (1975). *5 readers reading.* New Haven, CT: Yale University Press.

Iser, W. (1978). *The act of reading: A theory of aesthetic response.* Baltimore, MD: Johns Hopkins University Press.

Lakoff, G. and Johnson, M. (1980). *Metaphors we live by.* Chicago, IL: University of Chicago Press.

Rosenblatt, L. (1938). *Literature as exploration.* New York, NY: Appleton-Century.

Rosenblatt, L. (1978). *The reader, the text, the poem: The transactional theory of the literary work.* Carbondale, IL: Southern Illinois University Press.

Rosenblatt, L. (1985). Viewpoints: Transaction versus interaction—a terminological rescue operation. *Research in the Teaching of English, 19,* 96–107.

Travers, D.M.M. (1982). Problems in writing about poetry and some solutions. *English in Education, 16*(3), 55–65.

Wellek, R. and Warren, A. (1949). *Theory of literature.* New York, NY: Harcourt, Brace and Co., Inc.

Wimsatt, W.K., Jr. (1958). *The verbal icon: Studies in the meaning of poetry.* New York, NY: Noonday Press.

8 To Teach (Literature)?*

Anthony Petrosky
University of Pittsburgh

Part I: Prologue—A Brief Argument
Against Teaching Models

Problem-posing education, as a humanist and liberating praxis, posits as fundamental that men subjected to domination must fight for their emancipation. To that end, it enables teachers and students to become subjects of the educational process by overcoming authoritarianism and an alienating intellectualism; it also enables men to overcome their false perception of reality. The world—no longer something to be described with deceptive words—becomes the object of that transforming action by men which results in their humanization.

> —Paulo Freire, *The Pedagogy of the Oppressed*

Men were not intended to work with the accuracy of tools, to be precise and perfect in all their actions . . . if you will make a man of the working creature, you cannot make a tool. Let him but begin to imagine, to think, to try to do anything worth doing; and the engine-turned precision is lost at once. Out come all his roughness, all his dullness, all his incapability; shame upon shame, failure upon failure, pause after pause . . .

> —John Ruskin, *The Nature of Gothic*

Re-vision—the act of looking back, of seeing with fresh eyes, of entering an old text from a new critical direction—is for women more than a chapter in culture history: it is an act of survival. Until we can understand the assumptions in which we are drenched we cannot know ourselves.

I have hesitated to do what I am going to do now, which is use myself as an illustration. For one thing, it's a lot easier and less dangerous to talk about others.

> —Adrienne Rich, *When We Dead Awaken: Writing as Re-Vision*

* My sincere thanks to Judith Langer, David Bartholomae, and Jean Grace for reviewing the drafts of the original paper and recommending revisions.

Adrienne Rich is speaking to and about women; it appears that Freire and Ruskin are speaking to and about men, and their exclusion of women is painfully obvious. So to begin, I would like to draw attention to this problem, because it will recur later in this paper in a different context, and I would also like to proceed by suggesting the transformation of men and women in these passages into "people," so I might then put the emphasis on a human drama that includes issues of gender and, for my argument, issues of transformation and enactment where, as we'll see later, I, as a teacher, become a subject as Rich does for her study of her own writing.

It's necessary to do this, because the very concept of "teaching models" (those replicateable structures of how to teach in particular ways) displace one of the subjects of teaching, the teacher, and replace her with an abstracted notion, a model derived from theory or research, of what ought to go on in classrooms. Models, derived from theory and research, informed sometimes by practice, are presented in a discourse at once removed from the theories that bear responsibility for their construction and also from those who created them; as "models" they are allowed to exist in a space estranged from their derivers and attributable to others, to the theorists and researchers. Models, in other words, lack responsibility—their successes and failures, too, are always attributable to others, to those who adopt or use them; and although this is unsettling it is also symptomatic of a larger problem that involves the relationships of theory and practice and who is allowed to enact those relationships.

Let me cycle back. Teaching is a human drama, not a mechanical device, not a static space, as models force it to be, because it involves people interacting with people. But who are the subjects of teaching? We tend to think of the students as subjects, and this is only partly correct. Teachers are also the subjects of teaching, and traditionally they have not been allowed to establish and enact and assess the links between theory and practice; instead, they have been offered (and continue to be offered) teaching models, structures, and schematics that can be replicated no matter what the teachers' understandings of teaching and learning might be, no matter what their students might be like, and no matter what their agendas, their intentions, might be. Teaching models—the worst of which are lock-stepped in unalterable sequences like Madeline Hunter's Mastery Teaching (1984),[1] or the chapter-by-chapter study of novels (and the subsequent testing of students' recall of chapters) which seems so prevalent in schools, or the still strictly restrained instructional approach defined by the language of plot, character, and setting[2]—erase possibilities rather than create them by linking "individuals to certain types of utterances while consequently barring them from all others" (Foucault, 1972, 226). They effectively remove teachers and students from possibilities outside of the model. In the past, models have led to and been responsible for teaching being reduced to formulas which in turn are reproduced in textbooks, teacher-proof materials, and tests. Models, especially when they propose that they represent "right" or "true" ways of teaching, are strictly exclusionary, unlike local strategies (i.e., posing problems, initiating discussions, designing writing assignments or projects, etc.) which are context-variable and can be inscribed in dialogues, in interactive learning, with colleagues and students. Models shut down the field of play and they make re-visualizing and rethinking difficult, if not impossible. The very concept of models of teaching literature, in other words, encloses itself in a möbius strip from which it can't escape. And this is the "teaching model circle" that I would like to disrupt by proposing, as John Dewey once did,[3] that the link between theory and practice is one that must be recreated over and over again by individual teachers in concert with colleagues, including students.

But before going on to the report, "The Original Paper," of this semester's long enactment of theory in practice, let me further explore this argument that places the responsibility for the enactment with teachers and implies, I think, a sense of irreplicability (except, perhaps, in a most global way) and a shying away from models that locate the subject of teaching in a thing, a procedure, rather than in a person asking questions about how particular theories, whether they're literary or psychological or linguistic, might inform teaching and, then, a changing "consciousness" of teaching and learning. This stance, one that interrogates theories for what they might be brought to say about teaching and learning, is not a given in theoretical study and is particular to teachers, for it is quite likely that unless these questions are being asked of theory, the teaching of theory will proceed as the dominant notions of knowledge allow it—as transfer and acquisition— in what Freire refers to as the "banking concept of education."[4] The theory is delivered, in other words, from the theoretician (or the theory's interpreter) to the student of theory the way peas are put in a bowl without consideration for how this theory (in the case here, postmodern critical theory) might be brought to bear on questions of pedagogy. This is an important distinction, because it begins to define the space in which teachers can interrogate theory—one not likely to be occupied by theoreticians (or other students of theroy) who approach theoretical work as a body of knowledge to be mastered and interrogated in a conversation that proceeds primarily by relating it to other theoretical work.

Throughout this report, especially in the section to follow, called "The Original Paper," my posture (at least the one I intend) is that of a teacher grappling with and trying to enact a pedagogy derived from my questioning particular writings of Roland Barthes (1977), Jacques Derrida (1970, 1976), Julia Kristeva (1986), Michel Foucault (1972), and Edward Said (1975)—a questioning that has gone on (and continues to go on) for a number of years. I begin by positioning Barthes and Derrida against E. D. Hirsch (1988), not as a simplistic representation of the field, but to create a "thinking machine" (a term for which I thank Ellen Bishop, a graduate student in our English Department) posited between these poles, a dichotomy that allows me to generate an argument between oppositions. This allows me to locate the kinds of rote learning and drill, including the regurgitation of received knowledge, that I observe in teaching in my children's schools and in my university, in a space occupied also by Hirsch who over-defines himself by his insistence on iterating necessary knowledge through a dictionary or lexicon without much attention to pedagogical method. When Hirsch does turn to pedagogy, he takes a position commensurate with his views of knowledge and situates acts of interpretation, whether they are students' or critics', in a narrow field defined by a quest for intended meanings. On the other hand, this "thinking machine" allows me to situate Barthes and Derrida (and Said's shadow) in a pedagogical space defined by its dedication to multiplicity.

This multiplicity invites a field of play that opens literature and interpretations to close readings through various lenses, particularly those offered through self-reflexivity in language and discourse. And I'm interested in how my teaching of literature might for us—for my students and myself—open "a field of possible options" and enable even "various mutually exclusive architectures to appear side by side or in turn" (Foucault, 1972, 66) in our writings about and discussions of literary selections. I'm particularly interested in understanding the classroom as a space where a multiplicity of interpretations might exist in a tentativeness open to examination and re-examination from multiple perspectives, including those offered by postmodern literary and language theory.

This possibility seems intriguing to me because a place to play with multiplicity is never without knowledge, for interpretive activities with groups of students always proceed from texts, whether they're written or visual or oral, but the opposite case is not so. Rote learning and referential knowledge (of which I am positioning Hirsch as a representative) do not often involve interpretation, especially as they're used in the schools and turned into such things as prescribed curriculum content that must be covered on exercise sheets of multiple choice and fill-in-the-blank questions that teach and assess the retelling of received notions. Just as knowledge is always present in interpretive activities, so too it is not just knowledge about literature that these activities teach but also ways of working, methods. The space which allows for multiplicity, for multiple points of view, is also a space that encourages the study of a multiplicity of readings and methods. (The scope of learning here, as compared to the scope offered by the space occupied by a representative Hirsch, is both large and particular; it includes not only knowledge but also the presentation and study of multiple readings and methods.) And it has as one of its "possible options" the study and understanding of the positions of the subjects involved in the field of play, for the teacher and the students are always situated in beliefs and identities which are at once ideological and political.

Let me turn now to a discussion of my methods. This prologue was written after "The Original Paper," which you are about to read, and at the same time the epilogue was written. Both were done in response to reviewers' comments. And since I have all along wanted to present myself as a teacher enacting a position that eschews teaching models in favor of teaching strategies and individual experiments and personal reports, I haven't revised "The Original Paper," which I see as a personal report, except for editorial matters. This prologue and the epilogue that follows the paper are, then, further digressions in the conversation, points of departure in part made possible by reviewers' comments and in part by my own rethinking a year later of that semester's worth of teaching I represent in "The Original Paper."

You should expect the opening section of "The Original Paper," the section where I begin the discussion of the theory that informs the activities and choices I make with my class, to be difficult to follow. The sentences are long, a tension which I take to be necessary. The theory I interrogate for pedagogy is difficult, my understandings of it hopelessly flawed and incomplete, and the long, rambling sentences are an indication of this. "You can see Tony piling on clauses," my friend David Bartholomae once said of my writing in a similar situation, "desperate to figure out what the hell he is doing." And while I think this is so, I don't want to apologize or leave you thinking about the opening of the original paper as a moment of self-indulgence where you have to watch me fumble through a process, but as an indication of what happened when I set about "seeing" theory in practice. I offer it as an example of ways in which students and teachers can explore multiple interpretations through interaction—when they focus on ideas and texts, and each other, and themselves.

You should also expect to read long excerpts from my students' writing. It's possible for me to create the class conversations, but in a study of dialogues that involve interpretations, we need more than that, and the simple "flavor" of a piece of writing (as one of the readers put it) isn't enough. You need to see as much of what I saw as is possible to present in a paper (and still keep it readable) to enable you to think not only about my claims but also about the things I miss and can't see. And you also need to be attuned to my mistakes, to missed opportunities, to contradictions and inattentions, for as much as their opposites are involved in teaching, so are they. In the epilogue I'll discuss these mistakes and missed opportunities in more detail.

Part II The Original Paper: TO TEACH (LITERATURE)?

> Holden . . . One short, faintly stuffy, pedagogical question. Don't you think there's a time and place for everything? Don't you think if someone starts out to tell you about his father's farm, he should stick to his guns, then get around to telling you about his uncle's brace? Or, if his uncle's brace is such a provocative subject, shouldn't he have selected it in the first place as his subject—not the farm?
>
> Yes—I don't know. I guess he should. I mean I guess he should. I mean I guess he should've picked his uncle as the subject, instead of the farm, if that interested him most. But what I mean is, lots of times you don't know what interests you until you start talking about something that doesn't interest you most. I mean you can't help it sometimes. What I think is, you're supposed to leave somebody alone if he's at least being interesting and he's getting all excited about something. I like it when somebody gets excited about something. It's nice. You just don't know this teacher, Mr. Vinson. He could drive you crazy sometimes, him and the goddam class. I mean he'd keep telling you to unify and simplify all the time. Somethings you just can't do that to. I mean you can't hardly ever simplify and unify something just because somebody wants you to. You didn't know this guy, Mr. Vinson. I mean he was very intelligent and all, but you could tell he didn't have too much brains.

> —Mr. Antolini and Holden Caulfield,
> *The Catcher in the Rye*

Holden's position, in response to Mr. Antolini's pedagogical question, questions the educational enterprise of his schooling, the enterprise of conformity, the one that insists on language learning and use "as series of one-way interactions with no reciprocity and all the authority coming from the top down" (Bishop, 1988, 6). Mr. Antolini and Mr. Vinson both embrace a monologic paradigm; they would like Holden to know ahead of time where he's going, and to stick to his course once he has embarked. But the protagonist disagrees:

> Holden had the wit to know and be able to say to Mr. Antolini that you don't always know what you're interested in until you run into what you're not interested in. He also had the awareness to sense that the process of discovering what you are interested in, what does matter to you, is something that you can discover in the process of telling stories. (Bishop, 1988)

Holden, for all his lack of language and certainty, knows (without being aware that he knows) that everyone had "a backside they can't see . . . that no one is omniscient, all seeing, all knowing" (Bishop, 1988, 6), and that the notion of thinking and communicating as simplification and unification is naive. However, of course, we all know that it is requested frequently in literature classes, but at the expense of opening up, as opposed to shutting down, interpretations and discussions. Requests for simplification and unification can be read as monologic strategies that honor the well-made and documented position that begins with and comes to a point. Such strategies differ substantially from the exploratory narrative conducted with self-reflexivity and attention to multiple perspectives, including those, like Holden's, that emerge from and fracture singular subjects or monologues (learning what interests you, for instance, by digressing to what doesn't).

Holden's insight offers an opportunity to ask questions about literature, including whether it is a subject, at least in the Hirschian sense of it as a body of knowledge about literature,[5] or whether it is a field of play—under the influence of imagination. In other words, does "to teach literature" circumscribe a subject or a field of play where languages, grounded in various personal and social histories, interweave, digress and turn back on each other?

In this second sense, engagement with a text is not a search for its meaning, but a disentanglement, a following of the threads and terms it both sets up and transgresses, at various levels from various perspectives. As Barthes (1977) puts it,

> In the multiplicity of writing, everything is to be disentangled, nothing deciphered; the structure can be followed, a "run" (like the thread of a stocking) at every point and at every level, but

there is nothing beneath; writing ceaselessly posits meaning ceaselessly to evaporate it, carrying out a systematic exemption of
meaning. (p. 147)

It is this posture toward literature study as a field of play that holds
promise of providing students the opportunities to do what we teachers
do with texts. It also invites writing and discussion as ways to think
and rethink perspectives and takes on texts.

There is also the question of various contexts. Would we say, then,
that "to teach literature" with elementary school students means what
it means to teach literature with high school or college or graduate
school students? How does "to teach literature" exist within various
contexts? Do both (purposely polarized) views, the one that offers "to
teach literature" as a body of knowledge about literature and the one
that offers it as a field of play, permutate or change or evolve in
consideration of various and diverse contexts, not just in what language
or texts might be considered "appropriate" in these various contexts,
but in the strategies offered or the opportunities available in the various
contexts (i.e., elementary students or college students)? Or might it be
that "to teach literature" is monolithic, varying only by texts or
languages, maintaining consistent strategies for "to know" or "to
interpret" no matter what the contexts?

These important questions and issues frame my proposal for considering "to teach literature" as a field of play, rather than a body of
knowledge about literature, as Hirsch would argue (for no matter how
willing he might be to consider "to teach literature" in a classroom,
his position is solidified by his insistence on referencing literacy to a
dictionary of knowledge and information about literature).[6]

The teacher's problem in opening up "to teach literature" as a field
of play is a multifaceted one of posing questions that might allow
students to formulate their takes on a text, constructing opportunities
for students to critically exchange their takes, and then posing questions
that beg self-reflexive readings of the already offered takes on the text
(perhaps by drawing attention to the language, especially to the
metaphors, of students' written or spoken readings for what they
might be said to say about their assumptions and beliefs). The notion
of scaffolding[7] allows us to imagine that in order for a novice student
to enter the field of play with a text, she first formulates an interpretation
that evolves single-mindedly, a posture that will become inimical to
the ranging and playing among perspectives once other interpretations
are brought forward, either from her individual reading and rereadings
or by a group of people reading and rereading in light of each other's
interpretations and the purposes of the teacher's assignments.

This opening up begins with students either writing or discussing (or both) their interpretations of texts. How this might proceed depends in large part on the text at hand and the questions that it might be said to open up and close down. It is in this sense that the procedures depend in large part on the text at hand, that response heuristics (like Bleich's,[8] for instance) formulate and privilege one way of reading, one way of constructing a take on a text. To open a field of play with a text, a multiplicity of readings enables the fracturing of individual readings and establishes the possibilities of self-reflexive rereadings of the text and of the individual interpretations of it. There are, then, no initial generic problems or questions for texts, except perhaps for the question that asks students to say what strikes them as significant in their readings, but even that question takes its cue from the text at hand, and the teacher's (or the students', if they are fortunate enough to be posing their own problems) immediate take with a text is to formulate the questions that offer students (and the teacher, hopefully) the opportunities to engage the text and each other in disentangling the problems and assumptions posed by or through it.

If this opening up is phrased in terms of general teacherly moves, the question or problem posed for students proceeds to offer them opportunities to learn first how to form their interpretations or takes on a text, and then how to critically exchange those interpretations, and finally how to self-reflexively trace and reread the text and their interpretations of it by paying attention to the ideology and the language of the text and their interpretations of it, as well as the questions posed by themselves or by the teacher. None of the elements of this scaffolding are easy, especially since they aggressively push against traditional notions of literature studies, including such heuristics as the conventions of plot and theme, that prescribe single, monolithic readings of texts. Students in high school and college generally aren't prepared to even formulate their own interpretations of texts, and very few of them are exposed to environments where they might be encouraged to critically exchange those either written or spoken interpretations, but the place to begin is with their readings of texts, and writing offers a retraceable track which is, I would argue, a necessity for carrying out this proposal.

Notions of Sequences and Assignments
That Pose Projects for Students

To turn literature study into a field of play is not an easy proposal, although we have been working with it in the form of project-posing

sequences of reading and writing assignments for about ten years at
the University of Pittsburgh.[9] Sequences can take many forms, but
their common characteristic is that they take nominal subjects like
"Growth and Change in Adolescence," or they pose problems like
"What Are We Talking About When We Talk About Love?" through
series of reading and writing assignments that build on and play off
of each other. The twelve-week-long sequence, "What Are We Talking
About When We Talk About Love," from which I'll draw my examples,
works with three texts (two short stories and an interview) and four
writing assignments (and eight revisions—two for each writing assignment). The first three assignments invite students to comment on
what different people talk about when they talk about love. In two
stories and an interview, several very different characters confront the
difficult subject of love. The characters in the Raymond Carver story
("What We Talk About When We Talk About Love") talk directly about
love, yet they seem to be stuck and the meaning of their conversation
is elusive. Ted and Ellie Graziano (from the interview with them by
Thomas Cottle) hardly ever talk about love, but they act out an
argument that might be said to say very much about it. The third
story ("A Silver Dish" by Saul Bellow) brings forward another enactment of love, this time through the eyes of a son who has just buried
his father. The fourth and final assignment asks students to conclude
their project by taking a critical stance toward the people they have
studied and what they, the students, have said.

Although this sequence was designed with short stories at its center,
sequences with a variety of kinds of texts can be designed to give
students other opportunities. A common move in our sequences is to
ask students to see an ideology or perspective on a problem through
another ideology or perspective. They might be asked, for example,
to read a psychologist's notions of "entitlements" (those personal,
social, and financial traits of children of wealthy parents) through the
self-reflexive perspective of a young black man in prison for murder.
They might also be asked to see the notion through their own
experiences, or through others' perspectives. The move here, no matter
how many takes on it are available, is to see through other readings
or perspectives. The move in the sequence on love is to construct
perspectives from puzzling readings, and to then critically and self-
reflexively read those perspectives.

All of this happens, of course, in the contexts of certain kinds of
academic discourse which privileges logical, documented arguments,
inscribed in a quasi-legal code of proofs—cases, arguments, evidence,
and conclusions; and the paradox, as I mentioned earlier, is that this

kind of writing becomes the beginning move for later self-reflexive moves. The most interesting and hopeful situation is one where students' interpretations proceed univocally but under constant pressure from other interpretations and from self-reflexive rereadings. And, of course, the teacher can help turn such workings into a problem by asking students to examine their methods and procedures, their language and its metaphors for what it assumes, implies, or privileges from various perspectives such as feminism or deconstruction. The field of play can shift and expand in multiple directions once students learn the initial move of forming their own interpretations.

The advantage of working with multiple texts and assignments in a sequence is that the project presents multiple interpretive problems around a nominal theme by putting students in the position of positing meaning in a continuing, yet bounded, field of play. Although much of this play is carried in writing assignments, a substantial part of it has to be sustained in conversations, in class discussions where the locus of attention gradually shifts from individual interpretations to a multiplicity of disentanglings, including those defined by individual subjects' situations and those defined by culture and language. The teacherly role is one of posing questions and tracking the conversations. It also involves the reposing of critical and self-reflexive questions for students to interpret their own and others' interpretations, so they might learn about the text and themselves and the forces at play in their constructions.

Let me turn to some examples of assignments and students' writings. Here's the first assignment (for the Carver story) from the love sequence. It poses the opening question and frames the overall project.

> It's possible to read this story a number of times and still keep asking, "What are these people talking about? How do they explain love?" Terri, Mel, Laura, and Nick all make a number of observations, but they never seem to reach any conclusions or agreements, and the precise nature of their disagreements is elusive. At the same time, it's possible to feel that much has been said here. The question, then, is what do they talk about when they talk about love?
>
> Write an essay in which you address these questions. What is love to each of these people? What are they trying to say to each other about it?

For the freshmen and sophomores in my classes where I used this sequence, this was an enormous problem, located, for them, as they say, "in the fact that there aren't any answers in the story." They are accustomed to deciphering stories and essays for such things as main ideas and plots and themes, and suddenly, after years of this locating and deciphering, they're faced with forming an interpretation, with constructing a reading in a space occupied by the text, their situations, language, and cultural forces. Generally, they proceed logocentrically, hunting for evidence to make what might be called "legalistic cases" based on hard evidence from the text, and a common move in this case-making is their claim that something in the text, like a passage or a piece of dialogue, "shows that" or "proves" a claim or point of view is accurate or true. Mike, for example, makes that move towards the end of his paper, which we'll see in a moment, right before his final quote from the Carver story.

Mike's paper is particularly interesting on a number of accounts. He begins by making strong claims that he can never pin down an equation for love, a position he reiterates throughout the paper. He then proceeds to develop a case for whose love, Nick's or Laura's or Mel's or Terri's, will survive. This is a personal relations problem, rather than a text or writing problem posed by the assignment, but one which clearly interests Mike. I think it serves his strong inclination to read for a point, in this case a judgment, beyond his disentangling who might be saying what about love. Here's Mike's paper:

> Talking about love, or trying to set it within definite parameters, is in my opinion, impossible. There isn't an equation that equals love, and there are few constants. I thought about these things as I read Raymond Carver's short story, "What We Talk About When We Talk About Love."
>
> Each of the characters in the story have their own idea of what love is, or what it should be. The characters consist of two couples, Mel and Terri, and Nick and Laura. During the course of the story, one sees pieces of these characters' personalities, and histories. Through these glimpses one can make some judgements as to what exactly love is to each of these people.
>
> Mel, who could probably be considered the main character in the story, as he dominates the conversation, is seemingly obsessed with "putting his finger" on love. The conversation begins with Terri telling the others of how Ed (Terri's ex-husband) beat, and dragged her around their apartment. Still, she insists that Ed loved her. Mel disagrees, arguing that abuse of this sort excludes Ed from possibly loving her. But what is Mel's definition of love? After reading the story four or five times, I'm still not sure. My uncertainty stems largely from the fact that I don't think Mel is sure what love is.
>
> In the beginning of the story we find that Mel thinks of real love as being "nothing less than spiritual." That's fine, pretty vague,

but that's "okay" too. A little later in the story he defines the love that each of them knows:

> Physical love, that impulse that drives you to someone special, as well as love of the other person's being, his or her essence, as it were. Carnal love and, well, call it sentimental love, the day-to-day caring about the other person.

He goes on to say that he doesn't understand how he could have loved his ex-wife so much, as he now hates her. He further explains this by noting that everyone in the room has loved and even been married before. He thinks that if either him or Terri would die that the other would love again, leaving only a memory of the love that was.

Later, Mel describes his idea of "real love" in the story of an old couple who survived an accident together. He states that because of their casts and bandages they could not see each other. It's this fact that depresses the older gentleman. Mel sees this as touching and vital to their conversation. Mel says, "I mean, it was killing the old fart just because he couldn't look at the fucking woman."

Besides sounding drunk, Mel seems confused. He gives three definitions of love, or three different viewpoints, and yet he doesn't adhere to any of them. He tells Terri he loves her, and yet he treats her poorly; he speaks to her in a condescending manner on a couple of occasions:

> Just shut up for once in your life.

> "Vassals, vessels," Mel said, "What the fuck's the difference? You knew what I mean anyway."

This obviously isn't the way one treats someone one loves, yet Mel does. One can draw a parallel between this relationship, and Ed and Terri's relationship in as far as the conflict of terms. In Ed's case it was, "I love you, you bitch, I love you." Mel's style is similar in that he repeatedly says he loves her yet he insists on treating her as less of a person.

Terri's personality is opposite to that of Mel's. She seems to be much more complacent and accepting. She responds to his biting criticisms with apologies, "Please, Mel," Terri said, "don't always be so serious, sweetie. Can't you take a joke?" From what I can gather about Terri, I find that her prerequisites for love and a successful relationship are few. I think her idea of love is simply having someone, a person to hold onto. Her dialogue shows her insecurity; it's almost as if she needs someone to approve of her:

> He did love me though, Mel. Grant me that, that's all I'm asking . . . You can grant me that, can't you?

Because of Mel's dominating nature one can tell little about her, except that she accepts passively.

Nick and Laura's idea of love seems to coincide. This makes sense as they portray a flirtatious couple still very caught up in their relationship after eighteen months of marriage. The description Nick gives about Laura is much more flowery than that of the others. He talks of the color in her cheeks, and the brightness of her eyes. I'm quite sure these aren't the things Mel would notice about Terri, which may show that love isn't a constant, as much as Mel may want it to be.

The talking that Nick and Laura do during the story is most always a response instead of a question. They aren't the ones questioning love; instead, they seem contented in it. Mel, on the other hand, talks endlessly about it which tells me he might be wondering exactly what love is, as he hasn't found it.

In comparing the couples and their action, I find that through their language Nick and Laura are saying that they've found, for the time being, what they're looking for. Conversely, Mel and Terri stand less of a chance of survival. The language Mel uses is that of dissatisfaction, and restlessness. An example of this is the way in which he states that he'd rather be a chef, or if he had the chance to transcend the boundaries of time, a knight.

Although I'm not a psychoanalyst, the conclusions I have come to are, in my opinion, sound. They are the result of careful observation, but still they are only my opinion.

Mike's paper, one of the best drafts from a class of twenty students, moves from his initial qualification of the impossibility of reducing love to an equation, to his second paragraph, where he's willing to "make some judgements as to what exactly love is to each of these people," to his case for Mel's confusion about love (and Mike's faulting him for not adhering to any of his definitions) and the poor way he treats Terri, to his case for Nick and Laura expressing their love flirtatiously, and then he quickly concludes that Nick and Laura have found what they're looking for, while Mel and Terri "stand less of a chance for survival." Then Mike adds his final move, a move which speaks to his discomfort trying to disentangle rather than decipher a text, when he insists his opinions are sound, "but still they are only my opinion."

I included the entire paper because it frames Mike's uneasiness with problems posed for puzzling texts that defy locating meanings as givens in texts. He knows he has to form an opinion. He's not comfortable doing that, especially since he believes "there are few constants" in love. He proceeds admirably, reading closely to make his case for Mel's confusion and Terri's insecurity and, finally, Nick's and Laura's contentment with their flirtatious love, only to conclude that this is only his opinion; he doesn't have the authority of a psychoanalyst, but his opinions are sound. The two moves here, his uneasiness at forming an opinion and his subsequent case, are typical of students' initial beginning responses to these kinds of open-ended tasks. They're uneasy, but then they proceed to make their cases, arguing to win, not admitting multiple possible readings, pointing to moments in the text as evidence that "shows" or "proves" something, and then finally concluding with propositions that shut down their possible rereadings or reinterpretations. Mike shuts down the four characters by offering judgments about their futures, judgments that take the position as the final word on their relationships so that he might be done with them.

What teacherly moves might encourage Mike to relocate himself in the field of play rather than in a courtroom? As it happened in this class, he had the opportunity to read and hear other takes on this story (because I duplicated papers with strong and various readings) while he received my comments both encouraging him to continue arguing his case and questioning his points. Still, the most pressure was brought to bear by his exposure to other readings quite different from his. (And here I would like to say again that although this opportunity to read and hear multiple interpretations can begin to open up a field of play, it does not by any means make its happening a certainty. Mike, for instance, never did play; he saw every other reading as evidence to be discarded or incorporated into his reading, so the opportunities to read and hear others became, for him, not an occasion for tentativeness but an occasion for judgment, although by the end of the semester he did play a little by shifting his judgments to focus on the variability of love and the variability of our readings of it.)

As Mike and others in the class moved to strengthen their interpretations, they struggled with their close readings because they weren't accustomed to moving among texts. They had a difficult time incorporating the story into their readings, and they had an even more difficult time incorporating other students' readings into theirs as a way of speaking from or along with or against those readings. But we have to realize, too, that all of this difficulty is framed by their resistance to and lack of familiarity with forming interpretations of texts from open-ended problems and questions.

The next assignment in the sequence plays off of an interview with Ted and Ellie Graziano that was done by Tom Cottle for a book he did with Stephen Klineberg on people's perceptions of time. Here's the assignment:

Ted and Ellie Graziano touch on one sensitive subject after another in their interview, but they never talk directly about love, even though they say they love each other. Sometimes they sound like Mel and Terri from the Carver story, and at other times, they seem more involved with each other in their arguments than any of Carver's characters.

What are the Grazianos arguing about? What are their disagreements? What do their disagreements have to do with love?

For this assignment, select three or four passages from the interview that you think best represent what Ted and Ellie talk about when they talk about love. Write an essay in which you discuss what these passages tell you about the Grazianos and how they understand love.

This is a more difficult assignment than the one for the Carver story, because there are no moments of direct talk about love as there are in Carver's piece, so the act of interpretation is more problematic, more open to play in the space it occupies—but students didn't see it that way. They began their initial drafts by sticking close to the text, by retelling it and then representing those retellings as their readings. It wasn't until we had discussed about ten different papers in class that they began to move away from close retellings to imagining possible readings of Ted and Ellie, their relationship, and their love. Here are excerpts from three early drafts of this assignment. The first two represent retellings as readings, and the last, Mary's, ventures quite a bold and tangled interpretive reading.

1.

Ted loves Ellie and his family in the way that he wants a better life for all of them. His desire is for them to have everything they want, and he worries about how to make everything work out for the best, especially financially. If he would happen to die, he wants to know that Ellie would not have to struggle through life, at least financially. Ted states, "We'll manage. Eight thousand years, and I'll have this house paid off, and when I die she'll be set up." I INTERPRET THIS TO MEAN THAT IN CASE TED WOULD PASS AWAY AT LEAST ELLIE WOULD HAVE SOME-THING, SUCH AS THE HOUSE, TO HELP KEEP HER AND THE FAMILY SOMEWHAT SECURE FINANCIALLY. SHE WOULD NOT BE IN THE BIND FOR MONEY BECAUSE THE MONEY FROM THE HOUSE, EVEN IF SHE WOULD HAVE TO SELL IT, WOULD LAST FOR A LITTLE WHILE, UNTIL SHE COULD FIND A JOB OR SOME OTHER ARRANGEMENT TO KEEP THE MONEY SUPPLY FLOWING.

2.

Ted also could not bear the thought of his family working in place of him if he would happen to become incapacitated somehow;

he would be humiliated, degraded. He states, "Many times I've
thought about what it would be like having your wife and children
working while you sat around the house, sick or something. That,
my friend, is another form of death." SOMETHING INSIDE OF
TED WOULD DIE IF HE COULD NO LONGER SHOW HIS LOVE
TO HIS FAMILY BY PROVIDING FOR THEM. HE WOULD FEEL
INFERIOR, LIKE HE HAS NOT DONE ENOUGH; HIS ACTIONS
WOULD BE INADEQUATE AND SO WOULD HIS LOVE BE.

3.

Ted Graziano's dream was to free himself and his family from
their gray monotonous lifestyle. Every day Ted's way of living
was a living nightmare. The loneliness, the boring newspaper job,
the lack of support and responsibility from his family developed
into a nightmare of reality. Ted states.

Everyday of my life I am totally alone, making it possible for four
human beings to lead their lives with a little dignity. Four ungrateful
human beings. I don't have a soul to talk to in this house. I see
the way people are living. I see the way people are dying, and
we're not getting any of it. Either one.

TED FEELS HE IS TRAPPED IN A TRIANGLE OF LIFE. IN
EACH CORNER OF THE TRIANGLE IS HIS LIFE, HIS DEATH,
HIS FAMILY, AND TED IS IN THE MIDDLE OF IT. When Ted
says, "I see the way people are living. I see the way people are
dying, and we're not getting any of it. Either one." Ted is talking
about the rich people and Ellie's father's death. IN ONE SIDE
HE SEES THE RICH LIFE AND HOW THEY BECOME SO
SUCCESSFUL AND ON THE OTHER SIDE HE SAW ELLIE'S
FATHER AND HOW HE LIVED HIS LIFE BY DRINKING HIS
PROBLEMS AWAY AND NEVER THINKING OR PLANNING
FOR THE FUTURE. TED SEES BOTH SIDES AND HE IS STUCK
BETWEEN THE BOTH OF THEM. TED SEES AND TRIES TO
REACH FOR THE LIFE SIDE, BUT HE CANNOT MOVE BECAUSE
OF HIS FAMILY. TED NEEDS THEIR SUPPORT AND STRENGTH
TO GO ON, BUT HIS FAMILY IS SO MUCH WRAPPED UP
INTO THEIR DAY TO DAY LIVING THAT HE IS AFRAID OF
FALLING BACK DOWN TO THE DEATH SIDE OF THE TRI-
ANGLE AND RELIVE ELLIE FATHER'S LIFE. He says, "If only
it worked that way. If only I could ever get ahead of it, instead
of always chasing, chasing, chasing . . ." Ted is chasing, but he'll
never get ahead because his family is not with him to share it. I
FEEL THAT'S WHY THE RICH ARE SO RICH, BECAUSE OF
THEIR FAMILY'S SUPPORT, IT'S LIKE A TEAM, EVERYBODY
CHIPS IN AND HELPS PLAN AND PREPARE THEIR FUTURE
TOGETHER, BUT TED'S FAMILY LEAVES TED TO DO EVERY-
THING, THE PLANNING, THE PROVIDING, ONLY HIM, THAT'S
WHY HE IS ALWAYS CHASING.

When we discussed these excerpts in class (after about six writing

assignments—mostly revisions—and eight one-and-a-half-hour discussions), my students were quick to recognize the interpretations that
weren't interpretations (papers #1 and #2), and although they appre-
ciated what Mary (paper #3) was trying to do in her last paper, they
took (almost to a person) another quasi-legalistic position towards the
paper by arguing amongst themselves whether Mary's interpretation
of Ted's being caught in the triangle of life was right. Was there enough
evidence to support this position, they wanted to know, and then,
immediately after this question, they (almost to a person again) took
strong stands on whether they agreed or disagreed with Mary. No
matter how I asked my questions (i.e., "Is it possible, for instance,
that there is no necessary right or wrong reading, that we see Ted
from different angles, and that it's these acts of seeing and how we
enact them that we might talk about?"), they insisted on keeping the
field closed, but they were beginning to open up at least to entertaining
multiple readings, and this assignment was the first occasion for them
(as I see it through their papers) to move away from the notion of a
correct or consensus reading to strong, individual readings (but, again,
framed by their quasi-legalistic notions rather than by any field of
play that might involve self-reflexive readings).

Here's Joyce's second draft of her very unpopular position on Ted
and Ellie. Notice how well she works the text from the interview into
her reading (even though she's still using large chunks of text instead
of weaving bits and pieces, she's learning to move between her language
and the text's), and the paper serves as a good example of her ease
with close readings. No one agreed with her and she came under
heavy criticism in class discussions for her position, which she finally
gave up, although not without conditionally qualifying her acquies-
cence. If, she said, everyone disagreed with her, then her reading was
probably wrong, but it was still her reading, and she told the class
that she felt entitled to it, no matter what they said.

> I feel that Ted not wanting Ellie to work displays his love for her
> in that he wants to keep her out of the work force in order to
> protect her from what he has had to endure most of his life. I
> believe this because Ted states,
>
>> If every day were the same, like it is, it would still be all right
>> if I didn't ever have to wonder about how all the days string
>> together. But it's the line of days, one after the other, each one
>> repeating, and then the ability to look down the road and see
>> exactly what's coming. Jesus, that's, that's . . . honest to God,
>> man, it just about frightens me to death, because it means I
>> can see the days leading right down to the end.
>
> When Ted says this he appears terrified because he can predict

his life up to the day he dies. Ted does not want Ellie to be able to predict her life and see the future like he can because it is harmful; it kind of takes away hope. Hope for something better is what keeps people going; Ellie still has hope; Ted has very little of it left. Concerning his own life Ted says,

> So now I got the problem of being born with a vision that looks down the road, and being able to see everything that's coming. They got lots of guys, I'm sure, give their right eyes to be able to see what's coming up for them. Well, I can see, and just being able to see is more of a curse than it is anything else. An evil curse.

Ted does not want Ellie to have such a predictable life like he does; he does not want it to curse her and make her as unhappy as he. He wishes her to stay the same even though he does not believe in living day to day or in God, but those two things at least give her hope, something that Ted never wants her to lose.

When Ted was in the army he enjoyed not knowing what was going to happen; he liked the suspense of it all. He states,

> I think that's why so many of us liked being in the army so much. Didn't anybody want to get killed naturally, but it was a change. Everything that led up to the army stopped once I got in, and what would come after no one could see. I thought about my future plenty then. Oh brother, we had a million conversations about the future. But no one could tell us the way it was going to be. The future was all mystery. I remember, that was my word for it, 'mysterious future.' It made you kind of scared. But now that I think about it, those jittery feelings were exactly the feelings I needed to get me going. They give you a kind of push, a motivation.

Ted realizes that some uncertainty in life is necessary to keep people moving along, always striving for more and better things. With his present job and life situation he does not have these feelings. He thinks he can see and predict everything to the end of his time on earth. He loves Ellie so much that he always wants her to have hope, and his desire is to spare her from this monotonous life he lives, especially in the work place where there is little hope for anything better.

Three of the women in the class immediately questioned Joyce about Ted's noble motives. How, they wanted to know, could he be concerned about Ellie's hope and the possible monotony of her life as a worker, when he refused to let her work, because a working woman wasn't his idea of a wife? And, they continued, wasn't her life as a housewife monotonous, more monotonous than his job?

I chose Joyce's paper to duplicate because I thought it would spark discussion and because it was such a strongly argued paper, at least according to the rules the class had set up for itself, and I thought we might, after the initial discussion of the paper's correctness, turn to what the paper said about arguments. So, I asked the class what they thought about the argument as an argument. How was it possible, I wanted to know, that a paper could be so well argued, so seamless, and yet spark such disagreement? The class puzzled over the questions and finally came to some agreement that logic was like statistics, that arguments could be built for any position and evidence could be mustered to support them, but that didn't make them right. Most of the students felt that it was possible to lie with logic like it was possible to lie with statistics, and they were, to a person, still holding tight to the notion of right or, as they said (following, I'm afraid, my lead), stronger readings; but things had changed from the first assignment where they either offered retellings or monolithic consensus readings—they were now willing to recognize various readings as long as they were supported with evidence from the text.

The next assignment (for the Saul Bellow story "A Silver Dish") asked for an even more open-ended reading than the Graziano interview did, because Woody Selbst, the main character, buries his father in the midst of his widening struggle with love for a number of people, and like the Grazianos, he never talks directly about love. Here is the assignment:

> In the Saul Bellow story, "A Silver Dish," Woody Selbst struggles with his love for his father, his wife, his mistress, and his family.
>
> Write an essay in which you characterize Woody's love for the different people in his life, especially for his father, Morris. Ask yourself how his love for these people compares to his love for his father. In what ways could it be said to be similar? different? What passages or moments in the story can you use to explain and illustrate these similarities or differences?

This assignment (about three-quarters of the way through the semester) was an important marker point in my students' writing and discussion. They were now actively looking for multiple possible readings of the story, and they began class discussion with questions to each other about their individual readings. "How did you see it?" they asked each other; and they were willing to be tentative, at least until all the readings were out. Then they could decide, they thought, which ones were strong and compelling. Although we weren't in an open field of play yet, my students were now open to multiple readings; they were reading each other's readings, and, more importantly, they were beginning to pay attention to the language of the story, not just the incidents or characters, the way they were paying attention to the language of their papers. What, I began to ask in the discussion, does the language of the paper, or the story, allow you to say about the paper or the story? Joyce's paper in response to the Graziano interview offered the metaphor and language of protection for Ted's position towards Ellie, and you, I said, read that closely to see how well it held up; now, I asked them, how do the metaphors in these papers portray Woody?

Wendy's paper, the first we discussed, reads the story in terms of its own metaphors and makes a remarkable move. She offers two quite different readings from the two different metaphors of love as a defensive shield and love as a peaceful offensive. In the second paper (excerpted here), Trudy reads Woody's language closely, within a given narrow context, to see if he literally means what he says, and she concludes that he doesn't, that Woody means almost the opposite of what he seems to be saying, and that his four words, "I got you, Pop," are the closest he comes to telling anyone his feelings. Here's the complete first paper, and the relevant part of the second.

1.

"The Silver Dish" by Saul Bellow has a lot of possible interpretations on love. I chose two of these to write about. In the first interpretation love is a defensive weapon, a shield (to expand on Bellow's metaphor). In the second interpretation love is Woody's peaceful offensive attempt to make the world a better place: a world of love. Both of these interpretations show why he loved everyone the way he did. It also explains why he shows more of this love to his father than anyone else.

In the first interpretation Woody uses love as a shield to protect himself from loneliness. He keeps himself busy loving others so as to shield himself from feeling lonely. Woody felt that solitude used the world as its reservoir. To keep from feeling the effects of the terrible solitude

> . . . there always is [was] some activity to interpose, an errand to run or a visit . . . a shield between himself and that trouble-some solitude which used the world as its reservoir.

As long he was doing things for his family, he had no time to feel lonely. Love shielded him from it. His schedule was full. Certain days he took care of his mother and sisters. Other days of the week he shopped for his ex-wife and his mistress. He bought his mother and sister clothes. He maintained their homes. He lent his father rent money which was probably never returned. He especially did a lot for his father. All the escapades that Woody lovingly followed his father on kept him too busy to be lonely. It didn't matter what Morris did to Woody or connect Woody into. Woody still loved him, he took up a lot of time. All of these loving actions kept him too busy to worry about solitude coming

after him and making him lonely. If one does not think about
something, it can't bother him.

The sudden absence of his shield shows how he was using it. On
the first Sunday after his father's death Woody felt lonely. His
shield was gone. Before Sunday all Woody had time for was an
"Oh Pop" mumbled under his breath. On Sunday he heard the
church bells ringing and grew sad and felt the impact of solitude.
He really never paid attention to the bells on previous Sunday
mornings. He was too busy getting up early to go visit with Pop.
He heard them and ". . . all at once he knew how heartbroken
he was." The bells melted his shield. He had a chance to think
during his new free time, where he didn't have anything to do
for anyone. "Heartache was deeply unpleasant to him." He did
not like to feel lonely. That was precisely the reason why he used
love as his shield. He didn't like the feeling solitude thrust on
him.

The second interpretation is that Woody uses love as an offensive
weapon to make the world a better place. Woody has a theistic
theory. He thinks God's idea was that this world should be a love
world, that it should eventually recover and be entirely a world
of love. It isn't too easy to see at first, because he thinks that it
is stupid and personal, therefore, he won't tell anyone about it.
"Nevertheless," Bellow wrote, "there it was at the center of his
feelings." If it is at the center of his feelings, it is important to
him. Also, if it is at the center of his feelings and is important to
him, it will govern his feelings and actions. He tries to give as
much love as possible to make the world fit his theory. He does
all the things mentioned earlier so that love is out in the world.

Woody shows the most love to the people who give him the least.
The top of his list is Morris. Morris took Woody's caddy money
that the poor kid saved from last summer to abandon him. He
stole a silver dish and said, "so what, kid?" when Woody got
blamed for it. Woody lost his job and someone to pay for his
school after that. Morris never made things right again for Woody.
Woody still showed the most love to him. It fit in with his theory.
He put as much love into Morris as he could, so he could make
it a better world. To make a world of love one has to put love
into it. He figured Morris needed more love, I guess.

Love can be both a defensive weapon for Woody to protect himself
with and an offensive weapon to help others. I think either or
even a combination of these shows why he loves everyone the
way he does. It also shows why Morris got the most love from
Woody.

2.

There is a similarity between his love for his father and for his
love for the others in his life with respect to duty. For example,
when his father and Halina needed help with the rent, Woody

gave it. And when his father was abandoning him, Woody gave him the money that made it possible, or as Woody put it, he had "bankrolled his own desertion," because he realized that his father "couldn't get away without his help." It seems to me that Woody did these things out of a sense of duty, just as he did with the others, his dependents.

But Woody's love for his father stands apart from his love for the others in his life for the most part. The very fact that Woody mourned his father's death and the fact that "all at once he knew how heartbroken he was" gives evidence to me that there was more intensity of an emotion present in his love for his father. Also, the fact that Woody insisted on dressing the stiff himself and shoveled the dirt on the grave himself shows me Woody's devotion to his father. Unlike his relationship with the others I have mentioned, Woody shows a dependence on his father. When his father is talking to him about going to Mrs. Skoglund to ask for money, he says, "You're practically a man and your dad has a right to expect help from you. He's in a fix. And you bring him to her house because she's bighearted, and you haven't got anybody else to go to." To this statement, Woody immediately answers, "I got you, Pop." I think that for Woody to answer so directly that he has his father to go to he must have strongly believed that he really does have his father to depend upon in some way. I really don't believe that Woody meant he could go to his father for money, which is the context in which his father was making the statement, but that Woody took that statement, ". . . you haven't got anybody else to go to," and generalized it, took it out of the context in which his father was speaking, and thought immediately, "I got you Pop." I also think this statement was a kind of expression of love on Woody's part. I believe that Woody was trying to tell his father, in his own way, that he loves him. Throughout the story, this is the closest that Woody ever gets to verbally telling anyone about his feelings for them.

When we discussed these papers in class, my students once again approached them with the language of strength and strong readings. They wanted to argue about which reading was the strongest, and I deeply regretted introducing that metaphor at the beginning of the semester in my attempts to move them from retellings into strong interpretations, but (luckily) Wendy and Trudy refused to go along with the terms of the discussions, and argued instead for their multiple readings being equally strong and valid and possible because of the story's ambiguity. Wendy's paper came under the heaviest criticism because it seemed to offer two irreconcilable readings of the story. How could his love be both a defensive weapon, students asked, and a peaceful offensive at the same time? Wendy argued, with Trudy's help, that it could, because the situation of Woody's was so complex, so subject to different influences, and that the story's language revealed this complexity by portraying Woody as a character whose feelings and actions didn't fit one mold. It was here, after this week's worth of discussions on these two papers (and another not included here), that the monolithic sense of a reading began to fracture, and I think we entered a field of play with these papers and discussions. But it was to be, as I'll demonstrate, constrained and bounded by a willingness to consider and fret out multiple disentanglings but not by a willingness to be tentative about them, to hold them all in the air as readings to be read self-reflexively, although Mike, whose paper on the Carver story I used earlier, did move to what I would call a beginning self-reflexivity in his final paper that we'll look at in a moment.

These papers, this sequence, and my teaching with these students pose an intriguing problem that is brought forward by my students' discussions of Wendy's and Trudy's papers. Their insistence on arguing for the best interpretation, or what they considered the strongest reading, presupposed a hierarchical sense of discourse and interpretations, where writings and readings exist in competition with each other rather than in concurrence or cooperation. Reflecting this, our discussions shifted their valency, like tides of agreement, with whatever interpretation held sway, and these last two papers (for the final assignment) demonstrate this by the ways they position other people's writings as readings to be agreed or disagreed with, or, as in the case of Mike's paper, as true or not true readings. It was often the case, especially past mid-semester, that students would rewrite their readings, sometimes drastically, to embrace a winning position or perspective, and this seemed to me as puzzling as their initial reluctance (up until around mid-semester) to reconfigure or reconsider a reading once it was written. I think my students understood the language and situation of tentativeness as momentary, as a perhaps useful staging ground for their conclusions, not as a continuing occasion for keeping a story or its various interpretations open to the play of writing and discussion. Wendy offers a description of this understanding in the opening page of her final paper:

> There has been so much that could be done with these three stories we read this semester that it was very confusing to come up with an opinion of my own. Each time I reread a story, I thought of something new to add or I changed my ideas completely. Each time another student spoke or I read another student's paper, I doubted my own interpretations. After reading Michelle's first draft to this final paper, I decided to go back to my original idea from the beginning of the semester. When I read her paper, I realized what I really believed to be true. I was too busy trying

to change my interpretations to fit with the rest of the class's. Or I wanted to come up with something new and completely different. I lost track of the interpretations I originally had. Despite all the confusion or different interpretations, the one I really believe to be true has come to the surface. As a matter of fact, the different interpretations brought up have helped me to strengthen my first one.

The final assignment asked students to take a position in relation to the characters from the stories and the interview. Originally, for the first draft, I presented it as an occasion for them to draw conclusions from the texts and their characters, but after reading these papers, it was clear that I had made a mistake and that I was working against establishing a field of play by asking for conclusions. So I reworked the assignment for the final drafts and asked students to account for the various characters' enactments of love and to take into consideration the various readings of these enactments that we discussed in class. But it was too late, and, as you'll see from these excerpts from three papers, Wendy's (#1), Mike's (#2), and Trudy's (#3), the course was already set by the first draft of the assignment. There is still, I think, something to admire in these papers. All three of the students work with other students' readings. Although their major moves are to decipher the texts and other readings of them, they appear to be trying to balance and disentangle multiple possible meanings, and they are appropriating text from other texts—mostly weaving rather than chunking it.

Perhaps it is that these moves, however unsophisticated they appear, are necessary before play and reflexivity can be established. Here's a section of Wendy's paper that continues after the opening description of how she worked. Notice how she writes back to other students' readings in the shadow of a dialogue, as opposed to a straight monologue. She manages it within the contexts of an unequivocal meaning, one she says that she lost in the tangle of multiple readings but that she finally recovered by considering another student's reading of the unselfishness in Mel's feelings about Terri (as we'll also see Mike doing later in his paper). This unselfishness becomes, for Wendy and for Mike, the truth to hang a final conclusion on.

> Why did I like Terri's and Mel's relationship the best? There are a number of reasons. One major one is the fact that they put each other before themselves most of the time. When one really loves another, she or he is willing to sacrifice for that other.
>
> Mel put his life in danger to be with Terri. Her ex-husband, Ed, was a crazy man. He threatened to kill Mel. The threat was so real and terrifying that Mel even contacted his brother, an ex-

Green Beret. He told him who was responsible, if anything happened to him. Terri said that they even lived like fugitives, and "(we) they were afraid." Mel said that he bought a gun, which wasn't in his nature. He used to break into a sweat before he even got to his car on dark nights. He was afraid Ed was going to jump out at him. Mel said he was "capable of wiring bombs, anything." Ed would call Mel's service, and when Mel returned the call, he'd say, "Son of a bitch your days are numbered." Mel was afraid. Mel said of Ed, "Little things like that. It was scary, I'm telling you." It is obvious that Mel was afraid for his life. So, why would he put up with that for any woman? Terri has to mean a lot to him, if he was risking death for her. She must have been pretty special for him to do that.

Others have said in class that Mel just doesn't want to be lonely. That is why he is with Terri. If he was just lonely, he could have at least found someone who didn't have a crazy ex-husband. And believe me, Mel could have had other women. He is a doctor, a cardiologist even. I work at a hospital, so I see it. There are women who would go after any doctor no matter what he looked or acted like, because doctors spell money . . . So, if Mel can have a lot of other women, there has to be a reason why instead he decides to be with one who has a crazy ex-husband who is trying to kill him . . . Therefore, Mel loves Terri because he puts his life in danger for her when he didn't have to, because he could have had other women . . .

I don't recall most characters in the other stories putting themselves before others. Morris certainly did not. All Morris cared about was himself . . . The result for his son, Woody, was the loss of a job and financial backing for seminary school . . . Morris's reaction to this was, "So what, kid." Morris certainly did not put himself before his son . . . Some people have said that this taught Woody a lesson. Sure it did. It taught him what his father was like . . . Woody is the one who put his father before himself. He took the blame for his father. So, I think Woody shows love to Morris by taking the blame in the same way Mel (to a more drastic degree) risks his life to be with Terri.

Ted is too caught up in the American Success dream to worry about putting others before himself. There is no way to tell if Ellie puts others before herself. The same is true of Nick and Laura.

Wendy, you'll remember, wrote the paper on the Bellow story where she read the characters through the metaphors of the defensive shield and the peaceful offensive offered in the story itself. The reflexivity of that reading has been overwhelmed by this convenient and powerful aphorism of, as she says later in this paper, "putting others before oneself," and for this she completely abandons her metaphorical reading of Morris and Woody and turns instead to cast their story and the other pieces in terms of personal relationships. The aphorism gives her the frame, the certainty, that makes this later reading more attractive to her (partly because it is more attractive to others in the class) than her original metaphorical reading. When we discussed her paper in class, and when I asked her why she abandoned her other reading of the Bellow story, she returned again, as she does in the paper, to this aphorism, to its truth, as others did also, and the discussion quickly became a grand gesture to rationalize the aphorism as an overarching principle or frame rather than, as I had hoped, a conversation about its displacement of her attention to the language of Bellow's story. I believe my students understood my moves and questions in a way opposite of what I had hoped they would, and no matter how much I protested and tried to open up the discussion to Wendy's earlier reading of the Bellow story, the conversation steadily reduced itself to an argument in favor of this certain and safe frame. As I saw it, my only option was to take an even harder, insistent critical stance towards their quickly developing consensus, and I decided not to do that, to let them go where they would, because they had made the class their own, and preserving that seemed important.

Mike's writing latches on to the same aphorism as Wendy's does, and although both of them give over substantial space (Wendy's paper is eight pages, while Mike's is ten) to considering other readings, they are essentially similar in the privilege they give to this monolithic reading. Here we pick up Mike's paper about halfway into his argument. Notice how similar it is to Wendy's and how he channels himself into the paper by means of the power of the aphorism.

> I believe that Woody loves his family. He shows this in the way in which he cares for them. It has been a part of his everyday life since he was a teenager. What I feel started as a way of proving a point to all of those who doubted his character, ended up as routine. This routine became a part of his already compassionate personality. This routine equals love for those who benefit from it.
>
> I understand the love Woody holds for his family because, finances permitting, I intend to do the same for my family. For some unknown reason I feel very comfortable taking care of the people who did so much for me. I realize that the circumstances differ greatly from Woody's, but still, we share the desire.
>
> Why do I agree with the love Woody gives his family? The answer stems from an in-class discussion. It came to my attention that one conditional characteristic of love may be found in whether or not the person who supposedly is giving love is unselfishly

willing to put that person in front of himself. After thinking about it, I realized that this was in fact true, especially for Woody.

Out of the seven or eight people I really love in this world, I would put everyone of them in front of me in certain situations. Try to understand what I'm saying. Sure, every once in a while anyone can be selfish with those people he/she loves, but ninety percent of the time I think you'll find that I'm true to my word. Woody is the same. Seemingly everything he does is done for a loved one. I have no reason to doubt that Woody would gladly trade spots with his father in the hospital room. I feel this is true with the rest of his family also. Much like Woody buys, he loves—with a "broad hand."

We came to call this class discussion, the one that seemed to reconfigure everyone's thinking, "the infamous unselfishness," and its influence is again apparent in Mike's writing, not only in his mentioning it, but in his allowing it to reduce his reading and his personal connection to one rock-solid aphorism about personal relationships. He moves away, too, from the story as story, as language and writing (something he struggles with in his first paper that we looked at earlier), to the story as personal relations.

Trudy's paper makes many of the same types of moves that Mike's does; she weaves in comments on other students' interpretations and she quotes from the texts as well, but it's all done to present one rock-solid, seamless point of view that reduces other readings (and the stories) to statements on personal relations with which she either agrees or disagrees as she constructs the proof of her argument. All three of these final drafts also represent the class conversations. Students moved initially from these being occasions to argue for single, monologic consensus interpretations (no matter what) supported by "proof" from the texts under study to these woven discussions that encouraged various individual interpretations (still supported by the texts or now by others' readings of them or some point of consensus) but bounded by this quasi-legal code of proofs and positions of agreement or disagreement. The move to reflexivity seems to have allowed students (like Wendy and Mike and Trudy) to take critical postures towards various interpretations, including, at times, their own, but it doesn't seem to have allowed them much depth or tentativeness beyond these postures, for they continually push their "burden of proof" arguments for the final say, the complete conclusion of these readings. They aren't willing to leave the question of meaning up in the air while they consider various interpretations for what they might say about the texts or the readers or the language and culture. Still, they are willing to invite individual readings, and they are willing to consider them critically. This seems to be a necessary move through the scaffolding—of learning to make interpretations, learning to examine them critically, and learning to take reflexive stances towards those interpretations so that writings and discussions might be more a field of play.

Here's an excerpt from Trudy's final paper. Notice how she weaves quotes and references other readings from class discussions and papers into her paper, but how it's all done within the "evidence" to make her interpretation and to appropriate others' for her use or to dismiss others' if they don't support hers.

> Terri also made no comments on or appeared to even relate at all to Mel when he spoke about real love, the old couple's love. When Mel was describing his feelings and beliefs to the others, Terri responded, "Mel, for God's sake, . . . are you drunk?" I interpreted this comment to mean that she had no concept of what Mel was talking about when he described his idea of real love. I believe Terri is perfectly content with what she had and believes that it is love. I, however, have to disagree.
>
> Nick and Laura, on the other hand, don't really verbalize their thoughts on what love means to them. Laura says, "Nick and I know what love is . . . For us, I mean." When she tells Nick that it's his cue to say something, he instead "made a big production out of kissing her hand." Nick and Laura openly express their affection for one another by physical contact. Jeff argued in class that this proves that they love each other since they openly show their love to others. I disagree with his interpretation. This type of open display is stereotypical of newly-weds and says to me that they are insecure about their partner's love and must be assured of the love of their partner by their repeated physical contact.
>
> In class, Jeff argued that Nick and Laura are quiet because they are secure. But Nick and Laura have only been married for eighteen months and their "courtship," as Nick calls it, was sudden which leads me to believe that they may not have known each other very well before they got married. I think that their love is too new and still in the honeymoon stage where everything is wonderful and there are no problems. However, once they hit reality, perhaps having their first real fight or run into a serious problem, that will be the true test of the strength of their "love." I don't have enough information to make a judgement whether or not they love each other. I can see that they think they do but it's all too early in their relationship to be able to judge.
>
> I did agree with something touched upon by Nick in describing his relationship with Laura. He says, "In addition to being in love, we like each other and enjoy one another's company. She's easy to be with." For Nick, being in love is apart from liking each

other and enjoying another's company. I agree with Jeff when he
said "friendship and love should go hand in hand." I see being
"In love" as the irrational, newly-wed part of the attraction, like
Nick and Laura. But a part of "love" for me is being friends with
that person; its more than an infatuation or like a blind love in
which the person can do no wrong. But for me love is being
friends with the person, enjoying his company, and accepting that
person's faults. I believe I hold these views from the way I was
brought up.

For me, Trudy's paper stands both for what was possible in this
class and for its failures. Her interweaving of various readings and
her willingness to at least begin to move to self-reflexivity towards
the end of the paper, however superficial a move it is, offer a glimpse
of what a more full-blown, more reflexive and critical class might have
moved to. She's caught, however, in the burden of proof code, and
she allows herself to be silenced by the received talk about "the true
test" of Nick and Laura's love. Consequently, the end of the paper
seems to give itself over completely to those received aphorisms.

Taken together, these three papers demonstrate what I would call
fundamental or beginning moves. But even though there are solid
signs of these students appropriating texts, considering other students'
interpretations, relating their comments to their values and assumptions, they are only the barest moves. I would say that their efforts
are superficial, except my sense is that, for these students, they are
not, partly because they haven't thought carefully about what they've
been saying, and also because this kind of interpretive activity with
texts and with each other's interpretations is genuinely new to them.

Reflections on the Semester

It was difficult for my students to allow that multiple interpretations
of texts might exist alongside each other without one being better or
more truthful than the other. Although they finally, towards the end
of the semester, allowed individual readings, to a person they took
the position that any tentativeness in judging the best interpretation
was simply an occasion to withhold judgments until all evidence—all
the interpretations—were in. Self-reflexivity, a necessary element in
opening literature study to what I was calling a field of play, was also
difficult for my students, partly because their postures within the quasi-
legal code begged closure and partly because they didn't read texts,
including their own, very closely. Our class discussions of the texts

and of their papers were similar to their writings—the same posturing for unified, rational statements of meaning seemed to be at work.

Overall, then, my sense of the scaffolding in the context of reading and writing sequences is that students learn to do the thing itself, the monolithic interpretation inscribed in a quasi-legal code of claims and proofs, before they learn to undo it in a field of play. My moves, my insistence on their working for "strong interpretations," rather than for a way to imagine and develop multiple interpretations early in the semester, played to the kinds of monolithic readings I tried to displace or at least fracture, and as certain as I am about this, I am just as uncertain as to whether we would have worked any differently if I had proceeded by first asking for multiple readings and self-reflexive attention to those readings. This is an interesting problem that has to do with my proposal that students scaffold through learning the thing itself before learning to undo the thing. This is partly, I think, because of our cultural inscription in monologic discourse, and partly because a field of play exists to ceaselessly posit meaning only to "evaporate it," and the positing of meaning can take various forms, including quasi-legalistic, rational arguments. But the question remains: would my students have played more with multiple interpretations, with discussions of their origins, if the assignments asked for them, or would that have been even more difficult for my students, since they had such a hard time forming single interpretations and accepting others' interpretations? Is, in other words, the monolithic, burden-of-proof code so overwhelming that it has to be done before it can be undone, or can it be undone immediately by asking for multiple interpretations of a text and discussions of their possible origins by individual students?

My feelings now, after having written most of this paper, are that my students might have "played" if they had had opportunities to form interpretations and critical readings of texts and their interpretations earlier in their schooling. When they might have begun this is certainly an important issue, and although I wouldn't want to make a case based on grade levels, it does seem to me that they could have learned to do these interpretive activities during high school without much difficulty. My notions of using sequences of reading and writing assignments, with multiple readings (usually offering a number of perspectives on a question or problem posed by the sequence), and with writing assignments that build on and play off of each other should work in high school classes with time.

Part III: Epilogue

THERE'S SILENCE BETWEEN ONE PAGE AND ANOTHER**
There's silence between one page and another.
The long stretch of the land up to the woods
where gathered shadows
exit for the day
and nights show through
discrete and precious
like fruit on branches.
In this luminous
and geographic frenzy
I am still unsure
whether to be the landscape I am crossing
or the journey I am making there.
                              —Valerio Magrelli, translated from the
                              Italian by Jonathan Galassi

As I reread my paper now in the context of the prologue's remarks
on teaching models, I'm struck by how much my original sense of my
students' work seems situational, more connected to the context I
designed than any "developmental" progression. At first my students
practiced forming single interpretations. This was a task I set for them
and it seems questionable. Even given that they weren't practiced at
forming interpretations and began by retelling texts, I want to consider
why I didn't begin by asking them to form multiple interpretations
instead of the "strong reading," the monologic one asked for by the
assignments, that automatically positioned them in a way where they
had no choice but to write their single readings. This is an important
question. It underlies the paper's closing one about whether or not
they need to do the thing itself, the monologic reading, before they
undo it. I don't know how my students would have begun with
multiple readings, but I am sure they would have tried. To initiate
their multiple readings, I could have brought examples before them
of what those might look like, and it could have been the case that
those would have been examples I wrote. So, then, we might have
begun a discussion of the examples and the theoretical contexts from
which I was working. All of this is to say that I can imagine this now
but didn't then.

   A question that strikes me as adjacent to the one on how my
students might have proceeded with multiple interpretations has to
do with how much of what evolved during the semester proceeds

** From *Poetry* CLV, Nos. 1/2 (October/November 1989). Used by permission of *Poetry*,
Jonathan Galassi, and Valerio Magrelli. Grateful appreciation is expressed to Dana Gioia.

from my beginning monologic move. If, in other words, we had begun forming multiple interpretations, isn't it then the case that we would not have proceeded as we did with our ceaseless discussions of which interpretations were better or truer or with which ones we agreed or disagreed? This is partly what I am thinking of when I claim that the progression of the class through what seemed a scaffolding (from forming monologic interpretations, to considering them in relation to others, to appropriating and referencing others, to beginning to explain the origins of these interpretations, to the final level of getting caught in a received aphorism) is situational. And the situation, which is dominated by my desire to help my students learn to form their own interpretations in light of their desire to retell, is already, at its onset, caught in the discourse of monologic readings. It seems now, in hindsight, that if one begins there, then it necessarily will be difficult to enter a field of play with tentativeness about readings as one of its characteristics. But what if we did begin with individuals providing multiple readings? What might that look like? Would the monolithic discourse have fractured any other way, or would it have been similarly difficult to establish a field of play because the underlying process— forming readings—is identical and always already shaped by the dominant discourse that includes this desire for unified, "true" readings?

In an oblique way this brings me back to the opening argument against teaching models, for it reiterates the overpowering blindness of the monologic. The progression of what happened in my class was an occurrence that might be presented as a model if one were to take the scaffolding as a developmental progression. On the other hand, if one views what happened as an occurrence, always situational but never removed from the dominant discourse, then it becomes much more difficult to overgeneralize it as a model the way the discourse would have us do in its attempt to unify, simplify, and solidify. Once the overgeneralization about a situation's progression or development is made, often in terms of a "natural development," it becomes a möbius strip, in which people begin to see things in the model's terms, which are always the dominant discourse's terms. Then we even begin to design strategies for the model that perpetuate it, and it becomes "unthinkable" to see or do things differently. It seems to me that models always already reflect, as my teaching and sequence design do, a subject's desires, and as models they solidify that desire.

Paradoxically, my strategies and the situation they created could be said to have worked in somewhat the same way a model might have, only I didn't begin with a teaching model as such, as something presented to me in second-level, derivative discourse. I began working alongside theory and my interrogation of it for pedagogy, but I was already inscribed in an approach that I am here now, with the help of other readers and theory, questioning. And it's not as if there's an answer waiting to be discovered, for there isn't anything I could do that wouldn't be already inscribed in a dominant discourse. The problem is that my strategies, like meaning, can be helpful to me (remember I'm a subject in this also) and my students as people attempting to create a field of play only if they exist in a space that allows them to be ceaselessly constituted and then evaporated, like meaning. If I don't keep cycling back and over what I do, then what I do moves towards solidification as a model. When teachers are removed from theory and critical conversations of it and what they do with it, and when they are forced to deal with second-level derivations in the forms of teaching models, this space for play is shut down. And that is a major difference between enacting pedagogy with theory at one's side and teaching from a model. The former at least opens up possibilities by opening up a discourse and, then, "consciousness," while the latter shuts down discourse and "consciousness" to everything but itself.

Foucault would attribute the role of my pedagogy to an exteriority, to the regulations and rules of a discourse (including its contradictions and disruptions) (Foucault, 1972, 138); and while it certainly exists within that exteriority, I am uncomfortable with the completeness of this way of thinking, with its willingness to assign the statements that I make in the name of a pedagogy to only an exteriority in an enunciative domain. I am, instead, taken with Said's argument which allows will and intention to restore subjectivity to subjects in enunciative domains while positioning them also in the rules and regulations (including, of course, the discontinuities) of that domain (Said, 1975, 372–79). This move also allows the restoration of affection and emotions and, then, their enactments through will and intention by subjects in enunciative domains such as this educational one. This is an important digression from Foucault (1972) and Derrida (1970, 1976), because it allows subjects intention and will and emotion (which might be understood to exist alongside intention). These subjects are always situated, and any discussion of what subjects might construct would necessarily include a discussion of particular intentions and emotions. This speaking of and about intention is a substantially different move in a different domain than the interrogation of texts for authorial intentions, and it is often the case that these two acts are confused in a discourse that wants to unify them in the term "intention."

Working with theory like this in the contexts of an ongoing conversation about literature teaching allows me to reexamine my methods during the class, as I did with the example above where I questioned beginning students with single "strong" readings, and in the design of this sequence. As the problem has already been posed, there's a serious misrepresentation in this sequence. It privileges male voices and perspectives. The sequence also privileges one cultural perspective, and as I am redesigning it, I'm paying attention to representing women, other cultures, and issues of class differences. This is easy enough to do, but what fascinates me is how I constructed this sequence as I did. It's too simple a gloss to say I did it because I'm caught up in valorized male discourse. Although this may be so, glosses like this erase my agency as a subject who is always situated in particular circumstances.

I'm hesitant about continuing my explanation of how I composed the sequence, because I don't want it to seem as though I'm defending the sequence or rationalizing why it was written the way it was, but it's so obviously male, concerned as it is with issues of male love and the relationships between fathers and families, that, for me, it's a question of asking how it came to be constructed so I might study my history as a subject acting and creating pedagogy with other subjects. That's why this epilogue seems so essential to me; it extends the conversation and allows me to speak from a re-vision that includes the comments of my readers instead of, as is traditional to this kind of academic discourse, going back and fixing my representation of the pedagogy so it might be "truer" and less subject to its own inconsistencies and disruptions. This can lead to reformulations, although this change doesn't often proceed in a unified way. Like Holden, I can reconfigure my thinking by my digressions, and to represent that process as unified and replicateable is to misrepresent it.

So, now I would like to digress, to think about how this sequence was constructed. Obviously, the concerns of this sequence are my concerns—the relationships between men and women, fathers and sons—and they are located in the behaviors and discourse of my class, the working class, where the father is—central, responsible (by his and his culture's creation); sacrificial (a position he shares with women), in the sense that he gives up things and comforts for his children and family; and mysterious, in the sense that by his absence at work, often at two jobs, he is the least visible family member.

The father's attention falls on his son, usually before his daughter.

Attempts by the son to unravel that relationship, one that is so strongly coded as primary (as opposed, say, to the one with the mother, which is coded as secondary), turns to questions of male love and evolves, then, in an odd mixture of discourses at once bounded by class and by a class insistence that the subject of love is unbroachable. Here, then, are two different discourses, in that "odd mixture of discourses," creating tensions and playing off of each other. Neither one is "the truth," but together they both broaden the subject and narrow down interpretive possibilities. Juxtaposed like this, they ask you to play along.

14 WYANDOTTE: My house, one of those large two story wooden places, clapboard and shake-shingle, unfinished attic and basement, a porch, no lawn, in a block of identical houses on a street lined with huge elms. The rooms reeked a sourness of dogs. Directly down the hall from the front door, the kitchen floor warped under an iron sink and a door to the dining room. Up-stairs—green walls and more warped floors. It was a nasty piece of work and took years to remodel, and now the trees are gone and only my father is left.

When he talks suicide, I tell him there are reasons to live, and he tells me, with that voice, that I don't know what I'm talking about, that I don't know the pain he feels. He says it with the voice now inside of me, the one that speaks and snaps out when I am afraid or angry, and I have begun to hear it in my sons.

This is the voice that says it has had enough, it will do what it wants, stay away, listen, be

The working class saturates my life, and it wasn't surprising to hear one of my readers talking about the valorized male points of view in this sequence. From the outside I can see it that way, as sexist. Yet from the inside, as a subject of the working-class situation, it looks quite different. When this sequence was constructed, my attentions were turned to these issues, especially as I seem to me to be duplicating the language and behavior of my father in ways that I did not want. As I came to question this cultural inheritance, my desire to understand what had happened to me, and how what had happened to me was now happening to my two young sons, over-whelmed me in a discourse that was both paternal and single voiced. I became obsessed with these questions, and initially there were directed only at the father and son relationship, then at issues of male love, and only after I had spent years interrogating people, including my parents, and texts, did my attention warned, maybe to protect itself, to conceal the pain, or maybe it's only power or rage that wants to go on living, a survivor, misplaced from the Depression or war, trying to pass itself along, trying to find a place in my sons.

One of those sultry days before we had a car, we rode in my uncle's blue coupe to his place on the river. Ma stared ahead in the front. She must have distrusted us even then, when he imagined she couldn't handle money, and since she didn't have a job, she didn't have any. They shopped at discount stores, where he would let her buy little things—plastic containers, dish towels, cups and saucers—and when she left, they were stacked unopened in the cupboards and closets.

That night he came home from Scoops—Ma called it a "gin mill"—with a lopsided tree over his shoulder, the giant elms were covered with snow. She said (I remember her exact words), "your brain must be going bad, you can't even see straight anymore." Furious, he chopped it into pieces, then Ma went out, dragging me along.

Picture the two of us carrying a tree—Ma muttering under her scarf as the wind howled off the river, then imagine that the lord left his place and stopped at ours for drinks, and listened to our troubles then passed out while it

turn to considering the ways I wrote and talked about and considered my mother and sister as subjects in the larger picture. It's an odd experience seeing this from both the inside and outside, as both exteriority and interiority, as the force of culture and discourse and the force of intention and emotion. It seems inevitable to me that a feminist reading of this sequence and its construction is exterior to my working-class situation, which does not mean that it is irrelevant, but only that it is unlikely to come from within that working-class situation, for that situation constitutes itself and is constituted by codes and discourse that position feminism (and theory, as I will argue in a minute) outside of itself. And this points, too, to the odd space that class transformations create. My culture and language remain saturated with the working class, yet to understand this, I have had to pay attention to what lies outside of that situation,[10] and in so doing, another space opens, one that is at once saturated by working-class culture and overlaid with other, perhaps middle-class, culture and language.

When I think of an analogy, I think of theory and how it is possible for me, from the outside of working-class saturations, to be enthralled with postmodern critical theory, but from the inside feel strongly that what we've snowed for days and the windows froze, turning the trees and houses and light into refractions of themselves.

Marx said the increase in values is the result of self-valorization of capital; my father said his will is in the safety deposit box along with his CDs, and if I die before him, it all goes to the kids, so I shouldn't worry, and so there it is, death at 6 in the morning with weather threatening from the north, with this vague sense that the days and weeks have been going too quickly; maybe it's the month, maybe that's why my father called to say where the goods are, which brought death into every movement of the day. So, why if we're all going to, everything and all, are we here (such a simple question), but that supposes reasons, and who's to say they are more than inventions, like money and factories— the Great Pacific Paper, the Anaconda Brass, the General Motors—which invited my father to hand over his life for them, and he did.

The sun turns yellow in the window and already it's hot. My mother (in her pink housecoat) and I stand in the kitchens of different houses in different cities, eating. She stands next to the white stove as my son does here, and when we ask him to sit with us, he turns his head slightly, annoyed, squinting as I do.

got here is a bunch of elitist men talking about the theories of other elitist men.

My uncomfortable feeling in this entanglement has to do with what feels like a limiting möbius strip of male discourse, from that of my class to that of the theory which has allowed me to play with pedagogy, and the way in which it seems to desire to erase my connections to women, especially to my mother, and how I write and think about them. This is a discourse that moves me farther away from my mother, from the women I love, and allows me to erase them as subjects occupying positions related to the positions that I occupy. Goodbye identity—and the individual and cultural responsibilities attached to it. Said's shadow allows me to restore subjectivity to subjects, to say there is an odd space here, one that has to do with class and gender and subjects' intentions; and the theory that I am working alongside continues to marginalize these issues while, paradoxically, at the same time, making it possible for me to understand them in culture and language and, then, in my actions and enactments. How utterly disorienting. How stressful and far afield of teaching models and "truth." Yet how pertinent to questions of power. Who, then, does this theoretical discourse serve? Who does it empower by what it posits, by what it creates? And who does it marginalize by what it erases?[11]

Now the yellow mums among the red and orange or slightly brown ones remind me of my mother who always this time of year, the leaves falling, imitating colors, placed pots of them on the tables in the dining room (as I have) and, as we called it, the parlor, where she liked to sit with her lady friends to drink coffee and smoke Kents, and they would say, "Oh Bernice, such lovely mums," and it was easy to see why they liked each other so, talking about the neighbors as if they themselves were the mums, the interjected, the "Oh Betty, such a thing to say," or "Oh Bernice, you're a riot," and it seemed so comfortable in the presence of the mums with the lightest scent of bay and pine scattered here and there on small plates in the parlor in the smoke with the ladies, on a splendid, cold fall afternoon with an already noticeable low sun and its peculiar light on the white buildings. She is the woman in my dream, the one who announces in her old age that she is pregnant, then the man, the one drinking and digging in the yard, walks out (as she finally did), and I stand there opening my arms to hold her here where I have become my mother's most feminine of gestures, her presence in her hands shaping the once intimate space between her and Rosie and Betty with this idea of a self dissatisfied with herself, disturbed—the self of my mother myself isolated, outside, fashioning surfaces to be attractive and lovely, gesturing here to another woman—the one on the sofa listening to me in this place near the ocean—with my mother's long bony hands to hold the words to be held, and like her, my mother, not getting it right yet.

Coda: Change

A part of the transformation and change in this project over the course of a year's time is my assuming various points of view. I've learned from those actions that I do want to rewrite this sequence to include women's voice and matters of class.

A continuing conversation at various levels and in various enunciative fields has allowed me to reformulate a pedagogy and myself. The alternative, which one reader asked for, is silence. I could cut this degression and preserve "The Original Paper." But I am including the final section as an example, one set against exclusionary teaching, against models, an example of the usefulness of disruption/fragmentation. Intentionally so. I would like to begin to offer a different way of thinking about teaching and literature, one positioned in the continually stressful relationship of theory and practice.

Notes

1. Hunter proposes a teaching model which moves teachers through specific steps of direct instruction. The steps (i.e., setting anticipations, stating objectives, direct instruction, guided practice, testing for comprehension, etc.) become categories in lesson plans that are meant to evolve sequentially, in the teaching of skills. Once a skill is mastered, the teacher then moves on to another skill, following the same sequence of instruction. This has been a very popular program with strong advocates coming from school district administrators who see it as a way of ensuring identical instruction for all students and, in effect, making the sequence of instruction teacher-proof. My experiences with this in the Pittsburgh Public Schools have led me to consider this yet another attempt to take responsibility for teaching away from teachers and to locate it instead with a model of instruction that desires to be considered, as it is presented to teachers, as "objective" and "scientific."

2. It's easy to pass over the language of plot, character, and setting as "natural" to stories without considering that this too represents a model for teaching fiction, one that avoids, for instance, confrontations with issues of gender or class or culture and allows stories to exist in a field defined by these terms—plot, character, and setting. As a model, it has become hyper-attenuated by its application to increasingly smaller chunks of text. I saw a recent example of this in one of my son's schools where the students were asked a series of plot, character, and setting questions on worksheets for each chapter of a 130-page novel. Not surprisingly, it took the class almost two months to "cover" this short novel, and my son learned to hate it and the method in about one-third of that time.

3. Although Dewey insisted throughout his career that theory and practice flowed from each other, that teachers entered into theoretical experiments when they taught and had, then, a responsibility to inquire into the hypotheses they enacted and formed in this teaching, his progressive movement came to stand for today's equivalent of vocational education with the emphasis on providing students with work-related, "practical" experiences in schools. Perhaps his best recapitulation of his own position in response to this transformation is his *Experience and Education* (1963).

4. In *The Pedagogy of the Oppressed,* Freire develops what he refers to as "the banking concept of education," which represents the notion that knowledge exists like objects to be transferred or given to others by those who possess it. The *possessots,* according to Freire, are the *oppressots,* for they control literacy and consciousness not so much by the fact that they possess the knowledge as by the methods, the banking methods, with which they control learning by disallowing the oppressed the means by which they might pose and solve their own problems.

5. In *Cultural Literacy* (1988, 14), Hirsch asserts that people learn information by being taught it, and later (p. 30) he argues for "basic acculturation," a basic repertoire of knowledge, by age thirteen, and he bemoans recent disdain for memorization. His position seems to me to reflect the status quo of learning in the schools. Ninety-five percent of what my two children (ages 8 and 11) do in school is rote learning (by my literal account of a year's worth of written and worksheet "work"), and the great failure of their

education, as far as I am concerned, is this emphasis on information (and its testing) and their lack of reading books and stories, especially the absence of opportunities to write and talk about reading. Their understandings, their sense of knowledge about the world (and about texts, of course) proceeds like a spelling list of information, not as knowledge grounded in close readings of or engagements with texts (books, experiences, discussions, observations, etc.), including those texts they might produce themselves. This is how I read Hirsch's thinking about literature, as a body of knowledge about literature, and there isn't anything, in my experience, new in his position. It's status quo.

6. Hirsch's insistence on referencing literacy to a dictionary solidifies his position on what literacy might be to him. Lists of information pose literacy as a quantitative equation—the more one has, the more one is said to be literate. This metaphor, a "banking metaphor" of learning, as Freire calls it, creates a ground for oppressive relationships between those who have and those who do not, and so I think the implications of this way of thinking about "to teach" is incompatible with any way of thinking about "to teach" that values students doing the work of studying literature—interpreting texts and their own interpretations.

7. When I later refer to scaffolding, I am using the term in the sense that Vygotsky implies here. That is, that people learn not just a skill itself but a self-consciousness of the learning of that skill. I realize that scholars like Courtney Cazden use this term differently, but my sense of it is pretty strictly Vygotskian—the learning and the consciousness of self-reflexivity of that learning.

8. David Bleich's response heuristic (as he proposes it in his book *Subjective Criticism*) is as formulaic in what it asks students to do as, say, constructing themes and plots and symbols, only Bleich suggests that students' responses be grounded in their personal associations instead of simply in the text. Response heuristics like Bleich's (I'm using him to represent a field here) seem, finally, to preclude any sense of texts posing problems or problems being posed through literature by teacher- or student-made projects (like the sequenced reading and writing assignments that I'm so taken with). In calling for a field of play in the study of literature, I am more interested in the questions teachers and students pose of texts and of each other's readings of those texts, than I am in any heuristics for response that privilege certain formulas for response.

9. See Bartholomae and Petrosky's *Facts, Artifacts, and Counterfacts: Theory and Method for a Reading and Writing Course* (1986) and *Ways of Reading* (1987) for examples of sequenced reading and writing assignments. The "Growth and Change in Adolescence" sequence in *Facts* makes use of books like *I Know Why the Caged Bird Sings* by Maya Angelou, *The Catcher in the Rye* by J. D. Salinger, and *Coming of Age in Samoa* by Margaret Mead, while *Ways* offers sequences with essays and stories. The sequence on "What We Talk About When We Talk About Love" that I use for this paper is from *Ways*. The student papers are from a freshman course I taught during the Winter 1988 semester when I used this sequence.

10. In her essay, "Stabat Mater," Kristeva, in reference to the myth of the Virgin Mother, poses what are for me key questions about the privileges and

margins of my working-class situation. She asks: "What is there, in the portrayal of the Maternal in general and particularly in its Christian, virginal, one, that reduces social anguish and gratifies a male being; what is there that also satisfies a woman so that a commonality of the sexes is set up, beyond and in spite of their glaring incompatibility and permanent warfare?" (163). As I look into and out from my working-class position, the same questions— what gratifies the men and also satisfies the women—seem pertinent. From the outside, the marginalizing of women in that situation is oppressive, yet from the inside it doesn't seem that way and here is, apparently, something at play that allows satisfaction and the reproduction of the situation. Kristeva allows me to understand this as a complexity that implicates both men and women rather than as a simple attribution of oppressive moves by men.

11. I am also indebted to Kristeva's writing for the workings of these double-run pages. She makes use of this methodology in "Stabat Mater," and it seems to me useful to juxtapose adjacent conversations that might inform and disrupt each other when one is suspicious, as I am here (and I don't mean to imply that Kristeva is) of the totality of either (or both) texts. This is, then, another form of discursive play, something that is attractive to me.

12. Foucault (1972) refers to "a slow transformable unity" as "a plastic continuity, the movement of a meaning that is embodied in various represen- tations, images, and metaphors" (150). He says they may be thematic or systematic, explicit or not.

References

Barthes, R. (1977). *Image-music-text* (S. Heath, Trans.). London: Fontana.

Bartholomae, D. & Petrosky, A. (1986). *Facts, artifacts, and counterfacts: Theory and method for a reading and writing course.* Upper Montclair, NJ: Boynton/ Cook.

Bartholomae, D. & Petrosky, A. (1987). *Ways of reading.* Boston: Bedford Books of St. Martin's Press.

Bishop, E. (1988). *How to read The catcher in the rye.* Unpublished manuscript, University of Pittsburgh, Pittsburgh.

Bleich, D. (1987). *Subjective criticism.* Baltimore: Johns Hopkins University Press.

Derrida, J. (1970). Discussions. In R. Macksey & E. Donato (Eds.), *The language of criticism and the sciences of man: The structuralist controversy.* Baltimore: Johns Hopkins University Press.

Derrida, J. (1976). *Of grammatology* (G.C. Spivak, Trans.). Baltimore: Johns Hopkins University Press.

Dewey, J. (1963). *Experience and education.* New York: Macmillan.

Foucault, M. (1972). The discourse on language. In *The archaeology of knowledge* (A.M. Sheridan Smith, Trans.). New York: Pantheon Books.

Freire, P. (1984). *The pedagogy of the oppressed.* New York: The Continuum Publishing Corporation.

Hirsch, E.D. (1988). *Cultural literacy.* New York: Vintage Books.

Hunter, M. (1982). *Mastery teaching*. El Segundo, CA: Tip Publications.

Kristeva, J. (1986). *The Kristeva reader* (T. Moi, Ed.). New York: Columbia University Press.

Rich, A. (1978). When we dead awaken: Writing as re-vision. *On lies, secrets, and silence: Selected prose 1966–1978*. New York: W. W. Norton & Company.

Ruskin, J. The nature of Gothic. In E.T. Cooke and A. Wedderbrun (Eds.), *The stones of Venice, the complete works of John Ruskin*. London: George Allen, 1903–1912.

Said, E. (1975). *Beginnings: Intention and method*. New York: Columbia University Press.

Salinger, J.D. (1964). *The catcher in the rye*. New York: Bantam Editions.

Vygotsky, L. (1962). *Thought and language* (E. Hanfmann and G. Vakar, Trans.). Cambridge: MIT Press. (Original work published 1934).

Editor

Judith A. Langer is professor of education at the State University of New York at Albany, specializing in issues of literacy and learning. Her research focuses on how people become highly literate, how they use reading and writing to learn, and what this means for instruction. Her major works examine the nature of literate knowledge. She has studied reading and writing development, the ways in which understanding grows over time, how particular literacy contexts affect cognition and performance, and the effects of literacy instruction on academic learning. At present, she is studying the processes involved in literary understanding, the contribution of literature instruction to critical thought, and the underlying principles of response-based instruction. Langer has published widely. Her books include *Reader Meets Author: Bridging the Gap; Understanding Reading and Writing Research; Children Reading and Writing: Structures and Strategies; Language, Literacy, and Culture: Issues of Society and Schooling,* and *How Writing Shapes Thinking: Studies of Teaching and Learning.* Langer is codirector of the Center for the Learning and Teaching of Literature.

Contributors

Arthur N. Applebee is a professor in the School of Education, State University of New York at Albany, and director of the federally sponsored Center for Literature Teaching and Learning. Applebee specializes in studies of language use and language learning, particularly as these occur in school settings. Applebee's most recent studies have examined current practice in the teaching of literature in programs across the country. His previous studies include, *Tradition and Reform in the Teaching of English; The Child's Concept of Story: Ages Two to Seventeen; Writing in the Secondary School: English and the Content Areas,* and *Contexts for Learning to Write: Studies of Secondary School Instruction.* He is coauthor of *How Writing Shapes Thinking: A Study of Teaching and Learning,* and of a series of reports on reading and writing achievement from the National Assessment of Educational Progress. Applebee has had experience in program evaluation, high school teaching (English and drama), and clinical assessment and treatment of children with severe reading problems.

Jayne DeLawter is a professor of reading/language education at Sonoma State University. She also serves as regional director of the California Literature Project, where she oversees intensive institutes and follow-up sessions for K–12 teachers on the use of literature in a transactional curriculum. She taught elementary school in New York and California and is known for her whole language teaching and learning practices with adults as well as children. She has researched language use in multicultural classrooms, reading and writing with computers, and teacher roles in language learning; her journal articles and book chapters focus on the reading process and curriculum development. In 1978, she founded a teacher support group to explore whole language teaching and learning.

Patrick X. Dias is professor of education in the Department of Curriculum and Instruction, McGill University, where he directs the Centre for the Study and Teaching of Writing. A former high school English teacher and department chair, he has served as consultant to the Quebec Ministry of Education, conducted workshops for teachers all over North America, and lectured and published internationally on the teaching of writing, response to literature, and teacher education. His publications include three books: *Making Sense of Poetry: Patterns in the Process* (Canadian Council of Teachers of English), *Developing Response to Poetry,* with Mike Hayhoe, (The Open University Press), and, with four other authors *Writing for Ourselves/Writing for Others* (Nelson Canada). He is currently completing a report on the

International Response to Poetry Project, a study of response to poetry among secondary school students in four countries.

Susan Hynds is an associate professor in the Reading and Language Arts Center at Syracuse University, where she serves as program director of English education. She is a former finalist in the NCTE "Promising Researcher Competition," past chair of the NCTE Assembly of Research, and cofounder of the special interest group in literature for AERA. She has recently published *Perspectives on Talk and Learning* with Donald Rubin (NCTE) and *Developing Discourse Practices in Adolescence and Adulthood* with Richard Beach (Ablex). Her work has appeared in the journals *Research in the Teaching of English, The Journal of Teaching Writing, Focuses, JRB: A Journal of Literacy, The Reading Teacher, Contemporary Psychology, The Review of Education,* and *The English Record;* and she is a contributor to *The Second Handbook of Reading Research* (Barr, Kamil, Mosenthal, and Pearson, eds.), *Beyond Communication: Comprehension and Criticism* (Bogdan and Straw, eds.), and *Transactions with Literature: A Fifty Year Perspective* (Farrell and Squire, eds.). Her work focuses on social aspects of reading and writing within instructional contexts.

Anthony Petrosky is professor of education at the University of Pittsburgh, where he also holds a joint appointment in the English department. Along with David Bartholomae, he is the author of *Facts, Artifacts, and Counterfacts: Theory and Method for a College Reading and Writing Course* and the editor of *Ways of Reading* published by Bedford Books. He is also a poet and was awarded the Walt Whitman Award for his book, *Jurgis Petraskas,* from the Academy of American Poets. Currently, he is the principal investigator for the National Board for Professional Teaching Standards English Language Arts Assessment Development Lab, where he is designing the first national board certification for English teachers.

Robert E. Probst is professor of English education at Georgia State University in Atlanta. Before that he was junior and senior high school English teacher in Maryland, and Supervisor of English for the Norfolk, Virginia Public Schools. Interested in the teaching of both writing and literature, he has written *Response and Analysis: Teaching Literature in Junior and Senior High School* (Boynton/Cook) and was part of the team that prepared *New Voices,* a high school English textbook series (Ginn). His articles have appeared in *English Journal, Journal of Reading, Educational Leadership, The Clearing House,* and elsewhere. A member of NCTE, he has worked on the Committee on Research, the Commission on Reading, and the Board of Directors of the Adolescent Literature Assembly. He is also a member of the NCRE and a colleague of the Creative Education Foundation, where he has served as faculty member for their annual institute.

Alan C. Purves is director of the Center for Writing and Literacy and professor of Education and Humanities at the State University of New York at Albany. He received his AB from Harvard and his MA and Ph.D. in English from Columbia University. He has taught at Columbia and Barnard Colleges, The University of Illinois, and Indiana University before coming to Albany.

He has served in many professional organizations and has held office in the National Council of Teachers of English and The International Association for the Evaluation of Educational Achievement (IEA). He has written or edited some twenty-five books and seventy articles dealing with literature, written composition, reading, cross-national research and development.